TALERDDIG
IN GREAT WESTERN DAYS

'Duke' No. 3287 *Mercury* approaching
Commins Coch with the 12.40 p.m.
Aberystwyth-Birmingham (Snow Hill) train.
4 September 1937.
Ifor Higgon

TALERDDIG
IN
GREAT WESTERN DAYS

GWYN BRIWNANT JONES

First impression—1999

ISBN 1 85902 809 8 (hard back)
ISBN 1 85902 704 0 (soft back)

Printed in Wales at
Gomer Press, Llandysul, Ceredigion

Dedicated to
'AB' and Cambrian line colleagues
past and present.

Contents

Luckily for the lover of scenery, Providence has placed the travelling arrangements of the most beautiful parts of Wales in the hands of railway companies who do not run very fast trains, and who do not pay as much attention to punctuality as they might.

O. M. Edwards, who wrote in 1895, would surely have been impressed and enchanted by the progress of No. 7814 *Fringford Manor* as it approached Cemmes Road with the 'up' Cambrian Coast Express on 23 May 1963.

We now anticipate the early introduction of the latest, air-conditioned, 100 m.p.h. trains; may they serve the region by their speed, comfort and efficiency, and earn our respect and admiration as did the steam trains of yore.

(Photograph by John Gwyn Dewing)

Foreword

'Why this continued fascination with the Cambrian' it may be asked; 'surely after Grouping the magic went away'. This book provides the answer. Certainly, the Grouping of 1922-3 was a shock for enthusiasts; the old certainties of liveries and engine working had gone; what was a Great Central locomotive doing heading an express out of Kings Cross?

But the Cambrian was spared abrupt change. Its lines were so intensely local that they could not easily be squeezed into any outside mould. Great Westernising was gradual, though effective. The author has been able to illuminate these from his familiarity with the localities and wide reading of earlier days. Those who are familiar with the bare bones of history will find much fascinating new detail here.

The later period of nationalisation was less traumatic; the Second World War had already eroded many of the special features of the Groups; however, progression into the diesel era has its interest for the modern reader – more perhaps than those like myself who first travelled over the Cambrian in 1923!

Planning a book on an individual railway is not too difficult; the bounderies are fixed. It is more difficult when covering an area of country rather than a legal entity; the temptation to spread the bounderies as one proceeds is not easy to resist. The present author has clearly been conscious of this; where the narrative departs from the actual route through Talerddig there is good reason. Though laid out entirely beside beautiful coasts and splendid country, the Cambrian had its connections to less fortunate parts. Readers especially dedicated to the line, and those with wider views, will be equally rewarded.

Llandre, August 1999   R. W. Kidner

Acknowledgements

Talerddig in Great Western Days seeks to provide fresh information to extend existing knowledge rather than attempt a comprehensive account of the Cambrian line.

The text is based on official Cambrian and GWR records held at the Public Record Office, Kew (PRO), together with documents at the National Library of Wales Aberystwyth (NLW) and various Welsh County Record Offices. This information has been augmented by notes, based on personal observation, freely supplied by a host of good friends, professional railwaymen and lay-persons alike. Trevor B. Owen and W. G. Rear deserve particular mention but the principal source was the late Ifor Higgon of Arthog whose notes relating to the Barmouth Junction/Morfa Mawddach area probably form the single most detailed record of locomotive movements on the former Cambrian system.

Roger Kidner has always shared his knowledge of Cambrian matters most willingly; his books on the subject occupy a special niche in the telling of the Cambrian story and his contributions to this volume are equally appreciated.

Other valuable contributions and suggestions were made by: Denis Dunstone; Dr E. S. Owen-Jones of the Welsh Industrial & Maritime Museum, Cardiff; Hilary Malaws of the National Monuments Record Wales, Aberystwyth; Dr D. Huw Owen and colleagues at the NLW, Aberystwyth. Also Ron Cowell and W. H. Roberts, of Aberystwyth; Ken Davies, Neath; J. Horsely Denton, Welshpool; D. Bowyer, Murray Evans, E. Hughes, G. Hughes, R. Hughes, T. A. Hughes, Neville Pritchard and Gwyn Roderick, all of Machynlleth; David Evans Tywyn; Elwyn Jones, Ron Jones and E. H. Stephens, of Newtown; Bob Morgan, Mid Wales Tourism, Machynlleth, with Neil Owen and Ann Eleri Jones of Ceredigion Tourist Office; Aled Rees, Ruthin and R. C. Riley, Beckenham.

Public and service timetables have proved especially helpful, and Weekly Notices, where available, contain a wealth of additional information. Every effort has been made to use illustrations of a high standard, but where the choice lay between an unusual subject moderately recorded or a mundane topic impeccably photographed, the former option was generally taken. Photographs are credited in the usual manner and sincere thanks are extended to all contributors. I am grateful for permission to reproduce the map on p. 32, which first appeared in *Historical Survey of Selected G.W. Stations* by R. H. Clark & C. R. Potts, Oxford Publishing Company, an imprint of Ian Allan Publishing Ltd.

It should be noted that the spelling of station names in Chapters 1-5 generally follows the form commonly used during the period 1922-60, but the renaming of Barmouth Junction as Morfa Mawddach in 1960 signified an increased awareness of the Welsh language by the railways. This is reflected in the forms adopted in Chapter 6, although some anomalies remain.

Final thanks are extended to Dr Dyfed Elis-Gruffydd and all involved at Gomer Press, Llandysul.

Gwyn Briwnant Jones
Cardiff June 1999

Preface

The Newtown & Machynlleth Railway (N&MR) existed as an independent company for only a few years, just long enough to give title to that section of the former Cambrian Railways from Moat Lane, through Talerddig, to Machynlleth. In former days it could be regarded as the spine of the old Cambrian system, or, perhaps, as the bar of a crude letter 'H', linking the coast with the inland sections. Even today its role remains largely unchanged, despite closure of the Oswestry-Buttington and Moat Lane-Brecon lines. Nowadays, however, stations on the N&M section, as elsewhere, are reduced in scope, size and number; that at Newtown remains one of the few examples of early buildings which perform their original function. Although now occupied principally by a travel agent and taxi company, it still retains its loop-line, which ensures regular use of both platforms – one of the few crossing places so bless'd – but in common with most other locations along the line, the yard has closed and the signal-box, sidings and goods facilities are no more.

In contrast, the developments of recent years have focussed on Machynlleth, now established as the fulcrum of Cambrian operations; only here is

Machynlleth station before renovation, June 1979.

GBJ

Machynlleth station viewed from the 'rock', showing renovated roof, windows, walls and chimneys. The former main entrance now serves the head office of Mid Wales Tourism. Renovation, commenced in December 1993, was completed the following year.

Railway Heritage Trust

there any small semblance of the activity of the past. The station building, decaying slowly up to a decade or so ago and threatened with demolition, has been sympathetically restored through the combined efforts of Regional Railways, the Railway Heritage Trust, CADW, Mid Wales Tourism and various local authorities. Administrative offices of Railtrack and Central Trains now occupy most of the ground floor, whilst the headquarters of Mid Wales Tourism is located on the first floor, reflecting today's cohesive and corporate approach to tourism, in marked contrast with the pioneer days of 1869 when an Aberystwyth correspondent complained in the local press 'that tourists and sea-bathing seekers from the inland counties of England are systematically informed at the Machynlleth station . . . by agents from Barmouth and other sea-side towns, that illness is rife in Aberystwyth . . .' (*Newtown & Welshpool Express*, September 14 1869).

Machynlleth currently boasts the only sidings of any length and note on the present-day Cambrian. A DMU refuelling and stabling point (in the original N&MR engine shed of 1863), together with the Cambrian section's Building Services and Bridge Department, are established here, as is the radio signal-box controlling the whole line between Sutton Bridge Shrewsbury, Aberystwyth and Pwllheli.

Caersws, the only intermediate N&M station which remains open for passenger traffic, retains its single platform but the former signal-box controls only the adjacent level crossing; there is neither loop nor siding.

Oswestry – beyond the sphere of the old N&M – and where the Cambrian previously had its headquarters, lost its passenger service to the coast in 1965. The station building, however, survives as a hardware store, with private apartments above. Alongside, a disused, rusty track still wends its way between Gobowen and the Nantmawr quarries, optimistically awaiting a resumption of rail-bourne traffic, whilst the old goods shed – currently the home of the Cambrian Railways Museum – now stands on the threshold of new and exciting developments.

The elegant station building at Welshpool survives, happily in better condition these days although it too has changed its role. Regrettably, it no longer has any connection with the railway, which appears to have distanced itself in the face of such 'betrayal'. The town's bypass now occupies the old track-space; the rails have been moved due south to serve a new island platform, complete with glass shelter. Nonetheless, the grand old building endures to grace a new century; those responsible for its retention are to be congratulated on their achievement.

The junctions and associated branches at Afon Wen, Buttington, Moat Lane and Morfa Mawddach are no more – hardly a trace remains at any of these locations – yet Dyfi Junction somehow survives. The low, single storey building on the *gors* was never particularly elegant or attractive. It always appeared anxious, somehow, to press itself into the dark marshland in an endeavour to escape the harsh westerly gales, and seemed to lack sufficient confidence to rise much above its boggy surroundings. The primitive refreshment room which used to offer shelter and sustenance between trains has long gone and what nowadays passes for Dyfi Junction is largely ignored by many services. Machynlleth is now the main inter-change.

Newtown yard was still rail-connected but virtually empty—with the exception of the PW unit, far right—although the signal-box was still in operation at the time of this photograph, 22 November 1985.   *GBJ*

This June 1980 view shows the elegant Welshpool station building to be in good condition at that time, with the Prince of Wales feathers prominent above the main entrance. *GBJ*

Dyfi Junction and its exposed location; the buildings, (*far right*), do not intrude but merge into the landscape.

John Hillmer

The junction's isolated location, at the westernmost tip of the old county of Montgomeryshire remains within thrown-cricket-ball distance of neighbouring Ceredigion and Meirionnydd and still commands broad, ever-changing views of river, mountain and marsh. In the past, when lineside allotments were the cause of much friendly rivalry along the coast, one of the junction's station masters boasted that he grew his onions in Cardiganshire (as it was in those days) his carrots in Montgomeryshire and his potatoes in Merioneth. He apparently enjoyed considerable success in various shows with a variety of the latter known as 'Sharp's Express'. His colleague at Afon Wen – tired, no doubt, of hearing of the prowess of his rival to the south – was heard to retort, 'That was just about the only thing that ever came out of Dyfi Junction on time'!

The spacious terminus at Aberystwyth, one time mecca of holiday-makers from Birmingham, Bargoed, Tamworth or Treorchy, lies largely empty and abandoned. Railtrack has restored the early

Cambrian buildings and platform canopy on the former 'down' side, but the old 'up' or departure platform, together with the Great Western's 1925 concourse and offices, have been cordoned off 'awaiting development'. Elsewhere, down the coast, things are little better: Aberdyfi, Tywyn and Llwyngwril are little more than shelters; station buildings at Talsarnau and Penrhyn survive, but as private dwellings. Only at Barmouth, Porthmadog, Criccieth and Pwllheli do the station buildings remind us of their original purpose.

The Great Western, undoubtedly, put the Cambrian in fine fettle during its short reign, although the Second World War interrupted Paddington's plans for further development. Nationalisation came in 1948 and British Railways' Western Region management did their best to reinvigorate the system. Their crowning achievement was the restoration of the Cambrian Coast Express as a weekday restaurant car service from Paddington, and for the first time ever, its operation during winter periods. Modern

Aberystwyth station. The recently refurbished 1893 canopy contrasts with the earlier and currently neglected 1871 canopy on the right of the picture. The Great Western's 1925 extensions (beyond the white hoarding) are out of use and await 'development'. 9 September 1998. *GBJ*

locomotives and rolling stock were introduced, track was re-laid and a limited amount of bridge rebuilding also took place; signalling and other items of the infrastructure were generally in good order. In retrospect, the 1950s can be seen as good years for the railway in mid Wales.

British Railways boundary changes in 1963 coincided with the difficult transition from steam to more modern traction. The London Midland Region inherited the system in January that year, but Euston had other priorities than the Cambrian in those days, and the mid 1960s and 1970s witnessed a sharp decline in investment and morale. The fear of closure was real but little by little the Cambrian recovered, partly through improved management and partly due to some constructive badgering by the general public, well represented in parliament, and by the Cambrian Coast Action Group. Attentive monitoring by the various parties continues to be effective. Naturally, shortcomings remain but the sector survives and some aspects reflect steady progress, despite financial constraints.

The fascinating system that once existed can never return but the new, 'slim' Cambrian is undeniably better equipped for survival in the next century. As road congestion increases, so does the importance of our railways. Imaginative marketing, however, is vital in a competitive world but given attractive fares, suitable rolling stock, rapid and – above all else, perhaps – reliable services, the railway will not just exist but thrive again.

The line which runs beside the Severn, the Dyfi and along the coast remains an endless source of delight; hopefully, it will continue to serve the needs of this beautiful region of Wales for years to come.

Abbreviations used in the text

A&WCR	Aberystwyth & Welsh Coast Railway
B&MR	Brecon & Merthyr Railway
CWD	Central Wales Division
FSO	Fridays and Saturdays only
L&N	Llanidloes & Newtown Railway
LCGB	Locomotive Club of Great Britain
LPC	Locomotive Publishing Co.
LRGP	Locomotive & General Railway Photographs
M&M	Manchester & Milford Railway
MWR	Mid Wales Railway
N&M	Newtown & Machynlleth Railway
O&N	Oswestry & Newtown Railway
OE&WR	Oswestry, Ellesmere & Whitchurch Railway
PW	Permanent Way
RC	Restaurant Car
RR	Runs if required
S&MR	Shropshire & Montgomeryshire Railway
SE	Saturdays excepted
SO	Saturdays only
SOL	Superintendant of the Line
SRM	Steam Rail Motor
TC	Through Coaches

Shed Codes

ABH	Aberystwyth
BAN	Banbury
BCN	Brecon
CARM	Carmarthen
CHR	Chester
CNYD	Wrexham Croes Newydd
EXE	Exeter
MCH	Machynlleth
NPT	Newport (Ebbw Junction)
OSW	Oswestry
OXY	Oxley (Wolverhampton)
PPRd	Pontypool Road
RDG	Reading
SaLoP/SALOP	Shrewsbury
SRD	Stafford Road (Wolverhampton)
TYS	Tyseley (Birmingham)
MPD	Motive Power Depot

THE CAMBRIAN RAILWAYS.

Cambrian Railways time table map, 1912.

Chapter 1

The passing of the Cambrian, 1918-22

The scenically attractive but sparsely populated terrain of mid Wales held little appeal for Victorian railway promoters. The London & North Western Railway (LNWR) and the Great Western Railway (GWR) had both considered the area during the 1850s but were not convinced that any investment would be profitable. Their main concern, apparently, was to ensure that their rival gained no advantage. Both companies had reached Shrewsbury by that time, but neither ventured westward until 1861-62 when they operated a joint line from Shrewsbury, to meet the Oswestry & Newtown Railway at Buttington Junction.

As the English companies seemed reluctant to commit themselves, mid Wales provided an early example of railway self-sufficiency, as much of the finance and most of the protagonists came from Montgomeryshire. Thus were born the Llanidloes & Newtown Railway (L&NR) 1853,[1] the Oswestry & Newtown Railway (O&NR) 1855,[1] the

Newtown & Machynlleth Railway (N&MR) 1857[1] and the Oswestry, Ellesmere & Whitchurch Railway (OE&WR) 1861.[1] Although created as separate companies, they soon discovered the advantages of amalgamation and formed the Cambrian Railways in 1864. The process was completed by the addition of the Aberystwyth & Welsh Coast Railway (A&WCR) in 1865 and the Mid-Wales Railway in 1904 (the latter having been worked by the Cambrian from 1888).

The Cambrian was never regarded amongst Britain's more prosperous railways. Despite the promoters initial aspirations, the area failed to generate sufficient traffic to allow more than the most modest development. Had adequate finance been available, the railway would undoubtedly have been built to higher standards and a double track main line between Whitchurch and Aberystwyth, for example, would have been a priority. But the Cambrian was forced to build

Nineteenth century Cambrian. Photographs of general station views are less plentiful than those of locomotives but this fine view of *Dutton & Co.'s Patent Succession Lock with portable keys for sidings*, provides rare graphic information of Glandovey *c.* 1888. Noteworthy details include, *l-r*: the white-painted wooden 'up' platform (1872), minus shelter; the original 'down' platform, before lengthening in 1910; 2 Cambrian haystacks, smart bowler-hatted pointsman and an obvious lack of interlocking between the 'down' signal and siding.
PRO

A fascinating Great Central Railway handbill of 1914. As trains are advertised as calling at Ellesmere, the loop-line between the Wrexham and Oswestry lines would appear to have played no part in these arrangements.

GBJ Coll.

GREAT CENTRAL RAILWAY

STALYBRIDGE, MOSSLEY, DENTON and ASHTON WAKES.

Holidays in the Cambrian District.

On SATURDAYS, JULY 18 and 25, and AUGUST 8 & 15, 1914,

DEAN & DAWSON'S SPECIAL EXCURSIONS TO

Wrexham, Ellesmere, Oswestry, Llanymynech, Machynlleth, Aberdovey, Towyn,

BARMOUTH,

Harlech, Dolgelly, Borth
— AND —

ABERYSTWYTH

For 3, 4, 5 or 8 days, will run as under:

IMPORTANT NOTICE.

—

Saturday TO Monday TICKETS are now issued at a **SINGLE FARE** and a **THIRD** for the Double Journey, Between all Great Central Stations, including London, and between Great Central Stations and nearly all Stations in England and Wales. For particulars see Handbills.

AVAILABLE BY Any Train OUTWARD on SATURDAYS, RETURN on SUNDAYS (where train service admits, by any train after 5·0 a.m.) **or MONDAYS** (by any train).

Minimum Fares,

First Class.	Third Class.
4/0	2/6

STATIONS.	Times of Departure.	FARES THERE AND BACK. THIRD CLASS.									
		WREXHAM.		Ellesmere and Oswestry.		Llanymynech		Machynlleth		Aberdovey, Harlech, Towyn, Barmouth, Borth, Dolgelley, and Aberystwyth	
		3, 4 or 5 Days	8 Days	3, 4 or 5 Days	8 Days	3, 4 or 5 Days	8 Days	3, 4 or 5 Days	8 Days	3, 4 or 5 Days	8 Days
	a.m.										
STALYBRIDGE ...	9 35										
ASHTON (Park Par.)	9 38										
Dukinfield	9 40										
OLDHAM (Glod. R,)	9 37	5/6	6/9	7/3	9/6	8/6	10/0	9/0	12/0	9/0	12/0
,, (Clegg St.)	9 39										
Park Bridge	9 44										
ASHTON (Old. Rd).	9 48										
Guide Bridge	10 15										
Wrexham (C.) arr.	12 36										
Ellesmere ... ,,	1 20										
Oswestry .... ,,	1 39										
Llanymynech ,,	2a10										
Machynlleth . ,,	3 40										
Aberdovey .. ,,	4 7										
Towyn ..... ,,	4 15										
Barmouth .. ,,	4 50										
Harlech .... ,,	5 40										
Dolgelley ... ,,	6 30										
Borth ...... ,,	4 7										
Aberystwyth ..,,	4 25										

Passengers travel by Through Train from Guide Bridge.

a—Change at Oswestry.

3, 4 or 5 days' passengers return on the following Monday, Tuesday or Wednesday, and 8 days' passengers on the following Monday, Tuesday, Wednesday, Thursday, Friday or Saturday, from Aberystwyth at 12·25 p.m., Borth 12·45 p.m., Harlech 11·2 a.m., Dolgelley 9·45 a.m., Barmouth 11·45 a.m., Towyn 12·18 p.m., Aberdovey 12·31 p.m., Machynlleth 1·15 p.m., Llanymynech 11·2 a.m., Oswestry 3·42 p.m., Ellesmere 4·5 p.m., and Wrexham (Central) at 4·45 p.m., to MANCHESTER (Central) or GUIDE BRIDGE, going forward by first Ordinary Train after arrival.

The 12·25 p.m. train from ABERYSTWYTH is a THROUGH TRAIN to MANCHESTER (Central) and GUIDE BRIDGE.

Passengers also have the option on return of crossing the town of Manchester between the Central and London Road Stations, going forward from London Road by any Ordinary Train.

FOR CONDITIONS UPON WHICH EXCURSION TICKETS ARE ISSUED, SEE NOTICES EXHIBITED AT THE STATIONS, AND THE COMPANY'S AGENCIES. Children under Three Years of Age, Free; Three and under Twelve, Half-fare.

Ask for Tickets (Ordinary, Tourist, Week-end, Long Date Week-end and Excursion), and consign Parcels, Goods and Coal by the GREAT CENTRAL RAILWAY.

Tickets and Bills of the above, and all Great Central Excursions, can be obtained any time in advance at any of the Company's Booking Offices and Stations; from Dean & Dawson's Excursion Office, 2, Mumps, Oldham, and the usual Agents.

All information as to Excursion Trains can be obtained from any of Messrs. Dean & Dawson's Excursion Offices; or from Mr. GEO. J. GIBSON, District Traffic Manager, Great Central Railway, London Road Station, Manchester.

Marylebone Station, London, N.W., July, 1914. SAM FAY, General Manager.

Via Manchester (Central), Chester (Liverpool Road), Wrexham and Cambrian Railway.

M.D. 502 "GLOBE" Deansmere Press, Stockport and London. 75/5,000

within its means and the lines were constructed with single track, although the masonry of most bridge and culvert abutments was optimistically constructed to allow for expansion at a future date. A few short sections were indeed laid with double track, in due course, but the system remained essentially single line, with all the problems this entailed. These became most apparent on busy summer weekends, when few trains ran to time. Even express services suffered frequent, unscheduled halts, to 'cross' trains moving in the opposite direction. Punctuality was rare; when a train lost a few minutes early in the day and failed to maintain its allotted place in the 'great plan', the loss could be converted into lengthy delays by that same evening.

This major defect in the Cambrian's infrastructure has remained through the years. The railway copes more or less adequately with the demands of local traffic during nine months or so of each year but matters can often deteriorate during the summer, when resources are strained. T'was ever thus on the Cambrian.

Nonetheless, passenger numbers increased steadily through the 1860s, as thousands of workers from industrial centres took advantage of the new transport and made for the mountains of mid Wales and the coast of Cardigan Bay. The Cambrian only began to make anything approaching a respectable profit when the summer passenger traffic began to flow but, unfortunately, this was confined mainly to weekends, causing considerable congestion. At such times, every available man and machine was put to use and all were hard pressed. Sufficient capital to relieve the situation could never be justified, so the Cambrian limped along for most of its existence, surviving successive periods of feast and famine. Freight traffic usually attained modest proportions, with the possible exception of the war years. Goods outward consisted of lumber and the products of various quarries in the region, augmented by the

No attempt has been made to trim the negative area of this well-known image, although the photographer rather spoiled his shot by inadvertently omitting half the young lady on the left in his anxiety to include both locomotives. Of the two engines, Cambrian 4-4-0 No. 66 (*centre*) excites no particular comment but the ex-Metropolitan Railway 4-4-0T on the right, Cambrian No. 36, was later converted into a tender engine and goes part way to dating the photograph as pre-1916.   *NLW: A. J. Lewis*

carriage of wool and livestock; inward traffic comprised mainly of coal, coke, building materials and manufactured goods – from pots and pans to agricultural machinery. Combined freight and passenger returns reflected only marginal profits.

By the end of the First World War the company, in common with most of the other railways of Britain, was in need of fresh impetus and investment. Many of its supporters and shareholders looked to the government for salvation although the possibility of nationalising the railways, which had been aired previously, was then thought too drastic a step. Eventually, a

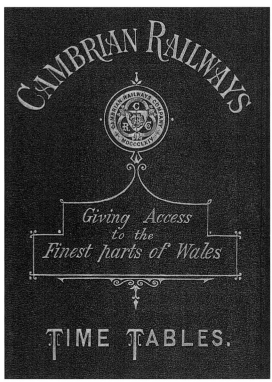

Gold-blocked hard cover folder for the company's timetables supplied to the larger hotels for display in reception areas.

Private Collection

Cambrian Railways publicity booklet, 1898.

IAH Coll.

compromise, the formation of four large companies, gained favour.

The first seeds for the 'grouping', as it became known, were sown during the latter quarter of the nineteenth century when parliament's desire for overall control of the nation's railways – vital during any national crisis – resulted in the passing of the Act of 1871 which empowered the government to assume full control during any such emergency. In 1912, largely as a result of the deteriorating political climate, the concept was developed through the formation of the Railway Executive, then charged with the creation of an efficient and cohesive national system. Within a few short years, the 1914-18 war was to provide the new organisation with its first major test. Amongst other achievements, the new regime quickly demonstrated its ability to move vast tonnages of coal by rail, to Cromarty Firth and Scapa Flow, for the Grand Fleet, which was then powered by Welsh steam coal. Every viable route between south Wales and Scotland was exploited; perhaps the most 'romantic' being the Brecon & Merthyr Railway's route through Pontsticill and Torpantau to Talyllyn Junction, thence along the former Mid Wales Railway to the Cambrian at Moat Lane, for Oswestry and the north.

The Cambrian's own war effort involved the transportation of thousands of troops to camps established in the area, usually along the coast but also inland, as at Rhayader, for instance. Without full documentation, we cannot now appreciate the density of this traffic, but sufficient information survives to provide an indication. We know that no fewer than twenty-two troop trains brought the Staffordshire, Worcester and Warwickshire Volunteer Brigades to Towyn for their summer encampment on Sunday, 2 August 1903. A corresponding number of empty trains returned later that day and the whole procedure was reversed a week later when the brigades returned home.[2] Activity of this nature increased during the period immediately before the Great War and the Cambrian eagerly seized such valuable traffic. Christiansen and Miller note that on 4 August 1912, no fewer than 13,000 territorials and 800 horses were transported to Bow Street station, in forty-five special trains; a massive achievement for a small company like the Cambrian.[3]

At one time, there were plans to convert the attractive Glaspwll valley, near Machynlleth, into an artillery range. Several War Office officials visited the area and started negotiations with local landowners, but the scheme was eventually abandoned.[4]

The demonstration of railway efficiency during the war led directly to the formation of a Ministry of Transport in 1919, charged with the

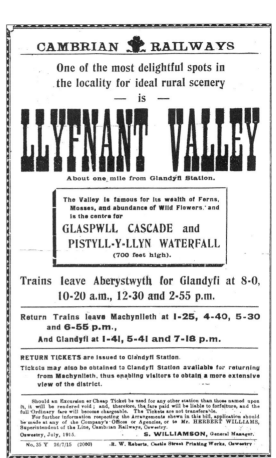

The Cambrian obviously capitalised on the 1912 decision to abandon a War Office scheme to create an artillery range in the Glaspwll/Llyfnant area. This handbill promoting the valley's scenic attractions was issued in July 1915. *Mike Lloyd Coll.*

development and integration of the railways in peacetime. Its efforts, under the chairmanship of Sir Eric Geddes, culminated with the Railways Act of 1921. The grouping became fully effective from 1 January 1923.[5]

Many in mid Wales were well aware that the old company had enjoyed a special relationship with the LNWR and felt that its successor, the new London, Midland & Scottish Company (LMS) might best serve the area, but eventually the

A group of Newtown staff pose for the camera. The style of the Cambrian uniforms suggests a date in the early 1920s and the photograph may well have been taken just before the grouping. The only persons identified are the two porters in the centre of the back row, W. Blayney and A. R. Davies and in the front row (*second and third from the left*) parcels clerk Harry Cooper and booking clerk J. E. Morris. *c. 1922.*
Courtesy R. A. Morris

Cambrian was amalgamated with the LNW's old rival, the powerful Great Western Railway. The Cambrian expired officially on 25 March 1922.

The GWR, alone amongst the four new companies, was allowed to retain its identity as it amalgamated with the Alexandra (Newport and South Wales) Docks and Railway, the Barry Railway, the Cardiff Railway, the Rhymney Railway, and the Taff Vale Railway, in addition to the Cambrian. Much as it might have wished otherwise, the Great Western was compelled to accept the foregoing as equal partners. Officially, at least, the companies were amalgamated, not absorbed. Each was represented on the new GW

Cambrian 4-4-0 No. 95, later destroyed in the Abermule disaster, is here banked in the rear between Machynlleth and Talerddig, with the 9.05 a.m. Aberystwyth-Whitchurch service, 15 August 1913. *LCGB Ken Nunn Coll.*

Board of Directors, which was increased in number from 19 to 25; the Cambrian's man at Paddington was Lt.Col. David Davies, MP of Llandinam, grandson of the railway pioneer.

As it happened, the new regime could not come quickly enough for the Cambrian, which had suffered a demoralising blow on 21 January 1921, when the 10.05 a.m. 'down' stopping train from Whitchurch collided, head-on, with an 'up' express, near Abermule. A seemingly 'impossible' accident had occurred which shocked railway companies and public alike. Single-line operation, supposedly safeguarded by rules, regulations and foolproof procedures, was scrutinised anew but the official Board of Trade Inquiry found that a series of slack practices had combined to create an accident of horrendous proportions in which seventeen persons lost their lives. During a visit to the area, as recently as 1998, it was gleaned that, perhaps, not all the facts emerged during the inquiry. For example, it

The small wooden building at Abermule, location of the first major misunderstanding which led to the 1921 disaster. Photograph, facing Montgomery, 23 August 1954.
H. C. Casserley

would appear that the Cambrian carried out a damage limitation excercise, when Abermule station staff were immediately called to Oswestry, before the inquiry took place. The enginemen of the 'up' train both survived, although they were away from duty for almost a year. Each was granted a bonus of £5.0.0 and allowed full wages until they resumed duties.[6] In June, both men were still attending hospital daily for treatment and J. C. McDonald, the locomotive superintendent, in his report of 2 November 1921 states that J. P. Jones, the driver, and J. Owen, the fireman, were 'still off' and paid weekly compensation.

An indication of the ferocity of the impact may be gained by learning that the boiler and firebox in the foreground were those of No. 95, the ex-Aberystwyth engine; they were wrenched from their main-frames (*l. and upright near the tender*) and turned through 180 degrees, facing whence they came. The tender of No. 82, the Oswestry engine, contributes to the dark mass in the centre of the composition.
Courtesy Dennis Jones, Abermule

Some pre-grouping tickets from the Cambrian and associated companies. The MWR ticket from Brecon to a destination on the Glasgow & South Western Railway, via Llechryd (Builth Road) is especially interesting, as are the tickets from destinations on the B&MR to various stations on Cardigan Bay.

Malcolm James Coll.

Most of those who died at Abermule were in the GWR composite carriage (No. 7730) here still on the track, centre of the picture. The Board of Trade report stated that Cambrian No. 324, a 1st and 3rd class composite tea car (whose remains are visible lying partly within the GW composite carriage) 'had telescoped through No. 7730, the frame and body of the former having swept the whole of the inside of the latter coach, including the passengers, into a mass of wreckage at the rear end' (nearest camera).   *WIMM*

There were proposals in March 1921 for a memorial stone to be erected at the site of the crash. McDonald proposed that this could be 'a large undressed block of limestone from Pant Quarry, about 10 tons or so in weight, with a brass inscription plate let into it. This stone weathers well and keeps its bright colour'.[7] The Cambrian's eventual reluctance to erect a prominent reminder of the tragedy at the site can be appreciated, but in other ways it is regrettable that a memorial to the victims of the accident does not exist in the locality. A tablet commemorating the assistance of doctors and nurses at Newtown Infirmary, for example, would have been most appropriate, for the Cambrian Board resolved that a donation of 200 guineas be made to the funds of the Montgomery County Infirmary, Newtown, 'in grateful recognition of the services rendered by that institution'.[8]

Amongst those tended at the Infirmary was Lord Herbert Vane-Tempest whose father, as Earl Vane, had been one of the foremost supporters of a railway through Talerddig. Lord Herbert's death at Abermule deprived Machynlleth and the Cambrian (he was then a director) of a prominent figure. Also killed at Abermule was Capt. Harold Owen Owen of Garthgwynion, Machynlleth; his family had established the successful stores of that name.

The shock of the Abermule disaster reverberated around the world. The introduction of new procedures and fresh investment were vital and the GW's greater resources succeeded in regenerating confidence in a manner which the old Cambrian would have found hard to equal.[9]

Somewhat surprisingly, the Great Western era lasted a mere 25 years. Yet, within that comparatively brief period, Paddington transformed the old line into an efficient part of the Western empire, despite the difficult financial climate of the 1920s and '30s.

PASSENGER SERVICES

A few carefully considered daily services served the area well for over a century, from 1863 until the demise of steam between 1965 and 1967. They required only minor modifications during that time, and successfully formed a basic pattern around which the more elaborate summer traffic arrangements were woven. Taking Machynlleth as an example, and quoting approximate times only, weekday 'down' services arrived around 6.30 a.m. (mail), 10.30 a.m., 1.10 p.m., 4.00 p.m., 6.00 p.m. and 9.00 p.m. 'Up' services left at 8.30 a.m., 10.45 a.m., 1.35 p.m., 3.40 p.m. and 7.00 p.m. (mail). Local services and connections to the coast fitted into some of the gaps, whilst through services to and from Manchester, Liverpool, Birmingham, London and south Wales were slotted-in during the period of the summer timetable.

Few of the through trains were sufficiently established to continue without some minor modification from year to year, reflecting the desire of timetable planners always to meet market requirements. Some of the basic services, together with the through trains, were run in two or three portions, if required; if the demand fell away, the service would be adjusted, perhaps to Monday or Friday/Saturday only, or a train could be listed as

Cambrian No. 94, an example of the 'Large Belpaire' class of 4-4-0 express engine, pauses at Machynlleth with a 'down' train. Judging from the position of the sun, this could have been a through train from Paddington, due at Machynlleth at 3.23 p.m. or a following service, the 1.50 p.m. from Whitchurch, due at Machynlleth at 4.08 p.m. *c.* 1920.   *J. P. Richards*

RR – runs if required. The Sunday timetable was more barren; usually just one mail train in each direction, with a coast connection worked from Machynlleth.

Although of limited photographic merit, this 'snap' nonetheless presents a rare view of the 'up' Cambrian mail train descending the bank into Borth station. The presence of Cambrian Post Office Van No. 293—distinguished by the long bulge for half its length—is sufficient to ensure the photograph's inclusion here. Cambrian 'Large Bogie' 4-4-0 No. 62. August 1921.
Revd. C. K. Douglas, courtesy of F. K. Davies

'Large Bogie' No. 11 at Barmouth Junction, working a Barmouth-Ruabon train, tender-first, as far as Dolgellau. *c.* 1921.

J. P. Richards

Through services, in particular, were curtailed during the First World War. Amongst the more obvious examples were the Rhondda-Aberystwyth trains, via Merthyr and Moat Lane. These, in common with most of the through services on the Cambrian, had developed from some of the early excursions of pioneer days. One such example is taken from a local paper of 1865, which reported:

> The first excursion trains, from South Wales, arrived here en route for Aberystwyth on Good Friday. There were no fewer than 30 carriages propelled [*sic*] by two engines. The South Walians were, in most cases, quite strangers to our North Wales scenery, and they appeared mightily gratified with their trip. During the ensuing summer, great traffic is anticipated between north and south Wales on the Mid Wales [Railway].[10]

This traffic was never as great as expected, perhaps, but each summer saw through trains plying between Treherbert and Aberystwyth. These commenced their journey by running down the Rhondda valley to Pontypridd before changing direction and heading up the vale of the Taff to Merthyr Tydfil, where another reversal and engine change took place, allowing progress to be made to Pontsticill and over the Brecon Beacons to the Mid Wales line at Talyllyn Junction. The through trains normally attempted to pass through mid Wales as quickly as motive power, track and other restrictions allowed, and usually stopped only at Builth, Rhayader and Llanidloes. Another reversal was called for at Moat Lane. Arrangements for further progress westward varied over the years. The south Wales trains usually ran independently, but at other times they were joined to convenient Whitchurch-Aberystwyth expresses. The frequency of the service also varied; some years the trains ran daily throughout the period of the summer timetable, or they were confined to Mondays, Fridays and Saturdays only. With the outbreak of the First World War, the service apparently disappeared from the timetable after 1915, but had certainly reappeared by 1920, when it ran on Mondays and Saturdays only. It was listed only in the mid Wales section of the timetable and appeared not to be drawn to public notice at all, between Moat Lane and Aberystwyth, at this time. (Table I).

Table I: Part of the Mid Wales section of the Working Time Book for 12 July-30 September 1915 showing the passage of the South Wales Express between Talyllyn Junction and Moat Lane.

IAH Coll.

UP. (Continued.)	26	28	30	32	31	36	38	40	42	44 South Wales Express, Mons. & Sats. only to Sept. 18th.		46 Goods		48
	Pass.	B.&M. Pass.	B.&M. Goods.	MID. Goods.	MID Pass	Pass	Pass.	Pass	Pass	arr	dep	arr	dep	B.&M. Goods.
	a.m.	a.m.	a.m.	a.m.	a.m.	a.m.	a.m.	p.m.	p.m.	p.m.		a.m.		a.m.
Brecon ......dep.	...	7X45	8 10	8 50	10 30	...	10 40	...	...	...	...	...	11 10	11 35
Brecon Junction ,,	...	7 47	8 12	8 52	10 32	.	10 42	..	...	...	...	...	11 12	11 37
Talyllyn ....{ arr.	...	7 55	8 20	9X 5	10X40	...	10X50	...	...	...	...	11X20 U	...	11 45
Talyllyn ....{ dep.	...	7 59	8 35	9 30	10 50	...	11 0	...	...	...	1J17	...	11 50	
Trefeinon ...... ,,	...	...	...	...	...	...	11* 6	...	...	...	...	11X57	12 0	
Talgarth ...... ,,	...	...	...	9 45	11X 1	...	11XT13	...	...	X	...	...	SR	..
Three Cocks..{ arr.	...	..	...	9 52	11 6	...	11 18	...	...	1X33	...	12 30	...	...
Three Cocks..{ dep.	...	...	...	10 30	11 8	...	11 20	...	...	...	1 36	...	...	...
B'rood & Llyswen ,,	...	...	...	..	...	...	11 26	...	...	...	...	...	SR	...
Erwood .... ,,	...	...	...	..	...	...	11X35	...	...	...	...	1X15	1 25	...
Aberedw .... ,,	...	...	...	...	...	...	*	...	...	...	...	...	...	...
Llanelwydd Qy. Sdg.	...	...	...	...	...	...	...	...	...	...	...	...	...	...
Builth Wells { arr	...	...	...	...	...	...	11T50	T	...	2X 0	...	1X45	...	...
Builth Wells { dep	...	...	...	...	...	..	11 55	12 35	...	...	2 5	...	2 50	...
Builth Road { arr	9T 5	...	...	...	...	...	12 0	12 40	...	2 10 X	...	2 55	...	...
Builth Road { dep	9 10	...	...	...	...	...	12 25	...	..	T	2 15	..	3 10	...
Thomas' Siding ,,	...	...	...	...	...	...	...	...	...	...	...	...	...	...
Newbridge-on-Wye ,,	...	...	...	...	...	...	12 33	...	...	...	...	S	...	...
Watts' Siding .. ,,	...	...	...	...	...	...	...	...	...	...	..	...	...	...
Doldowlod .... ,,	...	...	...	...	...	...	12 41	...	...	...	...	3 X40	3 50	...
Elan Junction .. ,,	...	...	...	...	...	...	...	...	...	...	...	...	...	...
Rhayader ....{ arr.	...	...	...	...	...	...	12X50	...	...	2 37	...	4 5	...	...
Rhayader ....{ dep.	...	...	...	...	...	...	12 52	...	...	...	2 40	...	4 50	...
St. Harmons .. ,,	...	...	...	...	...	...	1 5 Sats.	...	...	..	...	...	...	...
Pantydwr .... ,,	...	...	...	...	...	..	...	...	...	...	...	S	...	...
Glanyrafon Siding ,,	...	...	...	...	...	. .	...	...	...	..	X	...	...	...
Tylwch .... ,,	...	...	...	...	...	...	1 T 13 / 1 15	...	...	...	...	5X25	5 40	...
Llanidloes { arr.	...	...	...	...	...	...	1T21	...	...	3 X 5	...	5 55	...	...
Llanidloes { dep.	...	...	...	...	11 55	...	1 24	...	...	...	3T10	...	8 45	...
Dolwen .... ,,	...	...	...	...	12 0	...	*	...	...	...	...	...	...	...
Llandinam .... ,,	...	...	...	...	d12 5 / d12 6	...	*	...	...	...	...	...	...	...
Moat Lane Jc.arr.	...	...	...	...	12 10	...	1 40	...	...	3 25	...	9 5	...	...

The through services to Manchester, Birmingham and Paddington were also gradually re-established after the war. Contemporary timetables, however, do not furnish a complete picture for they cannot feature the interesting extra trains. A Cambrian Railways Supplementary Train Notice, for instance, indicates an intriguing operation by a dining car (on Saturday, 14 August 1920) which made its way from Aberystwyth on an all-stations local train to Machynlleth. On being put off at Dovey Junction it waited in a siding to be joined by some through coaches from Towyn, until all were attached to a later Pwllheli-Birmingham train. This notice specifically stated 'dining car' which, therefore, most probably indicated a GW vehicle, and pre-dated conventional operation to and from Paddington by several years.

Trains to and from Paddington, immediately after the First World War, carried no refreshment vehicle. Through services, however, via both Whitchurch and Shrewsbury, were numerous. On summer Saturdays in 1920, for example, Machynlleth was visited by no fewer than four 'down' expresses within 2 hours (at 2.40 p.m., 3.23 p.m., 4.08 p.m. and 4.24 p.m.), a not inconsiderable achievement given the need also to find paths for 'up' services during this period. The first of these was amongst the most remarkable of the Cambrian's non-stop runs. It was a summer express (possibly ex-Manchester) which left Whitchurch at 12.25 p.m. It ran on Fridays and Saturdays only, between 30 July and 28 August. Although this was scheduled to cross 'up' trains at Abermule, Moat Lane Junction and Talerddig, if all went according to plan, it was not due to stop until it reached Machynlleth (75 miles, in 2 hours 15 mins) at 2.40 p.m.[11] After an essential 5 minute stop for water here, it journeyed to Borth where a

Cambrian Pride I. Cambrian No. 73 was the first of the 'Large Goods' class of 0-6-0s built in 1894 by Neilson & Co. The engine's general appearance and the attendance of so many bowler-hatted gentlemen suggests this may be a portrait of a brand-new engine. *c*.1894(?)
IAH Coll.

Cambrian Pride II. 'Large Bogie' No. 84, with admirers, at Oswestry. Date not recorded.
GBJ Coll.

further 5 minute wait allowed it to cross another 'up' train, before arriving at Aberystwyth at 3.35 p.m. This service was followed by a weekday train from Paddington which ran non-stop between Wolverhampton and Welshpool (via the Abbey Foregate Loop at Shrewsbury). Its next stop was at Moat Lane (19 miles in 32 mins) and further stops were at Machynlleth and Borth, before Aberystwyth was reached at 4.10 p.m. A third train from Whitchurch (or again, possibly, from Manchester) ran non-stop from Oswestry (dep. 2.27 p.m.) to Newtown (arr. 3.15 p.m.) arriving finally at Aberystwyth at 4.50 p.m. Lastly, a 'down' express ran from Welshpool (3.10 p.m.) to Aberystwyth by 5.10 p.m., stopping at Newtown, Moat Lane, Machynlleth and Borth.

The Cambrian was optimistically attempting to return to a 'normality' reminiscent of pre-war days, an optimism which saw it through 1920 but which was severely damaged by the events of the following January, at Abermule. This was to have been the Cambrian's final season as a proud and confident company, but it was never quite the same after the Abermule disaster.

FREIGHT TRAFFIC

Goods traffic was always less intense than the passenger services but although there were no great seasonal peaks, it at least provided work over the comparatively lean winter periods. Nonetheless, during the summer months, freight was frequently relegated to make way for the heavy passenger trains and the sturdy 0-6-0s released from these duties were quickly redeployed on the excursion trains. Freight services are described in greater detail in following chapters.

LOCOMOTIVES[12]

Whatever the merits of the Cambrian's locomotive stock at the grouping, the GWR showed little regard for it – with small wonder, perhaps, for the 1922 amalgamation saw the transfer of a very mixed bag of 97 engines to Great Western stock. Some dated from the 1860s whilst over three-quarters preceded 1900. The majority were well worn and some had already been laid aside by the Cambrian. A large proportion of the remainder required heavy repairs and a survey by Great Western engineers resulted in the immediate withdrawal of a quarter of the stock.

The only class to make a favourable impression on the new owners was the 'Large Belpaire' class of goods engines. These bore a strong resemblance to the Great Western's own Dean 'Goods' 0-6-0s and proved more acceptable than most. Together with a few older and lighter engines, which could still be gainfully employed in certain restricted locations, they represented the bulk of Cambrian locomotives deemed useful by the Great Western.

The proud old name was quickly painted over, in some instances even before the locomotives had gained their GWR number-plates. 'Large Belpaire Goods' No. 99 and crew pause and pose at Machynlleth, 1922.   *J. P. Richards*

'Small Bogie' No. 60, as GW No. 1112, with an engineers train at Barmouth Junction, before returning to Oswestry, 12 May 1927.   *Ifor Higgon*

The oldest locomotives handed over were four survivors of 1863-65. These Sharp Stewart 2-4-0 engines had not steamed for some time and were virtually condemned on sight in 1922. They were allotted GW numbers but these were never carried. During Cambrian days they had been superseded by six 4-4-0 locomotives, usually referred to as the 'Small Bogie' class. These were built in pairs, the first in 1878, the second in 1886 and the final pair in 1891; they had been rebuilt between 1910 and 1915 but were also showing their age by the time of the grouping. The Great Western assessed each engine individually, allowing each to run as long as it could without major expenditure; only one, No. 1118, received much in the way of repair by the GWR. In Swindon's eyes, they were non-standard, aged machines and all were withdrawn by 1930.

The following class introduced by the Cambrian, designated the 'Large Bogie' 4-4-0 class, proved to be the mainstay of passenger services during independent days. They too were Sharp Stewart engines, built between 1893 and 1898, with a final pair assembled by the Cambrian itself at Oswestry in 1902, bringing the total at that time to twenty-two. Only twenty-one were handed over to the GWR, as Cambrian No. 82 was destroyed in the Abermule accident: they served the old company well. The final passenger class was formed of the five 'Large Belpaire' 4-4-0s, constructed by Robert Stephenson & Co., in 1904 to the design of Herbert Jones at Oswestry. They were initially allocated to Oswestry and Aberystwyth sheds for working the principal trains to and from the LNWR at Whitchurch, but from 1915 also appeared regularly down the coast. They undertook the heaviest work on the system and were well worn machines by the end of hostilities. Two of them, Cambrian Nos. 94 and 96 had received new boilers by Beyer Peacock in 1920-21, whilst No. 95 was the second engine destroyed in the Abermule disaster. Of the four handed over to the GWR, only No. 98 (GW 1043) was considered worthy of any major expenditure. It entered Swindon in March 1923 but did not emerge until September 1926; repairs comprised a fairly extensive rebuild of the boiler, which included the fitting of a Swindon superheater. No.1043 was then sent to Aberystwyth and usually worked the 7.50 a.m. local passenger train to

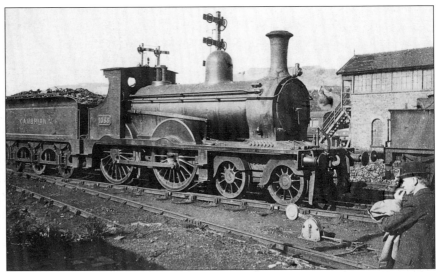

Cambrian 'Large Bogie' 4-4-0 No. 61 carries its new GW number-plate (1088) as it stands 'on shed' at Aberystwyth, c. 1923. The Cambrian livery of the tender was untouched.
IAH Coll.

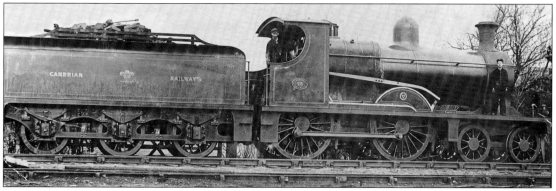

No. 98, one of the five 'Large Belpaire' 4-4-0s which bore the brunt of Cambrian express work during the decade before the grouping. They were superior to the incoming 'Dukes' in some respects but the latter, although nominally slightly heavier and more powerful engines, carried a greater proportion of their weight on the bogie than the Cambrian engines and as a result were more prone to slip under load. The better balanced Cambrian engines, however, were generally well worn by 1922, their numbers had been reduced to four and as non-standard designs they stood little chance of survival. Photographer and date unknown. *NLW*

Whitchurch and the balancing working, the 1.50 p.m. fast train home. This service carried through coaches from Liverpool and Manchester and picked up further through coaches from Paddington at Welshpool. No. 1043 worked this duty almost daily, in preference to the 'Dukes' then available. It was only relieved occasionally by classmate No. 1035, up to early 1928, when No. 1035 was withdrawn. Thereafter, No. 1043 was in sole charge of the duty until September 1928, when it was transferred to the coast.[13]

The Cambrian's 'Goods' engines found greater favour with the GWR and comprised two main classes, the 'Large Goods' class and the previously

Aston's 0-4-4T as GW No. 19, on station pilot duties at Aberystwyth, 30 July 1927. *Ifor A. Higgon*

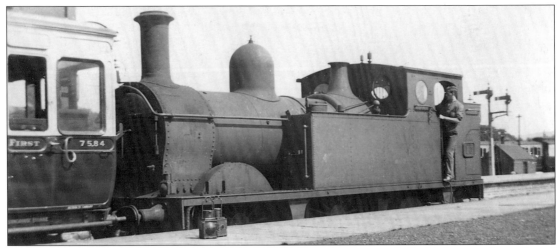

Another 0-4-4T (Cambrian No. 3 as GW No. 10) on similar duties at Aberystwyth. In this instance, the portion of carriage visible is possibly of greater interest than the locomotive. GW clerestory No. 7584 had no corridor connection with the remainder of the train, as is obvious by the location and design of the 1st class end-coupe in the photograph. The legend, just readable on the main frame indicates that the vehicle was fitted with the Westinghouse brake and there is also a painted instruction 'Return to Cardiff'. As the coach is standing at the main arrival platform (from Oswestry) it might be that No. 7584 arrived via Talyllyn and Moat Lane junctions. 4 August, 1928.

Ifor A. Higgon

mentioned 'Large Belpaire Goods' class; both were 0-6-0 types. There were ten of the former, designed by Aston and built between 1894 and 1899 by Neilson & Co. (5); Vulcan Foundry (3); and Neilson, Reid & Co. (2). In addition to their goods duties, they undertook many passenger turns during the busy summer periods, as did their successors, the 'Large Belpaire Goods'. Fifteen of these were built to the design of Herbert Jones by R. Stephenson (5), and Beyer Peacock (10). These sturdy engines were arguably the most successful Cambrian design; all were handed over to the GWR who considered them worthy of 'Swindonising'.

Remaining classes were generally small, physically and numerically. Amongst the more handsome were Aston's six elegant 0-4-4T engines, built originally by Nasmyth Wilson & Co., in 1895-99, for Oswestry-Ellesmere-Wrexham services. They later operated the Dolgellau-Barmouth services and the three survivors of the class ended their days at Aberystwyth, on carriage shunting duties and local trips to Machynlleth; the remaining trio were badly worn by the time the GWR saw them and were quickly condemned in 1922.

In 1905, another class of tank locomotive was purchased second-hand from the Metropolitan Railway, which proved to be more cumbersome and less useful. Indeed, the six 4-4-0Ts were decidedly unsuitable for Cambrian use, being too heavy for branch line work and lacking adequate water and coal space for any extended operation on the main line. Although two were later converted to tender engines in an attempt to increase their usefulness, they were largely regarded as white elephants and only purchased, apparently, because they appeared at a bargain price. Four were condemned in 1922, the last pair went the following year; of the six, only one is believed, with any certainty, to have carried a GW number (Cambrian No. 37; GW No. 1130).

18

Amongst the Cambrian's most interesting survivors at this time may be listed the 0-6-0 'Small Goods' class, constructed by Sharp Stewart between 1861 and 1865. Of the original thirteen, five survived to be handed over to the GWR; three were withdrawn at once in 1922, whilst the others lasted until 1935 and 1945. The class had been augmented by nine additional engines, from various sources, between 1872 and 1875; four of these survived to Great Western days, two being withdrawn immediately, with the final pair lasting until 1938 and 1947. They all proved to be useful machines for light work and, predictably, ended their days on such duties. Amongst the more interesting was that of station pilot at Portmadoc – a duty which took them over the lightly laid exchange sidings at Minffordd, but they mostly operated on branch lines around Oswestry where they shared this work with the ex-Lambourn Valley and Mawddwy Railway engines.

Small Sharp Stewart Goods engine (Cambrian No. 48/GW No. 908) shunting across the Cambrian turntable at Machynlleth, 28 May 1932.   *Ifor A. Higgon*

Much rebuilt GW 4-4-0 No. 3554 rests on the 'rock' siding at Machynlleth, 3 May 1930.   *Ifor A. Higgon*

Four ex-GWR engines were purchased by the Cambrian in 1921; two were 2-4-0 engines (Cambrian Nos. 1 and 10; GW Nos. 1329 and 1328, respectively) originally built in 1883, whilst the final pair Nos. 3521 and 3546, had a chequered history, eventually ending up as 4-4-0s.[14] The latter were purchased to replace the two engines destroyed at Abermule and were not renumbered by the Cambrian for this short period.

Also in 1921, Oswestry prepared designs for a mixed traffic 2-6-0 but the idea was shelved as talk of the grouping gathered momentum. Had the new engine been built, it would have provided the company with a versatile locomotive. Several variations were considered and interestingly, a drawing dated 31 March 1921 suggests proportions not unlike those adopted by Ivatt in 1946 and Riddles in 1953 (Table II). With a boiler pressure of 170 lbs per sq. in., cylinders of 18" dia. x 28" stroke and driving wheels of 5ft 6in. dia., tractive effort would have worked out at a useful 19,860 lbs at 85% boiler pressure. The Ivatt Class 2 had a tractive effort of 17,400 lbs and the Riddles Class 2, 18,513 lbs. For comparison, the tractive effort of the GWR '22' was 20,155 lbs.

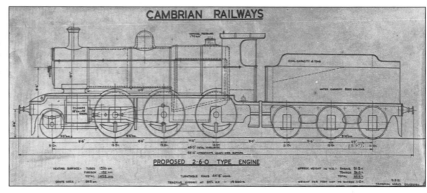

Table II: One of the Oswestry diagrams for the projected Cambrian 2-6-0 in 1921.
IAH Coll.

CARRIAGES

As with the locomotives, the Cambrian's carriage stock was of mixed quality. It included a good proportion of comfortable bogie carriages used on through services to Liverpool, Manchester, London and south Wales, contrasting with a number of smaller and older 4- and 6-wheel vehicles, most of which were quickly dispatched to the scrapyard by the new owners. Many of the latter would be prized by preservation groups or museums nowadays. Amongst the vehicles which 'got away' may be listed the small Cambrian 4-wheel saloons (Nos. 9 and 11) used by King Edward VII and Queen Alexandra at the inauguration of the Birmingham Corporation Waterworks in the Elan valley in 1904. The Cambrian also purchased two other vehicles with blue-blood connections. The more interesting, arguably, was the 6-wheel private saloon built at Oswestry in 1870 for Earl Vane (5th Marquess of Londonderry, from 1872). This vehicle was used primarily for travel between the Earl's principal residence at Plas Machynlleth, his estate in County Durham and town residence at Londonderry House, in London. It reflected the most advanced coach-building standards of the day but appears to have been little used by the family after the Earl's death in 1885. Its probate value was then set at £250.00 but it remained in the family's ownership until 1892, when the Marchioness of Londonderry eventually accepted the Cambrian Board's offer of £80.00. No photograph of it is thought to exist.[15]

The Great Western's photographic record of the Duke of Sutherland's saloon as Cambrian No. 1. It ended its days ignominiously as a Fruit and Parcels Van, in 1931. 27 March 1923. *WIMM/GW Coll.*

An official GW record of the Cambrian Observation Saloon, as GW No. 4072. *WIMM/GW Coll.*

Happily, the Cambrian's second 'aristocratic' saloon was recorded by the GW cameraman at the grouping, although it had by then been downgraded and displayed a nondescript appearance. It too was a 6-wheel saloon and had been constructed in 1895-96 for the Duke of Sutherland's private railway at Dunrobin, on the Highland Railway. When the Duke (who was also a director of the LNWR) commissioned a new bogie saloon from Wolverton Works in 1899, the smaller saloon was considered surplus to requirements. During the short period when both vehicles were in the Duke's ownership, it served to steady the riding of the larger carriage; later that year, however, the Highland Railway, acting as agents, sold it to the Cambrian. Thereafter, the Duke may have regretted this action, for the riding qualities of the large new saloon deteriorated, a deficiency which was so noticeable that a small 4-wheel 'day saloon' was specifically constructed at Inverness in 1908, primarily to rectify this matter.

The Duke of Sutherland saloon purchased by the Cambrian was given the number 1, but little is known of its Welsh duties. The Cambrian Registers record the cost as £550, indicating that it was in good order when purchased. As it was more modern than the older Londonderry vehicle, it may

well have been hired out occasionally to that family and perhaps also served during the early years as an unofficial director's saloon (the Cambrian had none). Otherwise, it is difficult to understand why it was purchased, as no account has been discovered detailing its use in Wales. At the grouping, it was allotted saloon No. 9215 by the Great Western but it would appear to have lost most of its prestige by that time and a few short years later (1925) it suffered a final indignity of conversion to a 4-wheel Fruit and Parcels Van (No. 1211); it was withdrawn in 1931.

Two interesting 6-wheel observation carriages constructed by Messrs Ashbury in 1894 and used extensively down the coast, were retained by the

Former Cambrian tea car No. 334 as GW No. 6334 brings up the rear of a Barmouth-Machynlleth train *c.* 1932. It was not withdrawn until 1946.
J. P. Richards

Two views of one of the small teapots distributed on trays from the small end-kitchen in the tea cars.

Private collection: GBJ photograph

Beautifully restored Cambrian composite carriage No. 238 on a low-loader at the Welsh Industrial & Maritime Museum, Cardiff before transportation to Nantgarw for storage. 28 August 1998.   *Dr E. S. Owen-Jones*

new owners and gave further valuable service until withdrawn in 1936, whilst a few of the older 4-wheel carriages served for a decade or so as mess or sleeping vehicles in breakdown or repair trains.

Most of the bogie stock survived to serve the GW well and no fewer than seventeen standard-gauge examples were handed over to British Railways in 1948. The last to be withdrawn from passenger service, on 27 February 1954, were GW No. 6327 (Cam. No. 306), a composite corridor coach of 1905 and No. 4135 (Cam. No. 314), a brake third of 1907. Amongst the more interesting Cambrian vehicles transferred to the GW were Cambrian Nos. 324-5 and 333-4 (GW Nos. 6331-2 and 6333-4, respectively). These were composite carriages in which the guard's compartment was converted into a small kitchen from which two girl attendants dispensed teas on trays. The coaches were then classified as tea cars – the nearest the Cambrian ever came to a specialist refreshment vehicle although they cannot be regarded as dining cars. The tea cars worked most frequently between Whitchurch and Aberystwyth, on the Manchester services.[16]

The only standard gauge Cambrian bogie carriage now in existence (Cambrian No. 238, GW No. 6277) survived as a result of the foresight and tenacity of the late Selwyn Higgins, of Liverpool, who purchased it from BR in 1969. After periods in store at various sites, restoration was carried out by the staff of the Welsh Industrial & Maritime Museum in Cardiff, the last major project undertaken by the museum in Cardiff Bay. The carriage was unveiled to the public on 4 October 1997.[17]

Erecting a rail-ramp for unloading. *GBJ*

No. 238 inches its way to its new accommodation. 28 August 1998. *GBJ*

Notes

[1] Dates of authorisation by parliament.

[2] Higgon Coll.

[3] Christiansen, R. & Miller, R. W.: *Cambrian Railways*, Vol. II, David & Charles (1967), p. 59.

[4] PRO RAIL 87/120 (1912).

[5] Simmons, Jack & Biddle, Gordon (eds): *The Oxford Companion to British Railway History*, Oxford University Press (1997), p. 197.

[6] PRO RAIL 92/96 p. 483.

[7] PRO RAIL 92/96 p. 619.

[8] PRO RAIL 92/96 p. 88.

[9] The GW suffered its own demoralising blow with the Friog accident on 4 March 1933, see pp. 99-101.

[10] In the Llanidloes column of the *Shropshire & Montgomeryshire Times* of Tuesday, 18 April 1865.

[11] Another non-stop run over this sector took place, in the opposite direction, in 1911, when two Cambrian 4-4-0s worked the 321 ton, 10 coach Royal Train between Machynlleth and Whitchurch in the creditable time of 2 hrs 10 mins (though with the assistance of a third engine to Talerddig).

[12] This broad sketch of Cambrian motive power in 1922 is not intended as an exhaustive survey of engines handed over at the grouping. Narrow-gauge engines, for example, are omitted but a detailed history of Cambrian engines, from 1922 until their final withdrawal, is in course of preparation.

[13] IAH Notes.

[14] Detailed in RCTS Part 10, pp. K78-80.

[15] Described in Briwnant Jones, G.: *Railway Through Talerddig*, Gomer Press (1990), p. 130.

[16] No. 324, although wrecked in the Abermule disaster of 1921, was not officially withdrawn until October 1925.

[17] Now in store at Nantgarw, Cardiff.

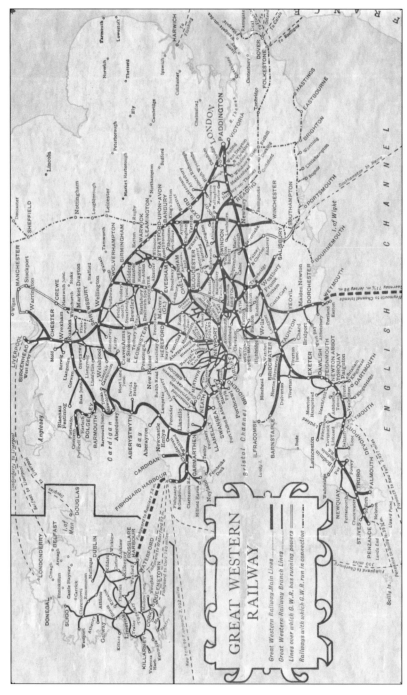

This would not have been the map published with a 1929 pocket timetable had the Great Western's initial response to a government appeal to create as much work as possible (to alleviate unemployment) been positive. Amongst proposals for central Wales were the construction of new routes from New Radnor to Trawscoed, Bishop's Castle to Montgomery and extension from Pwllheli to Morfa Nefyn (the Porth Dinllaen of Brunel's scheme of 1839).

IAH Coll.

26

Chapter 2

Paddington takes over, 1922-30

The waves of optimism which swept the country after the signing of the Armistice in 1918 were dispelled within a few brief years, as dreams and aspirations were quickly replaced by the realities of depression and contraction. Ambitious railway schemes had to be contained as a major new problem, in the form of serious competition from road transport, was encountered for the first time.

The war had accelerated the development of the internal combustion engine and its increased efficiency and reliability provided road competitors with a cheap and flexible source of power. Furthermore, the end of the conflict saw hundreds of cheaply priced army vehicles readily available for any who wished to buy them. Many of those trained to drive them during the war saw their opportunity and some vehicles were used directly, in ex-army condition, whilst others were stripped down to the basic chassis to receive new van or bus bodies. Their operation was completely unregulated for the first decade after the war as there was no compulsion to register nor licence commercial vehicles until 1929-30. Nor were the new hauliers obliged to transport all classes of goods, as were the railways. They could reject items which were heavy, hazardous or less remunerative and were free to concentrate on the more lucrative traffic; they increasingly helped themselves to the cream, leaving the residue for the railways.

Since the pioneering days, parliament had decreed that the monopoly of the railways should be controlled, and charges were rigidly fixed as a safeguard for traders. Since then, the railways had competed for traffic only amongst themselves and all had to abide by the same set of rules. Now they faced competition from outside the industry –

competition which was regarded as unfair as it was not bound by controls nor regulations. It could be argued that the railways have been fighting a rearguard action ever since; only rarely have they displayed any prolonged initiative or marketing energy.

The Great Western Railway was fortunate to emerge from the 1922 grouping comparatively unscathed. Indeed, not only did it avoid confrontation with another major company (or companies), it was actually strengthened by the whole process when it acquired, overnight, the vast dock and rail complexes of industrial south Wales. The few English companies which were simultaneously drawn into the GW net were relatively less important than the Taff Vale, the Rhymney and the Barry. These, together with smaller but only slightly less remunerative Welsh companies, such as the Rhondda & Swansea Bay, the Port Talbot Railway or the Alexandra (Newport

A 1924 cartoon reflects the GWR's pleasure with its latest acquisitions; the 'nurse' was Sir Felix Pole, General Manager, 1921-29.

WIMM/GW Coll.

& South Wales) Docks & Railway, served only to strengthen the GWR.

Initial changes concerned the rationalisation of some of the routes and services in south Wales. Many of the chief officers of the Welsh companies were integrated smoothly with the larger company (and were often promoted). They made valuable contributions to the new company and minimised the possibility of internal conflict, as beset the LMS, for example. The name of the Great Western did not change at all; only the creation of two new area divisions – the Cardiff Valleys Division and the Central Wales Division – indicate that anything untoward had occurred.

The Central Wales Division, 1922-30

A more obvious designation, the Cambrian Division, was apparently disregarded by the Great Western – probably a conscious attempt to stifle old Cambrian loyalties; the Central Wales Division (CWD) title was adopted instead. Over the years, this caused some confusion with that of the LNWR/LMS line from Craven Arms to south-west Wales, when the LMS chose to perpetuate the title of one of the original sectors of that line, the Central Wales Railway. More recently, new titles have helped to clarify the identity of both railways; British Rail used 'Rheilffordd y Cambrian' on its brochure/timetable for the winter of 1989-90 (without the English equivalent), whilst Central Trains, holder of the present franchise for the former Cambrian line, was happy to adopt Regional Railways 'The Cambrian Coaster' on its brochure for the winter of 1997. What remains of the former LMS route has been effectively marketed in recent years as the 'Heart of Wales' line.

The Great Western's aims were clear; the Central Wales Division had to be brought up to standard. But before larger and more powerful locomotives could be introduced, bridges and track had first to be renewed and the creation of longer sections of double line – long a dream of the old

company – was also still considered feasible. The economic constraints faced by the Cambrian had ensured that little had been achieved in this respect. Only the sections between Buttington and Welshpool (1863), Oswestry and Llanymynech (1900), and Newtown and Moat Lane (1912) had been doubled by the time of the grouping.

The new owners were thus happy to continue the scheme revived by the Cambrian after the First World War, the doubling of the Welshpool-Newtown sector. The stretch to Forden represented the first stage and although the old company had failed to complete this by the grouping, they were proud to have constructed a fine double-track bridge across the Severn at Cilcewydd. Further progress, however, continued to be slow, even under the GWR, and although the Forden section was duly completed, it was not commissioned until 1925.

Priorities had obviously been affected by the Abermule disaster. Prevention of a recurrence was of paramount importance. Although double track was seen as the obvious solution, it was considered too expensive and the more immediate recommendation of the Board of Trade Inquiry, the standardising and upgrading of telegraph and staff exchange apparatus, was given top priority. At many Cambrian stations these instruments were frequently divided between signal-box, telegraph-office or booking-office. The Cambrian had already started to carry out the recommendations of the Board of Trade, and the policy was actively pursued by the GWR. By January 1925, Fenns Bank, Llanbrynmair, Glandyfi, Bow Street, Tylwch, Pantydwr, Llansantffraid, Doldowlod, Newbridge-on-Wye, Llwyngwril, Dyffryn-on-sea, Llanbedr & Pensarn and Harlech had electric tablet or token instruments located within the signal-box but Carno, Cemmes Road and Bettisfield still awaited attention. The construction of a 'new' signal-box at Carno started in May 1927 and although the shell of the box (originally at Newton Abbot) was quickly erected, the work

These views of Llanaber Halt, taken expressly for the GW Engineer, amply demonstrate the vulnerability of many sections of line along the coast where Cambrian, GW and later BR engineers spent much time, money and effort strengthening the various sea defences. 7 April 1924. *WIMM/GW Coll.*

Harlech in 1925, by which time all token instruments were located within the signal-box. *Mowat Coll.*

Cemmes Road station. The presence of the little two-tone Dutton signal cabin half way along the 'up' platform helps to date this view as pre-1936, as the GW then erected a conventional signal-box virtually on the site occupied by the anonymous photographer of this view. *GBJ Coll.*

made no further progress until the summer timetable had ceased. Even then, the box could not be commissioned until relaying alterations were completed. The instruments were finally transferred into the new box and duly commissioned on Sunday, 4 March 1928.[1] The GW Board's intention to complete the doubling of the line between Buttington and Moat Lane junctions is supported by the allocation of £388,639 for improvements in the Central Wales Division during 1922-23; of this sum, £288,000 was for the purchase of land. In 1923, the board approved a recommendation that £52,200 be spent on station alterations and doubling of the line between Machynlleth and Dovey Junction. A scheme to widen this section was first presented to the Cambrian Board as far back as 1871 when George Owen, then the engineer, estimated the cost as £8,000.[2] Here, under the GW scheme, additional rails forming a new 'down' line would

have been laid south of the existing track, which would then have become the 'up' line. Older railwaymen at Machynlleth claimed that some materials were actually brought on site, but no evidence has been discovered to support this contention. Instead, the records show that delays occurred and that work was suspended 'awaiting approval of amended plan'. The scheme stagnated until November 1927, when it was officially 'deferred'.[3]

Some modifications of track and signalling at Dovey Junction were carried out in 1927 and Machynlleth, similarly, saw modest track improvements and improved freight facilities, which included provision of a 20T cart weighbridge (completed between June and November 1928) and a new 6T steel crane, installed in the lower yard by April 1931. But the opportunity for doubling the line had passed, never to return.

The dining-room built above the booking-office at Aberystwyth's new station, in 1925. It was not a commercial success and the area was later converted into the town's telephone exchange. 5 January 1926.
WIMM/GW Coll.

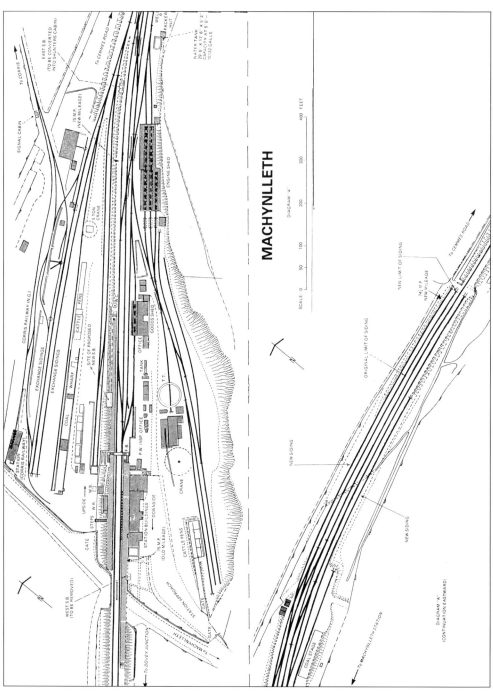

MACHYNLLETH

Chris Potts

The GWR's plan (c. 1923) on which R. H. Clark based this drawing contained several anachronisms, particularly the cross-over in the lower yard and the narrow gauge track layout, which reflects the situation before 1905 (See *Great Western Corris* pp. 16 & 34).

Nonetheless, the improved access between shed and running lines, the sidings proposals at the east end, and the projected location of the central signal-box, are all interesting.

The frailty of post-war optimism is well illustrated by expenditure forecasts which reflect the increasing economic difficulties facing the country as the decade advanced. The rising tide of labour unrest during the mid 1920s culminated with the economic crash of 1929 which affected projects other than railway plans for mid Wales. The recurring pattern of reduction of actual expenditure below forecast and the gradual overall decline in forecast expectation is illuminating, but this was common to the whole network and many a business outside the railway; the malaise was certainly not confined to the Central Wales Division. Capital expenditure for 1924 was forecast at £250,000 (a sum which probably included the Machynlleth-Dovey Junction doubling) but the actual expenditure was only £97,860, spent mainly on track and station improvements at Barmouth, Oswestry, Welshpool and Aberystwyth, where dramatic improvements took place. Here, additional sidings were provided for carriage cleaning and the station was virtually rebuilt. Platforms were extended, paved and provided with new verandahs, whilst a glazed roof was erected to protect a spacious circulating area. The station elevation facing the town was clad in Portland stone and boasted twin entrances and an impressive clock tower. A restaurant was located on the first floor, above the new booking-office and a refreshment bar (opened on 15 June 1925) was provided on the ground floor. All improvements were duly completed in time for that year's summer service, which commenced in July.

The GW photographer was busy in the area for many years, producing material for use by the publicity department. These views are typical examples; they depict Aberystwyth, in 1928 and Penhelig/Aberdyfi, the same year.

WIMM/GW Coll.

By 1925, the expenditure forecast appeared as a more modest £105,000 with actual expenditure much lower – just £40,123 – a graphic example of tightening the economic belt. Elsewhere in the Division, a new goods shed had been completed at Barmouth by the end of January 1925. This allowed the demolition of the old shed and subsequent extension of the 'up' platform; the work was completed by May that year.

The forecast for 1926 anticipated a further drop in expenditure to £58,000 but again the actual figure was markedly less, a mere £11,068. Yet, despite this, new cattle pens were constructed at Barmouth and a scheme was instigated for improvements at Pwllheli, when double track was laid from a point near the goods shed into the station. A new signal-box was built here but improvements planned for the locomotive department were suspended, pending purchase of land. At Newtown, signalling improvements and track relaying were completed by April 1926.

By 1927, capital expenditure forecast was further reduced to £29,005; in the event, actual expenditure was nil. Nil was forecast for 1928 yet, somehow, by the following year cash had started to flow slowly again – particularly where any investment was likely to create new traffic. Even the little Mawddwy branch benefitted from this policy, when a new private siding was constructed for Mr H. Wright to serve his silica mine at Nantcyff, near Aberangell. Earthworks were prepared by May and the siding was completed by 26 June 1929. The mine was not an enduring success, however, for it operated only until May 1935; the facility was withdrawn in 1937.[4] Further examples of the Great Western's adroit planning are provided by its ability to redeploy equipment made redundant on other parts of the system. When facilities were improved at larger stations, displaced equipment was frequently given a new lease of life in a rural location. Thus, in 1931, cart weighbridges from Birmingham Moor Street were relocated at Llanbrynmair (20T) and Llandinam (16T) and a further 20T example from Swan Village performed useful service at Llandre until freight facilities were withdrawn.

Little Girl (entering carriage with her mother and being glowered at by the occupants):
*'Mummy – next stop it'll be **our** turn to hate.'*

G. L. Stampa's charming original drawing for *Punch* magazine in 1924 portrayed a situation familiar to contemporary readers, that of 'defending' their compartment from 'intruders' who, in those days, had direct access from the platform.
Private collection

PASSENGER SERVICES

If improvements to rolling stock and infrastructure required time, changes to the passenger timetable could be tackled speedily, and the GWR gave this immediate attention. In order to maximise on the number of through carriages to and from Paddington, the basic timetable for the 1922 summer service – nominally five 'up' and five 'down' trains – was augmented by a few interesting additions. Perhaps the most fascinating at this time was not a London service but a 9.05 a.m. Birkenhead (Woodside) to Aberystwyth express which ran via Chester and Wrexham and, surprisingly, included a breakfast and luncheon car.

At Oswestry, a connection was made with a Manchester service (via Crewe and Whitchurch) and at Welshpool it combined with a long-established express from Birmingham (Snow Hill) and Wolverhampton (Low Level). This avoided Shrewsbury and ran direct to Welshpool via the Abbey Foregate Loop. Departure from Welshpool was at 11.25 a.m. and stops were made at Newtown, Moat Lane, Machynlleth, Dovey Junction and Borth, with arrival at Aberystwyth at 1.40 p.m. There was a connection from Dovey Junction for stations to Pwllheli. This is believed to be the only instance of a regular, advertised restaurant car service over the Cambrian which was not London-related. The

'Duke' No. 3271 *Eddystone* was declared 'a pleasure to behold' when it first visited the coast line in 1923. This photograph shows that its condition had hardly changed in three years, as it was recorded at Welshpool with the 9.58 a.m. Whitchurch to Aberystwyth service, on 6 April 1926.

LCGB/Ken Nunn Coll.

The 7.35 p.m. train from Aberystwyth to Machynlleth approaching Chapel Crossing, Borth, on 26 July 1924. The leading engine, Cambrian 4-4-0 No. 71 as GW No. 1104, survived little more than a year after this photograph was taken; Dean 'Goods' 0-6-0 No. 2449, however, lasted until January 1953.

H. A. White, courtesy R. W. Kidner

corresponding 'up' service left Aberystwyth at 10.15 a.m., arriving at Woodside at 2.36 p.m., and a timetable note for this service advises 'Luncheon Car Aberystwyth to Birkenhead. Through Carriages Aberystwyth and Towyn to Paddington'. The train proved successful and the service continued, with modifications, up to 1939 but from 1923 the dining car was diverted from the 'down' Aberystwyth portion at Gobowen, continuing instead to Paddington with a London portion.

Cambrian No. 73, as GW No. 875, approaches Aberystwyth with a train of mixed Cambrian and GW stock, the roof boards on the latter indicating they were through carriage workings. The four narrow gauge wagons on the right stand at the transhipment siding. c. 1929. *NLW/A. J. Lewis Coll.*

An unidentified 'Barnum' 2-4-0 leaves Barmouth with a train of GW stock, *c.* 1923. *J. P. Richards*

A second service to boast a dining car in 1922 was a Paddington-Aberystwyth through train which commenced on Friday, 14 July 1922. The roots of this service can be traced back to the earliest days of the Cambrian when excursion trains were run enabling city dwellers to enjoy the seaside, or country folk to sample life in the metropolis. In those days an excursion could take all day; the following account appeared in a local paper in August 1869:

> Day excursion to London . . . We beg to call attention to this, the latest marvel of the excursion world. It may at first sight appear a long and tedious journey, but in reality is not so when we consider the very convenient arrangements which are made. Most excursion trains from the neighbourhood occupy a day in passing the journey to London, the train having to stop at nearly every station along the line; but the arrangements in this case are such that the journey will only occupy six hours and no passengers will be taken after Shrewsbury. This has been agreed upon at the suggestion of the LNWR.[5]

Departure from Newtown (for example) was at 2.20 a.m. with arrival at Euston at 9.00 a.m. Excursionists were at liberty in the capital for no fewer than 15 hours, before returning at midnight; the fare was 14/- return in a covered carriage, with 28/- return, first class. Admittedly, the advertised times extend our credulity; six hours and forty minutes (if achieved) would have been a very creditable performance in 1869 but it would be rather surprising if the train could keep time. A century later, London trains reached Newtown in four hours and twenty-five minutes.

Over the years, a succession of excursion and seasonal trains plied between the Cambrian coast and the capital, and there was a constant service of through carriages to and from both Euston and Paddington. During the period preceding the First World War, there was a choice of two, sometimes three, through services daily during the summer period. These did not carry restaurant cars nor were they titled trains, although they were termed London Express in the Cambrian's public timetable and, confusingly, South Express in its Working Timebook. Those emanating from Manchester or Liverpool, via Crewe and Whitchurch, were known as the North Express.

The 1922 Luncheon and Tea Car train which ran that summer from the capital to the coast operated between 14 July and 16 September, and departed Paddington at 10.15 a.m. each weekday. It ran non-stop between Wolverhampton and Welshpool and arrived at Aberystwyth at 4.20 p.m. A second through service left Paddington daily at 10.40 a.m. (arr. Aberystwyth 5.00 p.m.) but this

A 1920s poster publicising Aberystwyth. *WIMM/GW Coll.*

Just arrived at

BARMOUTH

It's
FIRST CLASS
here

A picture postcard attempts to do the same for
Barmouth.   *GBJ Coll.*

train called at Shrewsbury, where it reversed
direction and the dining car was detached.

The return dining car service from the coast left
Aberystwyth at 12.00 noon and also ran non-stop
between Welshpool and Wolverhampton. There
does not appear to have been a second daily
through service in the 'up' direction, but a
Saturdays Only service left Aberystwyth at 2.30
p.m. An 'up' express destined for Leamington Spa
was also a Saturdays Only train; it left Aberystwyth
at 11.00 a.m. and connected with a service from

Towyn and Aberdovey. It appears that a better
service was provided for passengers anxious to
reach the coast than for those who needed to return
to work when their holiday had ended.

The 1923 timetable revealed an increase in the
number of through carriages and trains. The
services from Paddington, Birkenhead and
Birmingham were augmented by additional
through coaches from Manchester (London Road)
and Liverpool (Lime Street) and there were
frequent combinations of destinations within a
single train. For example, the 9.50 a.m. 'up' train
from Aberystwyth carried through coaches for
Birkenhead and Paddington and the 1.00 p.m. 'up'
train carried through coaches for Birkenhead,
Paddington and Manchester (London Road). From
the summer of 1923 the 'down' mail trains ran in
two separate (and advertised) portions from
Welshpool each weekday morning. The first to
leave Welshpool was the Shrewsbury portion (4.15
a.m.), followed at 4.24 a.m. by the north mail,
which had arrived via Whitchurch and Oswestry.
During the first years of this innovation, the
Shrewsbury mail stopped only at Newtown, Moat
Lane, Machynlleth and Borth, whereas the
Oswestry mail stopped additionally at
Montgomery, Caersws, Carno, Llanbrynmair,
Cemmes Road, Glandyfi, Llandre and Bow Street.
Sometime during 1933-35, the Shrewsbury mail
acquired the same stops as the Oswestry train. Each
winter, the service reverted to the original pattern
of a combined train from Welshpool; the format
was maintained until the outbreak of war.
Nonetheless, there were variations on this theme at
Christmas time, when the summer arrangements
applied. The expedient of running separate portions
west of Welshpool occurred with other services
also, particularly during the summer and the
practice was perpetuated occasionally during the
post-war period, although it was not advertised.

The most notable development in 1923,
however, was the appearance for the first time, of
the Cambrian Coast Express (CCE) title. Hailed as

a Luncheon, Tea and Dining Car Train, it left Paddington at 10.20 a.m. and arrived at Aberystwyth at 4.15 p.m. Again, Shrewsbury was omitted in both directions. The 'up' train left Aberystwyth at noon, stopped at Borth and picked up through coaches from Pwllheli at Dovey Junction. Thereafter, it stopped at Moat Lane and

Welshpool, arriving at Wolverhampton (LL) at 3.46 p.m., Birmingham at 4.15 p.m. and Paddington at 6.40 p.m. By 1924, departure from Paddington was established at 10.10 a.m. Wolverhampton was left at 12.55 p.m. and Moat Lane, the next stop, was reached by 2.38 p.m. A Machynlleth stop was omitted in favour of Dovey Junction, where the

The earliest known image of the Cambrian Coast Express, 'somewhere in England', drawn by 'Castle' class No. 4080 *Powderham Castle*. The dining car, seemingly a 70ft 'Dreadnought' vehicle, lies fourth behind the tender. The locomotive displayd no headboard but carriage roof-boards were well in evidence. 18 July 1929.
WIMM/GW Coll.

This well-known photograph by A. J. Lewis reflects the busy ambience of Aberystwyth in the late 1920s better than most and is happily used again. 'Duke' No 3277 *Isle of Tresco* pilots an unidentified Cambrian 0-6-0 on an 'up' express from Aberystwyth *c.* 1928-30. A second 'Duke' heads what may well have been a second portion of the same service.
NLW/A. J. Lewis

With the empty stock of the 10.10 a.m. ex-Paddington being drawn away by the station pilot—just discernable in the *r/h* distance – 'Duke' No. 3263 *St. Michael* is released from the main arrival platform. The roof-board of the Cambrian carriage (*extreme l.*) reads [Manchester London] Road, Oswestry, Welshpool and Aberystwyth. 22 August 1925.   *Ifor A. Higgon*

train was divided for the coast. The 'up' train now left Aberystwyth at 11.00 a.m., again omitted the Machynlleth stop, running through from Dovey Junction to Welshpool. Shrewsbury also was omitted; Wolverhampton was reached by 3.20 p.m. and Paddington by 6.00 p.m.

The arrangements during 1925 were generally similar but the service was disrupted the following year due to the general strike. The loss of the CCE title was a comparatively minor matter; it was not restored until 1927.

In addition to the foregoing, a considerable number of special and relief trains were run which featured in no public list, for it suited the operators to advertise a minimal train service and should greater numbers turn up for transportation at any given time, the railways saw to it that they were not turned away. Extra carriages were found to strengthen existing train sets and, where the need was even greater, additional trains were run. That these peak periods were confined in the main to weekends during summer months obviously

A fine trio of 'company's servants' – as railwaymen were generally regarded in the past: how regrettable that their names went unrecorded. Distant roof lines suggest the photograph may be of a Carmarthen-bound train at Aberystwyth, *c.* 1920-30.   *NLW/A. J. Lewis*

created problems but, generally, these were predictable and the railways took great pride in dealing with all contingencies. As far as the CWD was concerned, this caused intensive use of the system. It is regretted that no official account of a typical Saturday's operations on the Cambrian has survived – if, indeed, such a report was ever compiled – but some inkling of the effort involved during the 1920s may be gleaned from the few copied pages of a Weekly Notice (Saturday, 11 August to Friday, 17 August 1928). (Tables III(a) and III(b)).

SATURDAY, AUGUST 11th.

Carnival and Fete at Crewe.

Cheap Tickets, single fare for the double journey, may be issued to Crewe by any train between 10.0 a.m. and 3.0 p.m. from stations within a rail distance of 60 miles, available for return by any train after 3.0 p.m. the same day.

Criccieth Carnival.

Season Cheap Day Tickets will apply.

Period Excursion—Denton, Stockport, etc., to Aberystwyth, etc.

		a.m. arr.		dep.
Whitchurch	...	8 30		8 40
Bettisfield	...	8 54	X	8 57
Oswestry	...		9 20	
Welshpool	...		9 45	
Abermule	...		10 X 3	
Moat Lane	...	10 17	OW X	10 20
Cemmes Road	...	10 54	C X S	10 56
Machynlleth	...	11 4	X	11 16
Dovey Jct.	...	11 23		11 26
Glandyfi	...	11 28	C X S	11 35
Borth	...	11 47	X	11 49
Llanbadarn	...		X	
Aberystwyth	...	12 6		

		a.m.
Oswestry ... dep.	7‖ 0
Whitchurch ... arr.	7‖40

Passengers for Ellesmere, Oswestry, Llanymynech, Welshpool, Newtown, Llanidloes, Rhayader and Builth Wells change at Whitchurch and proceed by 9.58 a.m. ordinary train.

Passengers return Saturday, August 18th, by Through Special leaving Aberystwyth at 7.25 a.m.

Coast passengers proceed from Dovey Junction by first Ordinary Train.

Return Cadbury's Period Excursion to Bournville.

		a.m. arr.		dep.
Aberystwyth	...			8 25
Borth	...			8 45
Ynyslas	...	8 50	X	8 53
Dovey Jct.	...	9 5		9 12
Machynlleth	...	9 19	OW	9 23
Talerddig	...		9 56	
Carno	...	10 0	C X S	10 7
Moat Lane	...		10 X 20	
Newtown	...		10 28	
Welshpool	...	10 55		

Formation: 4 Thirds and Brake Third, Lavatory Stock.

To be worked with L. M. and S. stock of 3.7 a.m. Period Excursion, Whitchurch to Aberystwyth, the Coaches to be swept out on arrival at Aberystwyth.

Barmouth Portion.

		a.m. arr.		dep.
Barmouth	...			8 10
Barmouth Jct.	...	8 15		
Fairbourne	...		CR	8 18
Llwyngwril	...			8 28
Towyn	...	8 40		8 42
Aberdovey	...	8 50	X	8 54
Dovey Jct.	...	9 7		

Three Thirds and Brake Third, Lavatory Stock, to work through to Bournville attached to 8.25 a.m. ex Aberystwyth at Dovey Junction.

Table III(a).

SATURDAY, AUGUST 11th.—Continued.

Use of Telegraph and Telephones.

Commencing at once, and until the end of September next, no Telegram respecting General Matters must be despatched on Saturday, as it is essential that the Telegraph Lines should be free for Train Working and other important messages.

Relief Arrangements.

9.10 a.m. Birmingham to Aberystwyth.
Divided. Birmingham Engines and Guards to work through. Each train to make booked stops.

9.58 a.m. Whitchurch to Aberystwyth.
To run fast to Oswestry; attach Birkenhead portion, if this can be done to leave Oswestry at 10.53 a.m., and run thence to Aberystwyth in booked times.
Locomotive Department to provide Engine to be at the Passenger Station not later than 10.35 a.m. to work the Birkenhead portion separately.
A second portion to follow from Whitchurch, calling at all stations to Oswestry, thence taking up working of 11.0 a.m. Oswestry to Aberystwyth. Engine and Guard to leave Oswestry at 8.0 a.m. for Whitchurch. To be formed of Coaches of 6.0 p.m. Up Mail.

1.52 p.m. Whitchurch to Aberystwyth.
The Whitchurch portion of this train will be continued through to Aberystwyth independently of the 2.27 p.m. Shrewsbury if required.

12.55 p.m. Aberystwyth to Whitchurch.
To be double head Aberystwyth to Dovey Junction. The train to be divided from Dovey Junction to Welshpool, the Train Engine to work first part (South).
Formation: Van Third X, Compo X, Aberystwyth to Salop; Brake Compo X, Third X, Van Third X, Paddington; 2 Thirds X, Birmingham; (to form first part from Dovey Junction) Brake Compo X; Third X, Crewe; Two Thirds X, Compo, Van Third, Manchester; Third, Brake Compo, Birkenhead.
First part to attach in rear at Dovey Junction. Third X, Compo X, Van Third X, Pwllheli to Birmingham.
Second part to attach in front at Dovey Junction. Third Compo, Van Third, Pwllheli to Crewe.
A Relief to leave Welshpool at 3.18 p.m. for Whitchurch, making the booked stops. Formed Brake Third, Third, Compo, Brake Third. **This train to leave Welshpool to time.**

1.10 p.m. Oswestry to Gobowen.
If 10.15 a.m. Aberystwyth is running late and the 1.10 p.m. cannot leave Oswestry before 1.30 p.m. it will be extended from Gobowen to Chester. Loco. Dept. and Inspector Evans to be prepared.

2.25 p.m. Aberystwyth to Birmingham. Divided R.R. First portion to leave at 2.15 p.m. Worked by Engine, Guard and Coaches of first portion 9.10 a.m. ex Birmingham. Second portion at booked times.

10.25 a.m. Pwllheli to Dovey Junction. To be divided Barmouth to Dovey Junction.
First portion. Ordinary train set from Pwllheli, to leave Barmouth at 12.0 noon, stopping to pick up only and connecting at Dovey Junction with 12.20 p.m. from Aberystwyth.
Second portion to leave Barmouth at 12.20 p.m.
To be formed Third X, Compo X, Van Third X, for Birmingham; Third, Compo, Van Third for Crewe.

9.41 a.m. Ruabon to Barmouth. Divided. Engine and Coaches to return working first part of 2.35 p.m. Barmouth to Ruabon.

1.30 p.m. Ruabon to Pwllheli. Divided to Barmouth or Pwllheli as required.

3.5 p.m. Ruabon to Pwllheli R.R. Divided. London and Birkenhead portions to work through to Pwllheli separately. Coaches to be retained for the 11.30 a.m. and 12.15 p.m. Camping Specials ex Portmadoc and Barmouth, Sunday.

1.15 p.m. Barmouth to Ruabon (11.55 a.m. Pwllheli).
Divided from Barmouth to Ruabon.
First portion to leave at 1.5 p.m., formed of Van Third, Compo, Paddington 2 Thirds X, Barmouth to Birmingham, with 10th Birmingham Boy Scouts: Compo. Van Third, Ruabon.
Second portion as booked.

2.35 p.m. Barmouth to Ruabon. Divided. First part for Birmingham. Formed of Coaches working first part of 9.41 a.m. ex Ruabon, with one extra Third for Scouts. Arthog to Birmingham. Second part, ordinary train Coaches and two extra Thirds for Birkenhead.

Table III(b).

42

The Mondays and Saturdays Only through Treherbert-Aberystwyth trains via Moat Lane continued to be popular. During the 1920s there was, in fact, a second service between Treherbert and Aberystwyth, which commenced at the old Rhymney station at Cardiff (Parade) and travelled via Caerffili and Pontypridd to Treherbert. This would have left Treherbert in the opposite direction to the Moat Lane service, and used the Rhondda & Swansea Bay line through Blaenrhondda tunnel to gain the GW main line for Carmarthen and Aberystwyth. Passengers were not alone in finding central Wales attractive. Many footplate men from south Wales and elsewhere on the GW system – who had passed as drivers but found no vacancy in their home depot – applied as drivers in central Wales, initially for the summer period only; some chose to settle in the area.

Of the Welsh institutions which would have provided additional traffic for the railways in former years, mention must be made of the Royal Welsh Agricultural Show, the Royal National Eisteddfod of Wales and the annual eisteddfod of Urdd Gobaith Cymru, the Welsh League of Youth. These normally alternated between north and south Wales venues and, as each attracted thousands of visitors and lasted between 3 and 6 days, they earned a great deal of revenue for the railways. The Royal National Eisteddfod of Wales, for example, was held at Pwllheli between 3 and 8 August 1925. A booklet of special railway arrangements runs to 52 pages and lists, amongst other details, Presidents of the Day who included the Rt. Hon. Stanley Baldwin MP, Sir Alfred Mond MP, the Rt. Hon. David Lloyd George MP, and the Rt. Hon. J. H. Thomas MP, the one time general secretary

Two former Cambrian engines, as GW Nos. 1035 and 887 (facing camera) backing to the shed at Aberystwyth after their train (1.14 p.m. from Whitchurch) had been removed by the station pilot. That day, No. 887 banked several trains between Aberystwyth and Borth, in both directions; for return trips it was always 'inside', resulting in this tender-to-tender formation—a practice which endured to the end of steam. See photograph p. 164. 22 August 1925.

Ifor A. Higgon

Former Cambrian No. 97, as GW 1035, heads the 12.20 p.m. Aberystwyth-Moat Lane train, with through coaches for Merthyr and Treherbert. Compare the leading coach with that in the photograph on p. 18. 30 July 1927.

Ifor A. Higgon

of the NUR, later destined to play a key role in the following year's industrial conflict. Each day's programme attracted between eight and fifteen special trains, from as far afield as Blaenafon, Blaengarw, Fishguard, Swansea and Cardiff in south Wales, to Holyhead, Rhyl and Wrexham in north Wales. Perhaps the most surprising of all were two LMS excursions which arrived via Afon Wen, one from Blackburn on Tuesday, 4 August, with another the following day from Huddersfield. Normal freight arrangements were suspended for the week and replaced, in part, by special night-time operations. Even the stabling of the special trains at Pwllheli called for the goods yard there to 'be cleared on the night of Saturday 1 August, of all wagons except those which can be stabled on the Warehouse Road'. The week's arrangements were complex; Pwllheli will never see their like again. (Tables IV(a), IV(b) and V).

The Notice of Special Arrangements referred to above was issued privately by the Great Western and printed, in this instance by W.M.T. & Co., Ltd., Oswestry, a company which produced a great

many of the CWD special/weekly notices at this time. These were the only means by which staff could acquire details of operation and timings of additional trains not found in regular timetables. As such, each booklet was usually valid for one week only and consequently was either thrown out or destroyed at the end of that period to avoid possible confusion with the latest issue. The few survivors provide intriguing glimpses of the additional traffic catered for by the railways. Day, half-day and evening excursions featured frequently, as did many special trains for troops, scouts and guides, Sunday schools, Shrewsbury Fete, or agricultural events of all kinds.

An interesting example is provided by the fragment of Notice No. CW 22 which details a day excursion on Monday, 13 August 1928, from Tylwch, Llanidloes and Llandinam to Aberystwyth. (Table VI). The station at Tylwch still stands in its attractive location and is clearly seen by any motorist who takes the narrow, winding road from Rhayader to Llanidloes. Some, having knowledge of that Extra Trains Notice, are

Time Table of Trains leaving Pwllheli Station.
MONDAY, AUGUST 3rd.

Time of Departure.	Platform Number.	Stations.
6 5 a.m.	1	All Stations to Aberystwyth.
6 45 a.m.	1	Afon Wen and L.M. & S. Line.
7 30 a.m.	1	Afon Wen and L.M. & S. Line.
7 55 a.m.	1	All Stations to Dovey Junction, with connections to Machynlleth and Aberystwyth.
8 50 a.m.	1	Barmouth, Chester, Birkenhead, Manchester, Shrewsbury, Wolverhampton, Birmingham, Paddington.
9 10 a.m.	2	All Stations to Portmadoc, with connection to L.M. & S. Line via Afon Wen.
10 25 a.m.	1	All Stations to Barmouth, with connection to L.M. & S. Line via Afon Wen. Ruabon, Chester, Birkenhead, Manchester, Shrewsbury.
11 55 a.m.	1	Criccieth, Portmadoc, Minffordd, Penrhyndeudraeth, Harlech, Llanbedr and Pensarn, Barmouth, Ruabon, Chester, Birkenhead, Shrewsbury, Wolverhampton, Birmingham, Paddington.
12 10 p.m.	1	Afon Wen and L.M. & S. Line.
12 45 p.m.	1	All Stations to Dolgelley, with connections to Machynlleth and Aberystwyth.
1 30 p.m.	1	All Stations to Portmadoc, with connection to L.M. & S. Line via Afon Wen.
2 0 p.m.	1	Afon Wen and L.M. & S. Line.
3 35 p.m.	1	Afon Wen and L.M. & S. Line.
4 0 p.m.	1	All Stations to Dovey Junction, with connections to Dolgelley and Machynlleth, also to L.M. & S. Line via Afon Wen.
5 10 p.m.	1	All Stations to Ruabon (except Berwyn), and Stations between Barmouth and Machynlleth.
5 55 p.m.	1	Return Excursion to Aberystwyth, Pencader, Carmarthen, Ferryside, Kidwelly, Pembrey, Llanelly, Loughor, Gowerton, Cockett, Swansea.
6 15 p.m.	1	Return Excursion to Afon Wen, Criccieth, Portmadoc, Harlech, Dyffryn-on-Sea, Barmouth, Barmouth Junction, Fairbourne, Llwyngwril, Tonfanau, Towyn, Aberdovey, Dovey Junction, Machynlleth.
6 40 p.m.	2	All Stations to Dolgelley.
7 30 p.m.	1	Return Excursion to Colwyn Bay via Afon Wen.
8 15 p.m.	2	Afon Wen, Criccieth, Portmadoc, Talsarnau, Harlech, Llanbedr and Pensarn, Dyffryn-on-Sea, Barmouth, Barmouth Junction, Arthog, Penmaenpool, Dolgelley, Fairbourne, Llwyngwril, Tonfanau, Towyn, Aberdovey, Machynlleth.
8 30 p.m.	1	All Stations to Penrhyndeudraeth, with connection to L.M. & S. Line via Afon Wen.
9 40 p.m.	2	Return Excursion to Holyhead via Afon Wen.

Table IV(a).

MONDAY, AUGUST 3rd.—Continued.

Time of Departure.	Platform Number.	Stations.
9 45 p.m.	1	Criccieth, Portmadoc, Minffordd, Penrhyndeudraeth.
9 55 p.m.	2	Return Excursion to Rhyl via Afon Wen.
10 10 p.m.	1	Return Excursion to Bangor via Afon Wen.
10 20 p.m.	2	Talsarnau, Harlech, Llanbedr and Pensarn, Dyffryn-on-Sea, Barmouth, Barmouth Junction, Fairbourne, Llwyngwril, Tonfanau, Towyn, Aberdovey, Dovey Junction, Machynlleth.
10 25 p.m.	1	Return Excursion to Bangor via Afon Wen.
10 45 p.m.	2	Criccieth, Portmadoc, Minffordd, Penrhyndeudraeth.

TUESDAY, AUGUST 4th.

Time of Departure.	Platform Number.	Stations.
6 5 a.m.	1	All Stations to Aberystwyth.
6 45 a.m.	1	Afon Wen and L.M. & S. Line.
7 30 a.m.	1	Afon Wen and L.M. & S. Line.
7 55 a.m.	1	All Stations to Dovey Junction, with connections to Machynlleth and Aberystwyth.
8 50 a.m.	1	Barmouth, Chester, Birkenhead, Manchester, Shrewsbury, Wolverhampton, Birmingham, Paddington.
9 10 a.m.	2	All Stations to Portmadoc, with connection to L.M. & S. Line via Afon Wen.
10 25 a.m.	1	All Stations to Barmouth, with connection to L.M. & S. Line via Afon Wen. Ruabon, Chester, Birkenhead, Manchester, Shrewsbury.
11 55 a.m.	1	Criccieth, Portmadoc, Minffordd, Penrhyndeudraeth, Harlech, Llanbedr and Pensarn, Barmouth, Ruabon, Chester, Birkenhead, Shrewsbury, Wolverhampton, Birmingham, Paddington.
12 10 p.m.	1	Afon Wen and L.M. & S. Line.
12 45 p.m.	1	All Stations to Dolgelley, with connections to Machynlleth and Aberystwyth.
1 30 p.m.	1	All Stations to Portmadoc, with connection to L.M. & S. Line via Afon Wen.
2 0 p.m.	1	Afon Wen and L.M. & S. Line.
3 35 p.m.	1	Afon Wen and L.M. & S. Line.
4 0 p.m.	1	All Stations to Dovey Junction, with connections to Dolgelley and Machynlleth, also to L.M. & S. Line via Afon Wen.
5 10 p.m.	1	All Stations to Ruabon (except Berwyn), and Stations between Barmouth and Machynlleth.
6 15 p.m.	1	Return Excursion to Afon Wen, Criccieth, Portmadoc, Harlech, Dyffryn-on-Sea, Barmouth, Barmouth Junction, Fairbourne, Llwyngwril, Tonfanau, Towyn, Aberdovey, Dovey Junction, Machynlleth.

plus a further 12 services, up till 10.45 p.m.

Table IV(b).

Table V.
Stabling of trains,
Friday, 7 August 1925

Arrival Time of Ordinary and Excursion Trains at Pwllheli.		Where Stabled.	Departure time from Pwllheli.	Platform No.
... ...	... ...	No. 1 Platform ...	6 5 a.m.	1
6 35 a.m.	Ordinary ...	No. 1 Platform ...	6 45 a.m.	1
... ...	... ...	No. 1 Platform ...	7 30 a.m.	1
7 10 a.m.	Ordinary ...	No. 1 Platform ...	7 55 a.m.	1
8 35 a.m.	Excursion ex Portmadoc ...	No. 2 Siding ...	8 50 a.m.	1
8 43 a.m.	Ordinary ...	No. 2 Platform ...	9 10 a.m.	2
9 10 a.m.	Ordinary ...	No. 1 Siding ...	10 25 a.m.	1
9 32 a.m.	Excursion ex Portmadoc ...	No. 2 Siding ...	11 55 a.m.	1
9 37 a.m.	L.M.&S. Exn. ex Bangor ..	No. 1 Carriage Siding ...	10 10 p.m.	2
... ...	Retn. Period Exn. to Cardiff		9 30 p.m.	1
9 42 a.m.	L.M.&S. Exn. ex Holyhead	No. 2 Carriage Siding ...	9 40 p.m.	2
9 58 a.m.	Excursion ex Machynlleth ...	Goods Neck ...	6 15 p.m.	1
10 5 a.m.	L.M.&S. Exn. ex Rhyl ...	Cattle Siding ...	9 55 p.m.	2
10 21 a.m.	Exn. ex Wrexham ...	Passenger Neck ...	7 15 p.m.	1
10 50 a.m.	Ordinary ..	Empty Coaches to Portmadoc	11 35 a.m.	
11 16 a.m.	Ordinary ..	No. 2 Siding ...	12 45 p.m.	1
11 30 a.m.	Exn. ex Fishguard ...	Afon Wen ...	10 5 p.m.	1
12 35 p.m.	Ordinary ...	No. 2 Siding (Top End) ..	1 30 p.m.	1
1 10 p.m.	Ordinary ...	Passenger Neck ...	2 0 p.m.	1
1 29 p.m.	Relief ex Aberdovey ...	No. 2 Siding ...,	10 20 p.m.	1
2 0 p.m.	Ordinary ...	No. 1 Platform ...	4 0 p.m.	1
2 25 p.m.	L.M.&S. Exn. ex Colwyn B.	Afon Wen ...	7 30 p.m.	2
2 37 p.m.	Ordinary ...	No. 1 Platform ...	3 35 p.m.	1
2 55 p.m.	L.M.&S. Exn. ex Bangor ...	Coal Siding ...	10 25 p.m.	2
3 33 p.m.	Ordinary ...	No. 1 Siding ...	12 10 p.m. (next day).	1
3 56 p.m.	Ordinary ...	No. 1 Platform ...	5 10 p.m.	1
5 0 p.m.	Ordinary ...	No. 1 Siding ...	9 45 p.m.	1
5 45 p.m.	Ordinary ...	No. 1 Platform ...	6 40 p.m.	2
6 37 p.m.	Ordinary ...	Passenger Neck ...	8 30 p.m.	1
7 6 p.m.	Ordinary ...	No. 2 Platform ...	8 15 p.m.	2
8 56 p.m.	Ordinary ...	No. 1 Siding ...	10 45 p.m.	1
10 35 p.m.	Ordinary ...	No. 1 Platform ...	6 5 a.m. (following day)	1

The 6.25 a.m. ex Afon Wen to be divided at Pwllheli; One portion to be utilised for the 6.45 a.m. ex Pwllheli, and the other for the 7.30 a.m. ex Pwllheli.

Wrexham Cattle Market.

The usual arrangements will apply.

Day Excursion—Tylwch, Llanidloes, Llandinam, etc., to Aberystwyth.

	a.m.				p.m.	
	arr.	dep.			arr.	dep.
Llanidloes ...		6†40	Aberystwyth ...			7 10
Tylwch ...	6†47	7 0	Bow Street ...		C7χ21S	
Llanidloes ...	7 6	7 10	Machynlleth ...	7 50	0χW	7 54
Dolwen ...		7 15	Cemmes Road ...		8 5	
Llandinam ...	7 20	7 30	Llanbrynmair ...		8 16	
Moat Lane ...	7 35	7 43	Carno ...		8 31	
Caersws ...	7 46	χ 7 48	Pontdolgoch ...			8 40
Pontdolgoch ...		7 54	Caersws ...			8 45
Carno ...	8 3		Moat Lane ...	8 48	T	9 0
Llanbrynmair ...	8 15		Llandinam ...	9 5		9 10
Cemmes Road ...	8 27		Dolwen ...			9 16
Machynlleth ...	8 37	0χW 8 43	Llanidloes ...	9 21		9 25
Aberystwyth ...	9 30		Tylwch ...	9 33		9†40
			Llanidloes ...	9†47		

Formation: Brake Third, 6 8-wheeled Thirds, Brake Third.
Reserved accommodation: Three Thirds to be reserved for Church Schools from Tylwch, Llandinam, etc.; two Thirds for Chapel party from Llandinam. Coaches to be labelled at Llanidloes.

Table VI.
Notice No. CW22,
13 August 1928.

47

able to imagine country lads and lasses wending their way on foot to catch that special 7.00 a.m. departure to the seaside, in 1928. Today, Aberystwyth may be reached by car within an hour. During the winter, special services catered for football fans (lucrative business with no vandalism in those days), shopping expeditions to the Midlands or Merseyside, or various fairs and marts within the area.

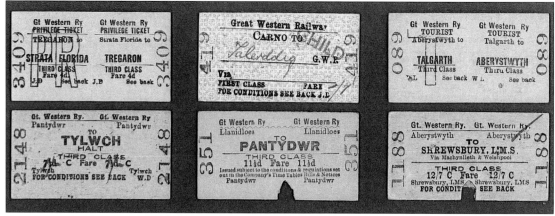

Some interesting GW tickets.

Malcolm James Coll.

Part of the front cover of the amended services timetable necessitated by the 1926 General Strike.

Courtesy C. R. Potts

Great Western Railway.

In consequence of Labour Troubles

THE

TRAIN SERVICE

advertised in the Company's Time Tables

WILL BE ALTERED,

AND UNTIL FURTHER NOTICE
THE SERVICE SHEWN IN THIS SPECIAL TIME TABLE
WILL, AS FAR AS POSSIBLE, BE ADOPTED.

WEEK-DAYS & SUNDAYS

COMMENCING SUNDAY, JUNE 6TH, 1926.

For particulars of Train Services over other Companies' Lines see the respective Time Tables.

Arrangements for the Cambrian Coast were advertised in this specially produced handbill. July 1926.
IAH Coll.

GREAT WESTERN RAILWAY.

ADDITIONAL EXPRESS TRAINS
TO AND FROM THE
CAMBRIAN COAST

DOWN TRAINS.		Fridays and Saturdays only.	Fridays and Saturdays only.	Fridays and Saturdays only, July 23rd to August 28th only.	Each Week-day.
		a.m.	a.m.	a.m.	p.m.
London (Paddington)	dep.	..	9 10	10 10	2 10
High Wycombe	"	..	9 42	10 46	..
Leamington Spa	"	8 W0	10 10	11 54	3 22
Birmingham (Snow Hill)	arr.	9W5	11 10	12 20	4 10
	dep.	9 10	11 15	12 30	4 15
Wolverhampton (Low Level)	arr.	9 30	11 35	12 49	4 35
	dep.	9 35	11 40	12 55	4 40
Wellington	"	10 0	10 H54		4 27
Welshpool	arr.	11 0	—	—	6 7
	dep.	11 5			6 20
Montgomery	"	11 18			6 33
Newtown	"	11 35			6 49
Moat Lane Junction	arr.	11 45		2 38	6 59
	dep.	11 50		2 43	7 3
Machynlleth	arr.	12 50		3 25	7 54
	dep.	12 55		3 33	7 57
Dovey Junction	arr.	—		3 40	8 4
Dovey Junction	dep.	..	—	3 50	8 25
Aberdovey	"	..	4 23	4 4	8 40
Towyn	"	..	4 11	4 11	8 48
Tonfanau	"	..	4 5		8 56
Llwyngwril	"	..	3 54	4 27	9 14
Fairbourne	"	..	3 44	4 36	9 17
Barmouth Junction	arr.	..	—	4 39	9 22
Barmouth	arr.	..	3 43	4 44	..
	dep.	..	3 50	4 50	..
Dyffryn-on-Sea	"	..	B	L	..
Llanbedr and Pensarn	"	..	B	L	..
Harlech	"	..	4 10	5 21	..
Penrhyndeudraeth	"	..	B		..
Portmadoc	arr.	..	4 31	5 40	..
	dep.	..	4 35	5 50	..
Criccieth	"	..	4 45	6 0	..
Pwllheli (for Nevin)	arr.	..	5 4	6 18	..
Dovey Junction	dep.	1 15	..	3 45	..
Borth	"	1 15	..	4 0	..
Aberystwyth	arr.	1 40	..	4 20	..

(Via Ruabon. Breakfast and Luncheon Car, Paddington to Ruabon.)
(Luncheon and Tea Car, Paddington to Aberystwyth.)

UP TRAINS.		Fridays and Saturdays, July 23rd to Sept. 4th only.		Fridays and Saturdays only.	Fridays and Saturdays only.
		a.m.		a.m.	p.m.
Aberystwyth	dep.	11 0	D	..	2 25
Borth	"	11 18		..	2 43
Dovey Junction	arr.	11 35		..	3 6
Pwllheli (for Nevin)	dep.	8 55		11 50	..
Criccieth	"	9 12		12 10	..
Portmadoc	"	9 26		12 25	..
Penrhyndeudraeth	"	9E34		K	..
Harlech	"	9 45		12 45	..
Llanbedr and Pensarn	"	9E54		K	..
Dyffryn-on-Sea	"	10E5		K	..
Barmouth	arr.	10 14		1 10	..
	dep.	10 20		1 15	..
Barmouth Junction	"	10 25		—	..
Fairbourne	"	10 28			..
Llwyngwril	dep.	10 37			2 30
Towyn	"	10 49			2 38
Aberdovey	"	10 57			2 55
Dovey Junction	arr.	11 12			
Dovey Junction	dep.	11 41			3 5
Machynlleth	"			—	3 15
Newtown	arr.	1 10			4 31
Welshpool	dep.	1 27			5 0
	arr.				5 10
Wellington	dep.	2 32	D		6 15
Wolverhampton (Low Level)	arr.	3 20		4 51	6 45
	dep.	3 30		5 23	6 55
Birmingham (Snow Hill)	arr.	4 0		5 28	7 17
	dep.			5 48	
Leamington Spa	arr.	4 26		6 0	7 47 / 8 0
London (Paddington)	"	6 0		6 26	8 15 / 8 20
				8 5	10 15

(Via Ruabon. Tea and Dining Car, Shrewsbury to Paddington.)

B—Calls to set down passengers from Ruabon and beyond on notice being given to the Guard.
D—Luncheon and Tea Car, Aberystwyth to Paddington.
E—Calls to pick up passengers for beyond Shrewsbury on notice being given at the Station.
F—Dining Car, Birmingham to Paddington.
H—From July 19th, Wellington depart 11.20 a.m. on Mondays and Fridays.
K—Calls to pick up passengers for Ruabon or beyond on notice being given at the station.
L—Calls to set down passengers from beyond Shrewsbury on notice being given to the Guard at Dovey Junction.
V—Also calls at Gogarth Halt to set down passengers on notice being given to the Guard.
W—Passengers change at Bordesley to arrive Birmingham (Snow Hill) at 9.5 a.m.

For complete Service see the Company's Time Tables dated September 21st, 1925, and also subsequent announcements.

PADDINGTON,
July 12th, 1926.

FELIX J. C. POLE,
General Manager.

As the decade progressed, labour problems throughout the country caused increasing concern, culminating in the 1926 General Strike. The actual period of the railway strike was from midnight on Monday, 3 May to Friday, 14 May, when terms of settlement were agreed. On Tuesday, 4 May, the first day proper of the strike, 86.4% of wages staff and 23.5% of clerical/supervisory staff withdrew their labour; the comparatively high percentage of clerical staff on strike being a surprising development. That day, the Chester Division was able to run Chester-Bala, Bala-Ruabon, Ruabon-Barmouth, Barmouth-Bala, and return Shrewsbury-Welshpool services, the latter with LMS men. In the Central Wales Division, the company's enginemen came 'out to a man' although, gradually, minimal services were operated largely by volunteers, some of whom were drafted in from London. On Sunday, 9 May, the district superintendent at Oswestry informed the Paddington-based Superintendent of the Line (SOL) that he could work trains 'all over my district within limits of one shift' – provided engines were available. The only serious accident recorded in the log of the SOL, features the CWD. It occurred on Saturday, 8 May when a morning auto-train from Gobowen to Oswestry, driven by a person from the locomotive stores department, ran into the block of the bay platform at Oswestry and ended up inside the parcels office. Remarkably, none of the passengers on board complained of injury.[7]

The railwaymens' Terms of Settlement, agreed on Friday, 14 May, failed to bring the dispute to a precise and neat conclusion, for many of the animosities born of the strike remained and festered. Members of staff accused of violent behaviour or intimidation during the conflict were brought to the attention of the general manager. In the CWD, these included the case of the Aberystwyth Acting Shed Chargeman (whose only offence was that he took part in the strike). Initially, his status was reduced to that of a driver, but his former position was restored after appeal.

'Stella' 2-4-0 No. 3508 at Barmouth Junction with the 2.40 p.m. Barmouth to Chester train. The first carriage is a through (composite) carriage to Paddington, forming a service frequently used, amongst others, by members of the Robertson family of Palé Hall, Llandderfel. Sir Henry B. Robertson was a director of the GWR. 13 March 1928.

Ifor A. Higgon

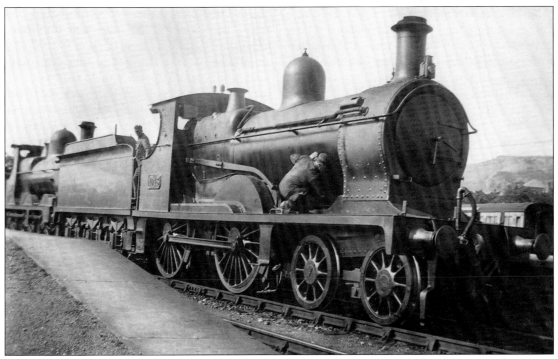

GW 'Large Belpaire' 4-4-0 No. 1043 at Aberystwyth, piloting a Dean 'Goods' on the 5.00 p.m. local train to Machynlleth. 4 August 1928. *Ifor A. Higgon*

The stationmaster at Llanbrynmair did not fare quite as well; he was accused of threatening behaviour toward his replacement during the strike, and after a period of suspension, was allowed to resume on 12 July 1926, but as a clerk at Builth Wells. Interestingly, according to RAIL 1025/224 at PRO Kew, the stationmaster's post at Llanbrynmair was then abolished.[8]

Settlement of the railway strike only ensured partial success, for the miners dispute was not resolved until the end of November, a vital factor which affected the railways both in terms of traffic and supply of coal to keep the trains running. Much of this was now imported and was generally deemed inferior to Welsh steam coal on which the GWR thrived.

Although a degree of normality was established after 13 May, services were not fully restored and a makeshift timetable was operated, based on that of the previous September. From Sunday, 6 June, this included four 'down' and three 'up' services per weekday, between Oswestry and Aberystwyth, with the usual mail trains on Sundays. Four services in each direction ran on the coast, with the motor services around Barmouth, Dolgellau, Llanbedr and Aberdovey. As the Cambrian Coast Express did not then feature in the winter service, special arrangements were made for a limited through service to and from Paddington on Fridays and Saturdays only, although the CCE title was not used. These services commenced on Friday, 13 July and continued to 4 September only, but a Birmingham (Snow Hill) to Aberystwyth service ran FSO from 16 July and a further Paddington to Barmouth service, in the 'down' direction only, ran via Welshpool each weekday from Monday, 12 July.

Broadly similar arrangements applied in 1927, with daily operation of the Cambrian Coast Express – with title restored – resumed on 9 July 1928. Departure from Paddington was changed to 10.20 a.m., a time which remained constant until the service was suspended in 1939.

FREIGHT TRAFFIC

Freight services continued to follow the time-honoured pattern based on decades of hard-won experience. Cambrian freight services had dovetailed with the requirements of both the Great Western and LNWR for over half a century and there seemed no valid reason for any major changes.

In 1924, the first train on the road was the 2.00 a.m. goods from Welshpool to Machynlleth, reached at 5.20 a.m. after stops 'if required to put off traffic' at Montgomery and Newtown; a twenty-minute stop at Moat Lane indicates regular exchange of traffic at this point. Five minutes were spent at Talerddig stop-board, pinning down brakes, and a pause of around ten minutes was allowed at Llanbrynmair, to 'cross' the 'up' 3.15

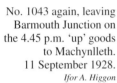

No. 1043 again, leaving Barmouth Junction on the 4.45 p.m. 'up' goods to Machynlleth. 11 September 1928.
Ifor A. Higgon

GW No. 1108 shunting at Barmouth Junction during the working of a cement special from Aberdovey to Trawsfynydd. 18 April 1927.
Ifor A. Higgon

52

GW No. 1090 on a ballast train at Barmouth Junction. 24 August 1928.   *Ifor A. Higgon*

A sheep special leaves Abermule for Kerry with GW 4-4-0 No. 1108 and 0-6-OST No. 2075, 13 September 1929. Special permission had been granted for the 4-4-0 to operate to Kerry in 1928 but the operating department abused this privilege by working the locomotive regularly on the branch, with consequent damage to the track. Special permission had again to be sought to operate in 1929; it was granted for two days only, 6 and 13 September.

Ifor A. Higgon

a.m. Newtown goods. This served as the final interruption before Machynlleth was reached at 5.20 a.m. A freight train for Towyn was then prepared at Machynlleth, in time for departure at 6.45 a.m. just before a second 'down' freight appeared. This was the only through goods in the 'down' direction, the 2.45 a.m. from Oswestry to Aberystwyth, and due at Machynlleth at 6.50 a.m.

It spent twenty-five minutes shunting there, before departure at 7.15 a.m. for due arrival at Aberystwyth at 8.25 a.m. Thereafter, local goods trains were the order of the day although there was another 'down' departure from Oswestry at 5.30 a.m. which ran only as far as Newtown, where the Oswestry engine spent from 8.00 a.m. until noon on shunting duties.

In 1924 there were two later 'down' goods trains from Oswestry to Machynlleth; the first at 3.20 p.m. (arr. Machynlleth 7.30 p.m.) was timetabled 'on Wednesdays to convey cattle traffic from Oswestry market to S & M Line'. The second Machynlleth goods left Oswestry at 5.40 p.m. and was scheduled to arrive at Machynlleth at 11.30 p.m. This service was authorised to call on Tuesdays at Llanbrynmair and Cemmes Road, 'if required to put off cattle traffic ex Newtown'. Interestingly, the Cemmes Road stop was also marked 'On Fridays will cross No. 57 Up season Excursion at Cemmes Road', which was a Fridays Only season excursion to the LMS (18 July to 12 September). This left Aberystwyth at 10.20 p.m. and stopped at Borth, Machynlleth, Newtown, Montgomery, Welshpool, Oswestry, Ellesmere and Whitchurch, where it left the CWD timetable. If it was a Manchester (only) train, it seems strange that the timetable did not say so; it might therefore have been bound for a different Lancashire destination each Friday.

Local goods trains are exemplified by two services at opposite ends of the system, the 3.30 a.m. from Oswestry to Whitchurch and the 5.30 a.m. from Aberystwyth to Machynlleth; they were typical of the short-haul goods which conducted much of the business in and out of country stations. Often, the working timetable carried a further instruction 'Not to convey more than 20 wagons'. Yet, these were the services which first reflected the intensity of the new road challenge. Up to 1924, for example, there were two 'up' and two 'down' local daily services between Aberystwyth and Machynlleth. From 1925, this was reduced to one service each way per day; the former frequency was never restored.

Elsewhere, Moat Lane, Newtown and Welshpool fed Oswestry with further freight trains and, at the end of each day, an 'up' through goods from Aberystwyth (dep. 6.30 p.m.) was followed, in 1924, by another from Machynlleth (dep. 8.55 p.m.) arriving at Oswestry at 1.30 a.m. the following morning.

Even though the Cambrian hardly impresed as a freight carrier, the working timetables of the 1920s and '30s reveal that goods trains made an important contribution to the viability of the line. Frequent banking of east-bound trains over Talerddig was called for as more powerful locomotives were still not sanctioned by the civil engineer. At times of intense line occupation, particularly weekends, less important freight services were suspended whilst others were re-timed to run early in the morning or late at night. Some of the more important freight trains were run on Sundays.

The lesson for the year 2000 and beyond must be that even a single (oil) train each week would attract vital revenue; one additional general freight train per day would help to secure the line's future. Finally, lest it be thought that interchange with continental railways is something new, Ifor Higgon noted an interesting Belgian State Railways covered van at Machynlleth on 6 March 1926, lettered:

'Sainte Belgo Anglaise' Louvain.
Hired by LNER.
Through traffic between
Great Britain and the Continent.
(without transhipment)
12000 Kgms. 'Etat Belge'[9]

LOCOMOTIVES AND ROLLING STOCK

The motive power situation was critical at the time of the takeover. The GWR would obviously have wished to introduce 'Bulldogs', 'Aberdares' or Churchward 'Moguls' to the area, as were employed along the valleys of the Dee and Wnion between Ruabon and Dolgellau, but they were prevented because Cambrian track was generally lighter and a great many of the smaller bridges and culverts were wooden affairs which dated from the opening of the railway. A renewal programme would take years to complete.

The short-term solution was to draft in some of the GW's smaller locomotives which, by that time,

Dean 'Goods' No. 2315 pilots No. 2468 with the SO 9.17 a.m. Barmouth to Paddington train, up the Dyfi valley towards Cemmes Road, on 7 August 1937. (Load, 10. 8s). *Ifor A. Higgon*

were also some of the company's older engines. Thus arrived a succession of 'Dukes', Dean 'Goods', 'Stellas' and 'Barnums'. All had been very capable engines in earlier times and had performed main-line duties elsewhere on the GW system but by 1922 many were already 25-30 years old.

The backbone of CWD motive power over the next couple of decades was undoubtedly provided by the versatile and ubiquitous Dean 'Goods' class. Nos. 2391, 2454 and 2528 were among the first immigrants; they and their sisters performed every task asked of them, from humble services on the most lightly laid branch line to double-heading some of the section's heaviest summer passenger trains. They were found everywhere. It must be recorded, however, that although they were no longer new machines they were, almost without exception, put through the works before transfer and were in fine form when they arrived in central Wales. Higgon records that they were a credit to William Dean and to Swindon. Because of their versatility, they moved freely around the Division and are amongst the more difficult to 'tie down' in terms of allocation.

A good but by no means exceptional example, is provided by engine No. 2323:

in January 1935 it was listed as a Machynlleth engine;
in February it went to Oswestry Works;
in March, it was listed under Pwllheli;
in April   . . . Portmadoc;
May   . . . Pwllheli;
June   . . . Pwllheli;
29 June   . . . Machynlleth;
27 July   . . . Pwllheli;
24 August   . . . Aberystwyth;
21 September . . . Machynlleth;

19 October   . . . Oswestry Works;
16 November . . . Portmadoc;
14 December . . . Pwllheli.[10]

Early in the new regime, Machynlleth shed received a pair of interesting 2-4-0s, Nos. 3239 and 3241. Their most unusual feature was the diameter of the driving wheels which, at 6ft 8½ins, probably ensured that they would be the largest ever to roll down the bank from Talerddig. Nos. 3232 and 3251 were two further representatives of this class, based at Oswestry; the Machynlleth pair spent much of their time down the coast.

The smaller-wheeled engines sent by Swindon were equally interesting and the 'Stellas' and 'Barnums', in particular, found great favour among the enginemen. Both classes steamed freely and were good runners; they rode well around the many curves and through the loops at stations, and with moderate loads of four or five bogie vehicles revealed a respectable turn of speed. They appeared all over the Division but the 'Stellas' (Nos. 3501 and 3519 being early examples) gravitated to the coast and Mid Wales sections.

The 6ft-8½ins driving wheels of GW No. 3241 show up well in this view of the 2-4-0 at Machynlleth. *c.* 1925.

J. P. Richards

Ex-Cambrian 'Large Bogie' No. 63 as GW 1091 at Machynlleth, after being displaced from the Mid Wales line, 1926-30.

Lens of Sutton

'Barnum' 2-4-0 No. 3210 after arrival at Machynlleth with an 'up' train. The original height of the platform is noteworthy. *c.* 1926.

J. P. Richards

'Barnum' No. 3216 carried a dome-less boiler when it first ran on the Cambrian, as depicted here alongside the pump house at Machynlleth, *c.* 1924. It regained a domed boiler in 1926.

J. P. Richards

'Stella' 2-4-0 No. 3511 replenishes its water supply at Barmouth, *c.* 1924.

J. P. Richards

'Stella' No. 3505 waits at Barmouth Junction with the 2.40 p.m. Barmouth to Chester service, 13 July 1929.

Ifor A. Higgon

The 'Barnums' had previously performed main-line express duties from depots such as Swindon, Wolverhampton, Oxford and Bristol but by 1922 were relegated to less demanding duties. As a result of the grouping they suddenly found themselves again on express work, on the Cambrian. They acquitted themselves well on Whitchurch-Aberystwyth services and down the coast; one example, No. 3213 was based at Llanidloes in July 1924. An indication of their achievement is provided by details of a run on 6 March 1926, when No. 3217 worked the 1.50 p.m. Whitchurch-Aberystwyth Buffet/Tea Car train, and turned an 8 minute late departure from Whitchurch into a punctual arrival at Machynlleth. This effort involved a rapid descent of Talerddig when speeds of over 50 m.p.h. were recorded (with maximum of 64 m.p.h. between MP 62/iii and 64/i) and a respectable 52 m.p.h. was calculated between Cemmes Road and Machynlleth (MP 72 and 72/i). The load (of 141T tare) consisted of Cambrian buffet car No. 6333,

one GWR composite coach ex-Liverpool, two LMS corridor coaches ex-Manchester (London Road) and one further GWR composite carriage from Paddington; a creditable achievement for a 37 year-old locomotive.[11]

The other class which gave invaluable service in central Wales at this time was the 4-4-0 'Duke' class. Amongst the early examples noted at Machynlleth (on 26 June 1924) were Nos. 3260 *Mount Edgcumbe*, 3269 *Dartmoor* and 3256 *Guinevere*. No. 3261 *St. German* was observed at Oswestry that day whilst, on 20 September 1924, No. 3278 *Trefusis*, No. 3285 *Katerfelto* and No. 3260 *Mount Edgcumbe* were in evidence at Aberystwyth.[12] At one time or another, all members of the class, save No. 3286 *Meteor*, were observed by Ifor Higgon on Central Wales duties but as he was inclined to focus his attention rather more on events around the Barmouth area, it is not impossible for *Meteor* also to have worked a Birmingham to Aberystwyth service, unobserved by Ifor, at least once during 17 years.

A well-known but none the less dramatic photograph of 'Duke' class No. 3264 *Trevithick* clearing its cylinders as it moves an 'up' train out of Aberystwyth, *c*. 1925.

NLW/A.J. Lewis

Ex-Cambrian No. 94, as GW 1014, with No. 3256 *Guinivere* backing to the shed at Aberystwyth after bringing the 1.50 p.m. from Whitchurch to the coast. 30 July 1927.

Ifor A. Higgon

The 'Dukes' also had previous express experience. Designed initially for the undulating lines of the west country, they soon acquitted themselves in central Wales. They were allowed to work through to Aberystwyth (and Llanidloes) and down the coast, where they generally worked only as far as Barmouth as they could not use the short 45ft Cambrian turntable then at Afon Wen. The first 'Duke' noted between Machynlleth and Barmouth Junction (only) was No. 3261 *St.*

Germans, on 1 June 1923, on 'extra freight' duty. By September that year Nos. 3254 *Cornubia*, 3260 *Mount Edgcumbe* and 3270 *Earl of Devon* had worked further 'extra freight' trains to Barmouth Junction, where they turned on the triangle. In October 1923, No. 3271 *Eddystone* ventured further along the coast on military specials to and from Portmadoc; it also had to return to Barmouth Junction to turn. Apparently 'the engine was a pleasure to behold, clean and polished'. At this

'Duke' No. 3266 *Amyas* (TYS) waits at Aberystwyth with the 2.25 p.m. FSO train to Birmingham (Snow Hill) on 21 August 1926.
Ifor A. Higgon

Three 'Duke' portraits: No. 3290 *Severn*, at Oswestry, 7 April 1936.   *IAH Coll.*

No. 3283 *Comet*, at Machynlleth, 10 April 1936.

No. 3268 *Chough*, alongside the pump house at Machynlleth. Photographer and date unknown.

time, the Ruabon-Barmouth Junction branch was worked entirely by Dean 0-6-0s and 'Stella' 2-4-0s from Wrexham Croes Newydd (CNYD) and Chester (CHR) sheds. The local Barmouth-Dolgellau passenger services, previously the province of the Cambrian 0-4-4T engines, were worked from the summer of 1922 by Great Western Steam Rail Motor Cars (SRM). These, at various times, also worked along the coast between Criccieth and Aberdovey, and for one season only, from Machynlleth also.

In September 1926, the section from Llanidloes to Three Cocks Junction, initially regarded by the GWR as a 'yellow' route, was redesignated an 'uncoloured' route, with a maximum permitted axle load of just 14 tons. A direct consequence was that the Cambrian 'Large Bogie' 4-4-0s (with maximum axle weight of 15 tons) were withdrawn from the Moat Lane-Brecon route, although one of the 'Small Bogie' 4-4-0s, No. 1118, worked auto services based on Builth and Llanidloes in 1927, after withdrawal of the SRMs. Two of the displaced 'Large Bogies' came to Machynlleth in September 1926 (Nos. 1082 and 1091); No. 1108 followed in October. With No. 1090 already at the depot, Machynlleth then had four examples of the class, all in near original condition. Two other displaced mid Wales sector 4-4-0s, Nos. 1100 and 1106, went to Oswestry.[13] The year 1927 was not particularly momentous on the main line between Whitchurch and Aberystwyth, but the Ruabon to Barmouth branch saw important developments. On 4 March, two pannier tanks from Chester Division, No. 1824 ('yellow' route category) and No. 1863 ('blue' route category) were run, coupled together, testing bridges along the route, including Barmouth viaduct. These tests had no immediate effect; traffic on the Ruabon branch was still handled by the Dean 'Goods' class and the 32xx and 35xx 2-4-0s, but by June 43/53/63xx 2-6-0s began to appear for the summer service but as far as Barmouth Junction only. They turned on the triangle there and worked 'up' services to Chester.

The smaller engines, however, regained their former duties when the winter service commenced but further tests were then carried out, in October, by a 2-6-0 and 39xx 2-6-2T on Barmouth viaduct and Barmouth tunnel bridge. This latter bridge proved something of an Achilles heel and 'blue' category engines were not allowed to cross this point until the bridge was largely filled in. The opportunity was also taken that winter to renew several other bridges on the main Ruabon-Barmouth Junction line, particularly west of Dolgellau. The most important of these was the old Cambrian trestle bridge at Arthog, which was replaced by a new girder structure in April 1930; this survives as part of a nature trail between Penmaenpool and Morfa Mawddach.

This route again saw the most notable developments of 1928, when No. 3314 *Mersey*, the first 'Bulldog' on the Ruabon branch, and a 2-8-0 made an appearance between Chester and Barmouth Junction. The filling-in of the bridge by Barmouth tunnel was complete by December, when the 43xx 2-6-0s began to work directly into Barmouth. In March the following year, 'Bulldogs' again made a welcome reappearance on Chester-Barmouth trains; No. 3445 *Flamingo* being the first to enjoy the privilege of working directly across the estuary and in August, the tests were carried a stage further when a second 2-8-0 tested the road and clearances between Ruabon and Barmouth Junction.[14]

Steam Rail Motors: the coast line.

Great Western steam rail car operation in central Wales has been largely unrecorded by contemporary railway observers and most of the following details are based on official records at the PRO, extracted by the late Ralph Tutton. The GWR had first launched their rail motors, as they fondly referred to them, between Chalford and Stonehouse, in Gloucestershire, in October 1903. Whilst not without a few shortcomings, they undoubtedly displayed operational advantages on

The new girder bridge at Arthog, before being winched into position. The wooden piles of the old structure are still *in situ* in the river. Arthog Halt features in the background. 13 April 1930.   *WIMM/GW Coll.*

A broadside view of the new bridge in position showing both winches . . . and the limited clearance at high water. 13 April 1930.   *WIMM/GW Coll.*

branch lines and secondary routes, such as their ability to return from a terminus without use of a loop line. Their initial success led to the construction of additional cars and the introduction of further services between, for example, Southall-Brentford, Plympton-Saltash and, in Wales, Wrexham-Gobowen and Ruabon-Dolgellau. When it became clear that the Great Western was to acquire the Cambrian, the powers at Paddington immediately tried the steam rail motors on the more lightly-used services. They were introduced with the summer timetable in 1922 'to work in the district for the purpose of augmenting the holiday traffic'.[15]

The Central Wales Division allocation, on 13 August 1922, was;

> Oswestry: Cars No. 74 & 85;
> Machynlleth: Cars No. 39, 40 & 58.

A month later, 10 September, these had been re-allocated;

> Oswestry: Cars No. 39 & 85;
> Dolgellau: Car No. 40;
> Llanidloes: Car No. 58;
> Machynlleth: Car No. 74.

The new arrangements were partly prompted by the fact that some of the cars encountered problems whilst negotiating the Aberdyfi tunnels. Although generally similar in appearance and profile, some of the cars were 60 ft long whilst others were 70 ft vehicles. The bores of the four tunnels in the Aberdyfi area were not over generous and matters were hardly helped by the fact that the railcars oscillated noticeably when under power – the movement being not unlike that of a small boat in choppy water.[16] The problem, apparently, appears not to have occurred on each and every trip through the bores, for car No. 40 – a 70 ft vehicle – continued to use the tunnels between May and December, when it was eventually replaced by car No. 75, a 60 ft car. Car No. 74, which originally shared the coast roster

with No. 40, was a 60 ft vehicle. The track-bed through the tunnels was later lowered a few inches but the immediate problem was solved by allocating only 60 ft vehicles to this service.

The Great Western had introduced the SRMs with commendable speed after the grouping; perhaps it is understandable that the clearance difficulties within the Aberdyfi tunnels were not obvious at the outset but emerged only with experience. The profiles of a 70 ft vehicle and the tunnels were obviously considered to be compatible but when the longer cars started to pitch and yaw on the curves within the tunnels, some contact with the walls must have occurred. The direction of travel, i.e. whether the car was being 'drawn' or 'propelled' by the power bogie, may also have been a factor. It could well have been that the 70 ft cars were capable of negotiating the tunnels safely, at very low speeds, but this obviously did not help with timekeeping.

The 1922 summer timetable shows that the SRMs supplemented existing services on the coast route by adding no fewer than four additional 'shuttles' between Dolgellau and Barmouth, some of which extended beyond the coastal town. This timetable also shows the first and only operation of a rail motor service from Machynlleth, which left at 6.10 a.m., arriving in Barmouth at 7.08 a.m. During the day, this car operated (in conjunction with the Penmaenpool car) a fairly intensive service from Barmouth, as far as Harlech to the north and Llwyngwril to the south, in addition to the more intensive Dolgellau service. No official diagram has been discovered for these workings but the timings suggest that the two cars had to be interchanged daily, and not at four-week intervals, as suggested by the official registers. The only return service through the tunnels to Machynlleth left Dyffryn Ardudwy at 4.15 p.m., arriving at Machynlleth at 6.07 p.m. The 70 ft cars could well have continued their visits to Machynlleth for maintenance purposes but no SRM operated a public service through the tunnels after 1922.

This small culvert at Arthog was typical of many similar structures which had to be strengthened to allow 'blue' category engines to pass in regular service. Here, No. 887 waits while a ballast train (from Llynclys, via Ruabon) is unloaded. 27 November 1938.

Ifor A. Higgon

From the start of the 1922-23 winter service, the SRM diagram for operation down the coast required one vehicle only, based at Penmaenpool. The timetable no longer included Machynlleth but the new arrangements extended, at various times, between Criccieth and Aberdovey. By the following summer (1923) the SRMs abandoned the Barmouth Junction-Aberdovey section but extended northern activities to encompass Criccieth. The Dolgellau-Barmouth motor services consisted of three 'down' and two 'up' trains per day. By the winter of 1923-24, Aberdovey had returned to the format, whilst operation to the north terminated at Llanbedr & Pensarn. This

This view, although out of date sequence, illustrates the measures taken to eliminate the weak tunnel viaduct on the southern approach to Barmouth. 2-6-0 No. 5319 (84J) passes with the 2.07 p.m. from Ruabon to Barmouth. 19 May 1956.

Ifor A. Higgon

emerged as the winter and summer pattern for the remainder of SRM operation down the coast. The summer 1924 timetable reinstated a service to Criccieth, whilst Aberdovey was again omitted (although a conventional train service was substituted here, if not to the exact times). A new innovation involved the first SRM of the day on the Dolgellau branch, which travelled 'light' as far as Drws-y-nant before commencing its trip to Barmouth. Any schoolchildren who took advantage of the motor in the morning, returned by a normal service train in the afternoon. Where the SRMs were most successful in generating new traffic, they were quickly made redundant as they could not cope with increased passenger numbers. They generally operated singly on the coast but a photograph existed of one towing a 4-wheel trailer – an unusual combination.

The timetable pattern of previous years was repeated during the winter of 1924-25; Aberdovey was again reinstated, with northen operation once more curtailed at Llanbedr & Pensarn. The 8.30 a.m. departure from Drws-y-nant continued through the summer of 1925, when Criccieth again reappeared as the northern limit of SRM operation. The service south was once more withdrawn until the start of the following winter's programme (from 21 September 1925). At this time, the Drws-y-nant experiment was dropped and the resulting pattern served, largely unchanged, for the 1926 summer service also. The foregoing presents a good example of timetable adjustment and fine tuning, from season to season.

An impression of the single car's intensive programme may be gleaned by listing its daily duties during the summer of 1925. According to the late O. B. James, of Machynlleth shed, there were few moments of respite during the working day. He was the only engineman who could recall in recent times the steam rail motors on the Cambrian. He was sent to Penmaenpool 'on relief' for a week to fire the rail motor, and had to sleep at night, as best he could, in the car itself or on a bunk at the back of the shed.

Table VII
> Steam Rail Motor roster: Penmaenpool Shed.
> 13 July – 20 September 1925: Shared by cars No. 30 and 76.
> The rested car was stabled at Machynlleth, for boiler washing and general maintenance.

Penmaenpool Shed		a.m.	dep.	7.50
			EM (Empty Motor)	
Drws-y-nant	arr.	8.15	d.	8.30
Barmouth	a.	9.14	d.	10.20
Llanbedr & Pensarn	a.	10.49	d.	10.55
Barmouth	a.	11.24	d.	11.29
			EM to Barmouth Jc.	
Dolgellau	a.	12.38 p.m.	d.	12.50
Barmouth	a.	1.26	d.	1.45
Llanbedr & Pensarn	a.	2.10	d.	2.25
Dolgellau	a.	3.26	d.	3.40
Barmouth	a.	4.04	d.	4.20
Dolgellau	a.	4.44	d.	5.00
Barmouth	a.	5.24	d.	5.55
Portmadoc	a.	6.50	d.	7.25
Criccieth	a.	7.36	d.	7.50
Portmadoc	a.	8.01	d.	8.25
Barmouth	a.	9.30	d.	10.05
Dolgellau	a.	10.29	d.	10.35
			Empty Motor	
Penmaenpool Shed	a.	10.40		

According to the official registers, cars No. 30 and 81 were allocated to Machynlleth and Penmaenpool between January and July 1927, but Ifor Higgon noted that in January the service was operated by former Cambrian 0-4-4T GW No. 19, which replaced motor No. 30. This was probably No. 19's final visit to its old haunts, before going to Aberystwyth as carriage shunter during February; it was replaced on the motor by 2-4-0 No. 1329. Gradually, 0-4-2Ts and 'Metro' 2-4-0Ts assumed control; the take-over was complete by June. Ifor Higgon's notes illustrate the value of personal observation.

Herbert Jones, the Cambrian's Locomotive, Carriage & Wagon Superintendent, when interviewed for the *Railway Magazine* (April 1901 issue) stated that 'the coast line runs around Cardigan Bay for 70 miles and practically on the beach for the whole way'. This 1950s aerial view of Barmouth amply supports this statement. The location of Llanaber, where the railway is compressed between the hills and the sea (and illustrated at the head of this chapter) is just visible at the top of this view. *c.* 1950-60.

WIMM/Tempest Coll.

Churchward's powerful 2-8-0 locomotives do not normally feature in a book on the Cambrian but this view of No. 2882 reminds us that the class first visited Barmouth Junction on trial in October 1928. Regular operation to the coast, however, did not commence until 1937, but they (and the Great Central 04 2-8-0s in the GW 30xx series) operated throughout the war and into the mid/late 1940s. Photographer and date unknown.
Photomatic Ltd.

Un-named 'Bulldog' No. 3426 stands at Barmouth, off the 9.00 a.m. Chester train, awating return to that city with the 2.35 p.m. service. 25 January 1930.
Ifor A. Higgon

MOAT LANE – BRECON

Unlike the coast workings, the introduction of SRMs to the former mid Wales section provided an opportunity to effect economies, as attempts were made to replace normal train sets, if only for part of the journey. One such example was the service from Llanidloes to Moat Lane at 11.35 a.m.: another was the 4.50 p.m. departure from Moat Lane to Llanidloes, to connect with a Brecon train which, hitherto, had commenced its journey from the junction. During the first winter of operation (1922-23) a new Llanidloes-Moat Lane service was introduced and later extended to Newtown. Such operations seem to have encouraged the development of SRM services on the Mid Wales, for by the summer of 1923 cars were also allocated to the southern section, when one was introduced to Brecon and another was stationed at Builth Wells. At the same time, the Llanidloes car was relocated at Moat Lane. This car additionally undertook a Moat Lane-Caersws and Caersws-Newtown service. The longest

69

journey in the section was undertaken by the Builth car, from Brecon through to Moat Lane. The 60 mile journey occupied some 2¾ hours, of which just over a quarter of an hour was spent at Builth, probably replenishing water and coal which, in the case of the SRMs, was easily undertaken at the platform, where supplies of pre-bagged coal were kept.

The flexibility offered by SRM operation caused a reduction of the service for the following winter. It came as no surprise. The service was trimmed and operated by just two cars, one at Moat Lane and the other at Brecon. No car now operated the entire length of the section but the Moat Lane car worked three round trips per day to Builth Wells, with the Brecon car working north to Builth Road twice a day.

1924 summer service saw further curtailment of motor operation when the Brecon car was withdrawn and all its services replaced by trains; the Moat Lane roster continued, but with minor adjustments. The 1925 summer arrangements saw the continuation of SRM operation south to Builth Wells but these services now originated and terminated at Llanidloes; their continuation the following year was prevented by the labour troubles. Broadly, the same pattern of operation was perpetuated in 1927 and 1928 but by that time all the cars had been withdrawn and the services were operated by auto-fitted trains.[17]

CARRIAGES

Virtually all the carriages of this period were wood-frame, wood-panelled structures, mounted on steel chassis. The majority were bogie vehicles but a considerable proportion of older 4- and 6-wheeled coaches – very much at home on the various branch lines – were frequently pressed into use down the coast and on the main line. Because the composition of many trains was thus a mixture of 4-wheel, 6-wheel and bogie vehicles, the accepted form of identification by railwaymen ignored the number of carriages in a train, but noted the number of wheels. A train of five bogie coaches would be referred to as 5.8s.

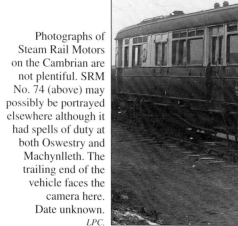

Photographs of Steam Rail Motors on the Cambrian are not plentiful. SRM No. 74 (above) may possibly be portrayed elsewhere although it had spells of duty at both Oswestry and Machynlleth. The trailing end of the vehicle faces the camera here. Date unknown.
LPC.

When the SRMs on the local Dolgellau-Barmouth service were replaced by more conventional auto-trains, the engines for this duty operated from Penmaenpool but visited Machynlleth at two-week intervals for boiler-washing and general maintenance. Here No. 1155 rests between turns in the bay platform at Barmouth Junction. 25 September 1929.

Ifor A. Higgon

Notes

[1]NLW Facs 687, GW Memo. Book: CWD Improvements 1923-48.

[2]RAIL 92/21. 8 May 1871.

[3]NLW Facs 687, GW Memo. Book: CWD Improvements 1923-48.

[4]ibid.

[5]*Newtown & Welshpool Express*, 24 August 1869.

[6]IAH Notes.

[7]RAIL 786, and in Potts, C. R.: *The GWR and the General Strike*, Oakwood Press (1996), p. 33.

[8]RAIL 1025/224 and in Potts, C. R.: *The GWR and the General Strike*, Oakwood Press (1996), p. 107.

[9]IAH Notes.

[10]PRO Register.

[11]IAH Notes (Barnum).

[12]ibid. (Gen. GW Locomotive notes).

[13]ibid.

[14]ibid.

[15]PRO (per Ralph Tutton).

[16]IAH. It will be interesting to see if the SRM currently being recreated by the Great Western Society at Didcot displays similar characteristics on completion.

[17]Most of the preceding SRM notes from PRO RAIL per Ralph Tutton.

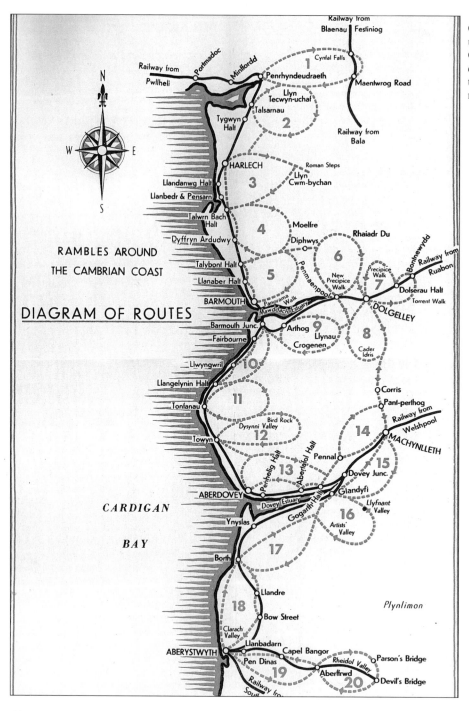

RAMBLES AROUND
THE CAMBRIAN COAST

DIAGRAM OF ROUTES

Copy of a map
used by the
GWR and BR to
encourage use of
the trains by
ramblers.

GBJ Coll.

N

W   E

S

CARDIGAN

BAY

Railway from
Pwllheli

Portmadoc

Minffordd

Railway from
Blaenau   Festiniog

Cynfal Falls

1

Penrhyndeudraeth

Maentwrog Road

Llyn
Tecwyn-uchaf

Talsarnau

2

Railway from
Bala

Tygwyn
Halt

Roman Steps

HARLECH

Llyn
Cwm-bychan

3

Llandanwg Halt

Llanbedr & Pensarn

Talwrn Bach
Halt

Moelfre

Rhaiadr Du

4

Dyffryn Ardudwy

Diphwys

6

Bontnewydd

Railway from
Ruabon

Pennaenpool

Precipice
Walk

Talybont Halt

New
Precipice
Walk

7

Dolserau Halt

Llanaber Halt

5

Torrent Walk

BARMOUTH

Panorama
Walk

Mawddach Estuary

DOLGELLEY

Barmouth Junc.

Arthog

9

Llynau

8

Fairbourne

Crogenen

Cader
Idris

Llwyngwril

10

Corris

Llangelynin Halt

Pant-perthog

Tonfanau

11

Railway from
Welshpool

Bird Rock

14

Dysynni Valley

MACHYNLLETH

Towyn

12

Penhelig Halt

Pennal

Aberdofal Halt

15

13

Dovey Junc.

ABERDOVEY

Dovey Estuary

Glandyfi

Gogarth Hall

Ynyslas

16

Llyfnant
Valley

Artists'
Valley

17

Borth

Plynlimon

Llandre

18

Bow Street

Clarach
Valley

ABERYSTWYTH

Llanbadarn

Capel Bangor

Parson's Bridge

Pen Dinas

Rheidol Valley

19

Aberffrwd

20

Devil's Bridge

Railway from
South

72

Chapter 3

Consolidation, 1930-39

The difficult economic situation stifled progress within the Central Wales Division, as elsewhere, but by 1931 the reinstatement of the relaying programme heralded the first signs of recovery. Nonetheless, the decade proved to be one of consolidation rather than expansion. The centenary which the GWR celebrated elsewhere on the system in 1935 with bullet-nosed 'King' and luxurious 'Centenary' rolling stock, had little or no relevance in central Wales. As far as the Oswestry Division was concerned, the Great Western directors confined themselves to cautious developments and prudent economies.

The programme of constructing additional halts continued wherever and whenever management thought appropriate. Llangelynin Halt was opened in 1930 and Commins Coch, the destination of one of David Davies's pioneer temperance excursions of 1862,[1] followed in 1931, although without the passing loop originally intended by the Cambrian. Penhelig and Penychain opened during 1933 with Abertafol and Llandecwyn following in 1935. The introduction during the early 1930s of motorised trolleys for permanent way workers, the Motor Economic System of Maintenance, was extended to the coast from 27 February 1933.

Relaying continued throughout the 1930s, finally enabling the larger engines to make their bow soon after the declaration of the Second World War. Whether the engineer was fully ready at that time, or whether the need was actually influenced by the Saltney munitions trains may never now be determined. Machynlleth relaying gang, 14 May 1934. *GBJ Coll/Courtesy W. Putt*

GREAT WESTERN RAILWAY

Day and Half-Day Cheap Tickets

ISSUED DAILY except where otherwise shewn.

JULY 7th TO SEPTEMBER 20th, and until further notice.

Cheap Tickets are issued.	Return Fares. 1st Cls. s. d.	Return Fares. 3rd Cls. s. d.
From Dinas Mawddwy to		
Aberangell	8	5
Aberdovey	4 9	2 9
Aberystwyth	7 0	4 3
Barmouth	8 0	4 9
Borth	5 0	3 0
Cemmaes	1 3	9
Cemmes Road	1 6	11
Llanidloes	6 9	4 0
Machynlleth	2 6	1 6
Mallwyd	5	3
Newtown	6 3	3 9
Towyn	5 6	3 3
From Mallwyd to		
Aberangell	5	3
Aberystwyth	6 9	4 0
Barmouth	7 9	4 9
Cemmaes	1 0	7
Cemmes Road	1 3	9
Dinas Mawddwy	5	3
Llanidloes	6 6	4 0
Machynlleth	2 6	1 6
Newtown	6 0	3 6
Towyn	5 3	3 3
From Aberangell to		
Aberdovey	4 0	2 6
Aberystwyth	6 3	3 9
Barmouth	7 6	4 6
Borth	4 6	2 9
Cemmaes	8	5
Cemmes Road	10	6
Dinas Mawddwy	8	5
Llanidloes	6 3	3 9
Machynlleth	2 0	1 3
Mallwyd	5	3
Newtown	5 9	3 6
Towyn	5 0	3 0

Cheap Tickets are issued.	Return Fares. 1st Cls. s. d.	Return Fares. 3rd Cls. s. d.
From Cemmaes to		
Aberangell	8	5
Aberdovey	3 6	2 3
Aberystwyth	5 9	3 6
Barmouth	7 0	4 3
Borth	4 0	2 6
Cemmes Road	4	3
Dinas Mawddwy	1 3	9
Llanidloes	5 9	3 6
Machynlleth	1 6	11
Mallwyd	1 0	7
Newtown	5 0	3 0
Towyn	4 6	2 9
From Cemmes Road to		
Aberangell	10	6
Aberdovey	3 3	2 0
Aberystwyth	5 6	3 3
Barmouth	6 6	4 0
Borth	3 9	2 3
Cemmaes	4	3
Dinas Mawddwy	1 6	11
Llanidloes	5 6	3 3
Machynlleth	1 3	9
Mallwyd	1 3	9
Montgomery	E 6 3	3 9
Newtown	4 9	3 0
Oswestry	C 11 0	6 6
Towyn	4 0	2 6
Welshpool	D 7 9	4 9

TRAIN SERVICE.

	a.m.	a.m.	p.m.	p.m.	p.m.
Dinas M'ddwy dep.	8 25	10 0	12 40	3 10	6 30
Cemmes Road arr.	8 48	10 23	1 3	3 44	6 53
Cemmes Road. dep.	9 0	11 40	1 20	5A 0	7 10
Dinas M'ddwy arr.	9 25	12 13	1 45	5A25	7 35

A—On the last Tuesday in each month, leaves Cemmes Road 5-30 p.m.

The Tickets will be available by any train, outward and return, on date of issue only.
C—Mondays, Wednesdays and Saturdays only. D—Mondays and Saturdays only. E—Thursdays and Saturdays only.

CONDITIONS OF ISSUE.

Children under Three years of age, Free ; Three and under Fourteen, Half-price.
Excursion and other Tickets at fares less than the ordinary fares are issued subject to the Notices and Conditions shewn in the Company's current Time Tables.

LUGGAGE ARRANGEMENTS.

Passengers holding Cheap Day Tickets may carry with them 60lbs. of marketing goods at Owner's Risk, free of charge, all excess over that weight to be charged for. Passengers returning from Shopping Centres may take with them, free of charge, at Owner's Risk, articles not exceeding in the aggregate 120lbs. (First Class), or 60lbs. (Third Class), which they have purchased for their own domestic use. Furniture, linoleum, musical instruments, cycles, mail carts, typewriters, and other articles of a similar character are excepted from these arrangements.
DOGS ACCOMPANYING PASSENGERS are charged for at the single fare for the double journey, tickets available on day of issue only.

For any further information respecting the arrangements shewn in this Bill, application should be made at any of the Company's Stations or Offices ; to
Mr. H. WARWICK, District Traffic Manager, G.W.R., Oswestry ; or to
Mr. R. H. NICHOLLS, Superintendent of the Line, Paddington Station, W

Paddington Station, June, 1930. **JAMES MILNE, General Manager.**

No. 130 (750) Oswestry, 7/6/30. Printed by Joseph Wones, West Bromwich ; also at Birmingham and London.

Before the GW withdrew passenger services from the Mawddwy Branch (1 January 1931) a determined bid was made the previous summer to explore the full passenger potential. The handbill was issued in June 1930.

WIMM

Abertafol Halt, newly constructed and photographed on 13 November 1935. The cottage alongside was for a PW lengthman or ganger.

WIMM/GW Coll.

Further economies were made with the closing to passenger traffic of the Mawddwy Railway from 1 January 1931, although the GW was clearly anxious to retain its hold on the goods service as it undertook to improve the Hendre Ddu Quarry tramway that year, at a cost of £100; the work was completed by January 1932.[2] Also in 1931, the cart weighbridge at Dinas Mawddwy was replaced by a 7 ton unit, previously at Paignton and, again in the interest of economy, the little engine shed at Dinas Mawddwy had to close. Enginemen J. Caffrey and J. Jones, with W. Davies and E. E. Evans, were transferred to Machynlleth.[3] Other economies occurred within the Division's Motive Power Department when the administration of Aberystwyth shed was transferred to Machynlleth, thereby also eliminating the ABH shed code. From 1932, all engines working from that depot carried the Machynlleth MCH shed code (later 89C and 6F), an arrangement which endured until closure in April 1965.

An interesting attempt to secure new traffic is illustrated by the construction of a small cattle dock, on the 'up' side of the main line, at Ynys Crossing between Dovey Junction and Gogarth Halt. The work, authorised to cost £140, was quickly completed during June 1934 and the facilities were brought into use from 3 July. The accommodation came under the control of the stationmaster at Dovey Junction and as no siding was provided, livestock were loaded directly into the wagons of 'up' or 'down' coast freight trains. If time did not permit, empty (or loaded) wagons could be propelled from the Junction with brake-van leading; the engine had to remain coupled to the wagon until it was returned to Dovey Junction.[4] Many other modest improvements were carried out to both passenger and freight; the latter was certainly not neglected. Cart weighbridges were renewed throughout the Division; replacement units were brought in from places as diverse as Truro, Bath, Malvern Link and Buckfastleigh, for

75

The warehouse at Towyn forms a backcloth for this charming 1930s view of mixed Cambrian and GW rolling stock. At that time, 4-4-0 No. 3204 sported an original 'Duke' cast-iron chimney, with its distinctive taper. 15 September 1937.   *John Gwyn Dewing*

example, and installed at Criccieth, Borth, Caersws and Talsarnau, respectively. A new goods warehouse was provided at Llandre (1930) and a 60 ft x 15 ft corrugated iron warehouse was erected at Portmadoc in 1931. Goods facilities at Aberystwyth warehouse were also extended during 1931 and an additional building was completed by October 1934; a further extension was erected in 1936. Nor were the smaller stations disregarded: Pontdolgoch warehouse was replaced in 1935 and that at Towyn in 1937. Although traffic at Glandyfi did not warrant a warehouse in 1931, a sound 29 ft carriage body was found to replace the former store, which was condemned.[5] Passenger traffic was stimulated by the provision of improved waiting-rooms at Criccieth in 1930, and work at Moat Lane, authorized in January 1937, included

the establishing of a chief inspector's office. Much of the control of the division, particulary during the busy summer months, was then undertaken from Moat Lane. The impending visit of the Royal National Eisteddfod of Wales to Machynlleth in 1937 prompted raising the height of the 'up' platform at an estimated cost of £340 which, together with construction of a new footpath and waiting-shed, was completed by late July. The eisteddfod traditionally takes place during the first full week of August and the accounts reflect the amount of overtime paid (£105) to overcome additional work necessary to meet the deadline.[6] During 1937 the construction of a detached house for the district permanant way inspector was also planned for Machynlleth, at an estimated cost of £600.

Criccieth station. 1935. *GBJ Coll.*

From 1934, the GW refurbished redundant carriages for use as Camp Coaches. These were located at the ends of quiet sidings in suitable holiday areas; this example was photographed at Talsarnau in July 1934. *WIMM/GW Coll.*

A larger, bogie carriage was established at Aberaeron by September, 1935. *WIMM/GW Coll.*

Some of the heaviest expenditure, however, was again earmarked for Aberystwyth. A contract was let to E. Taylor & Co. for demolition of the existing engine shed and construction of a new shed for an estimated £10,250. By 24 November 1938 this figure had risen to £16.947 and by 28 June 1940 the chairman of the Locomotive Committee had approved further expenditure of £747 regarding the shed. With a view to improving facilities for more powerful locomotives, particularly on the main lines from Whitchurch and Shrewsbury, larger (65 ft) turntables were planned for Whitchurch, Welshpool and Aberystwyth. Eventually, in 1938, it was proposed to erect a turning triangle at Aberystwyth as 'it is anticipated that there will be a saving of about £110 p.a. in the cost of maintaining a triangle as compared with the cost of maintenance of a new 65 ft turntable'.[7] Machynlleth's old Cambrian 45 ft turntable was also due to be replaced. Originally, the plan here was to bring in a replacement table

from Old Oak Common but it eventually proved more economical to relocate the 55 ft table, then at Aberystwyth, 'as the 55'-0" turntable at Aberystwyth is too small for the engines working there'.[8] This, patently, was not so, for the longest engines then working into Aberystwyth were the 'Dukes' and 'Earls', with a wheelbase of just over 46 ft but it may have been anticipated that the 'Manors' with a 'drawing-board' wheelbase of just over 52 ft might prove difficult (or even impossible) to turn on a 55 ft table. In which case, if such a turntable was considered adequate for Machynlleth, it could be that it was not then expected that the '78s' would work down the coast. The 'Manors' did not enter service until January 1938 and there was obviously an element of 'trial and error' when a '78' was first driven onto a 55 ft table for turning – wherever and whenever that may have been. The first time it happened in the CWD was at Machynlleth[9] but the authorities at Oswestry must by then have learned

ROYAL
NATIONAL EISTEDDFOD of WALES
AT MACHYNLLETH
AUGUST 2nd to 7th, 1937

PROGRAMME:

MONDAY, AUGUST 2nd.

Brass Band Competitions.
Second Choral.
Ambulance Competitions.
Evening Concert—Massed Bands.
Operatic Trio of Soloists.
Florence Austral, Heddle Nash,
Watcyn Watcyns.
Conductor: W. H. Reed, M.V.O.

TUESDAY, AUGUST 3rd.

Crowning of Bard.
Second Male Voice.
Ambulance Competitions.
Evening—Children's Concert.
Choir of 750 voices. String Orchestra.
Conductor: Bumford Griffiths.

WEDNESDAY, AUGUST 4th.

CHIEF CHORAL COMPETITIONS.
Presentation of " Fine Prose " Medal.
Evening Concert:
Full Symphony Orchestra (composed of
Members of the London Symphony Orchestra
and Welsh Symphony Orchestra).
Leader: W. H. Reed, M.V.O. (Leader of the
Orchestra at the Coronation).
Montgomery County Music Festival Choir.
Guest Conductor - Sir Adrian Boult.
Solo Pianoforte - Harriet Cohen.
Vocalist - Mary Jarred.
Drama in the Town Hall.

THURSDAY, AUGUST 5th.

Ladies' Choir Competitions.
Chairing of Bard.
Evening Concert:
Montgomery County Music Festival Choir,
Full Symphony Orchestra and Artistes.
" Elijah " (Mendelssohn)
Soloists: Isobel Baillie, Mary Jarred,
Parry Jones, Harold Williams.
Guest Conductor - Sir Adrian Boult.
Drama in the Town Hall.

FRIDAY, AUGUST 6th.

Children's Day.
Evening: Miscellaneous Welsh Concert.
Eisteddfod Choir (500 voices).
Full Symphony Orchestra.
Conductor: W. R. Allen, A.R.C.M.
Artistes: Megan Thomas, David Lloyd,
Owen Bryngwyn, Ted & Frances Richards
(Penillion) Solo Harp: Rhiannon Jones.
Drama in the Town Hall.

SATURDAY, AUGUST 7th.

CHIEF MALE VOICE COMPETITIONS.
Rural Choirs.
Evening Concert: Gold Medal (" Blue
Riband ") Competition
and Eisteddfod Choir.
Drama in the Town Hall.

ARTS AND CRAFTS EXHIBITION OPEN DAILY

CHEAP TICKET FACILITIES

From Monday, August 2nd, to Saturday, August 7th (inclusive), CHEAP TICKETS Third Class at about the Single Fare for the return journey (First Class at approximately 50% above the Third Class fares) will be issued to

MACHYNLLETH

from stations where the train services permit of passengers travelling out and home the same day.

Third Class MONTHLY RETURN TICKETS available for return on any day, within one month, are issued to MACHYNLLETH, from any station, at about the Single Fare and a third. FIRST CLASS TICKETS are issued at approximately 50% above the THIRD CLASS FARES. (Minimum Fares—3/9 1st Class, 2/6 3rd Class).

WEEKLY SEASON TICKETS.

11/6 First Class, 7/6 Third Class, will be issued from Newtown, Llanidloes, Aberystwyth, Barmouth and intermediate stations to MACHYNLLETH. The tickets will be available during Eisteddfod week, for unlimited travel by any train to and from Machynlleth.

FOR PARTICULARS OF EXCURSIONS—SEE OTHER ANNOUNCEMENTS.

In Wales, *eisteddfodau* were an excellent source of additional revenue. This is part of a handbill advertising the National Eisteddfod held at Machynlleth in 1937. Excursions organised for the event necessitated the production of an 8-page booklet.
Powysland Museum

from Swindon (or elsewhere) that it was feasible to turn a 'Manor' on a 55 ft table, before Nos. 7807 and 7819 were sent down to Machynlleth to return with two important troop trains in 1944. Some of the enginemen present on that occasion were decidedly sceptical at the outset.

The cost of this work makes interesting reading: the new 65 ft turntable at Welshpool was estimated at £4,278; Aberystwyth's turning triangle worked out at £3,085 (Chief Engineer £2,140; C.M.E. £820; Signal Engineer £125), whilst the replacement 55 ft table at Machynlleth emerged as the best bargain of all – the table itself was valued at £350 and the cost of installation totalled £1,890 (Chief Engineer £1,100; C.M.E. £790).[10] Many other facilities were improved throughout the Division during the 1930s; engine pits, crew cabins, sand driers, etc, but a full inventory is not attempted here.

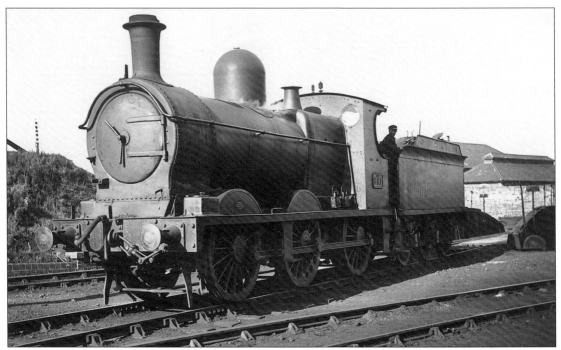

The GW turntable at Aberystwyth on 19 September 1936, before relocation at Machynlleth at the end of the decade; the locomotive is former Cambrian 0-6-0 No. 887.   *F. K. Davies*

PASSENGER SERVICES

Local passenger services followed the accepted, well-established pattern whereas through services, with a few minute adjustments here and there, showed a slight increase in number by the end of the decade; this despite the occasional loss of the through Treherbert train, as a separate service, between Moat Lane and Aberystwyth. From 1932, this 'down' train, depending on the load, could be combined at the junction with a preceding Manchester-Aberystwyth express which arrived at the coast some twenty-five minutes earlier than if the Treherbert portion had waited for its own path from Moat Lane. Also in 1932, an additional through service was introduced from Manchester,

A Treherbert-Aberystwyth train makes its way past Commins Coch in charge of Dean 0-6-0 No. 2388. 10 August 1935.
Ifor A. Higgon

which left London Road station at 8.35 a.m., calling at Whitchurch at 9.45 a.m. before running non-stop to arrive at Moat Lane by 11.25 a.m. Further limited stops at Machynlleth, Dovey Junction and Borth contributed to an Aberystwyth arrival by 12.58 p.m. It featured in the timetable as a Holiday Ticket Train, dedicated to economy ticket holders only. As such, it would appear to have been successful for by 1936 an 8.35 a.m. train from Manchester was timetabled as a regular service, with connections shown from Preston, Warrington, Leeds, Halifax, Huddersfield and Bradford; arrival at Aberystwyth was at 1.00 p.m. By 1937, it was scheduled to stop at Oswestry (dep. 10.23 a.m.) before running non-stop to Machynlleth, arriving at 12.08 p.m. The time of 1 hr 45 mins, meant that the 56¾ miles were covered at an average speed of 32 m.p.h., a seemingly unimpressive figure unless it is realised that it was influenced, in part at least, by no fewer than fifteen speed restrictions of 15 m.p.h. and others of 30, 40 and 50 m.p.h.

A set of '8.8s' – possibly all ex-Taff Vale Railway non-corridor stock – forms a 1937 version of the same service, at the same location: 4-4-0 locomotive No. 3204, 31 July 1937. A general instruction, included in an Extra Trains Notice (week of 29 July-5 August 1938) is of interest:
Every effort is made to provide corridor and lavatory accommodation on long-distance trains, but in some exceptional cases such provision cannot be made, and in these circumstances Station Masters at points where time is scheduled for locomotive etc., purposes, should arrange as far as practicable to ensure that time is allowed passengers for lavatory purposes. *Ifor A. Higgon*

Nameless 'Duke' No. 3257 (formerly *King Arthur*) leads No. 3265 *Tre Pol & Pen* into Aberystwyth on an ex-Birkenhead excursion, 16 April 1932.

Ifor A. Higgon

An unidentified 'Duke' heads an 'up' train at Commins Coch. Although no details accompany the print, this formation is similar in appearance to a 2.45 p.m. ex-Aberystwyth train frequently referred to in contemporary railway circles as 'the first mail'. Date unknown.

E. E. Smith/Courtesy W. G. Rear

Tickets mainly from the 1930s (with the exception of the Penychain and Dovey Junction tickets.)   *Malcolm James Coll.*

The 1936 timetable shows two additional SO 'down' evening trains, one from Welshpool and one from Moat Lane. Previously, at this time of day, the only through train was the 5.30 p.m. stopping train from Shrewsbury, which carried through coaches from the Paddington 2.10 p.m. service. By 1936, this was improved by new timings for the Monday-Friday service (five minutes earlier arrival at Aberystwyth) and the introduction of a SO 'fast' connection with the 2.10 p.m. Paddington, which stopped only at Welshpool, Newtown, Moat Lane, Machynlleth and Borth, enabling it to arrive at Aberystwyth at 8.15 p.m. thereby reducing the journey time by thirty minutes. To compensate for this on Saturdays, a stopping train was put on from Welshpool, and matters were further improved (SO) by providing a connection from Moat Lane to the last 'down' service of the day, a Whitchurch-Llanidloes train (which also connected at Welshpool with the 4.07 p.m. from Paddington).

These innovations were obviously successful for they were retained until the outbreak of war. Additionally, in 1939, a new through train left

The year-old 4-4-0 No. 3213 could have been called *Earl of Powis* (sic); the name had been allocated but was never carried. This glorious view is of No. 3213 on an Oswestry-Aberystwyth service between Clatter and Carno. 18 July 1938.   *John Gwyn Dewing*

Paddington at 2.05 p.m. This carried a buffet car to Wolverhampton and, after an engine change, continued direct to Welshpool, via the Abbey Foregate Loop at Shrewsbury. The following 2.10 p.m. from Paddington (to Birkenhead) still included through coaches to Aberystwyth in its make up. These were removed at Shrewsbury and, remarkably, even after calling at all stations to Welshpool, were only eleven minutes behind the 2.05 p.m. at that stage. The times for both these services from Welshpool were identical, which suggests that, if loadings were light, they might have been combined for the remainder of the journey; if loads were heavier, they could have followed one another down to the coast.

The Cambrian Coast Express enjoyed its last pre-war season as a daily service in 1930. It commenced on Friday and Saturday, 11 and 12 July, then operated daily from 18 July until 21 September. The following year, it ran only on Fridays and Saturdays during the period of the summer timetable. Nonetheless, these services,

together with the Birmingham and Manchester through trains, were frequently run in more that one portion. There were three timetabled through trains to/from Manchester on summer Saturdays (one to/from Victoria station and two to/from London Road) plus through coaches by other services. On average, there were three through trains to and from Birmingham with, additionally, the CCE and two or three other through coach services working to and from Paddington. The 9.05 a.m. service from Birkenhead to Aberystwyth, introduced in 1922, continued to convey through coaches from Manchester (London Road) up until the war and the Treherbert-Aberystwyth trains endured, with only minor modifications over the years. Up to 1933, at least, it was not unknown for the Treherbert train, at times, also to run in two portions. Ifor Higgon noted 0-6-0 No. 2483 with the main train (5.8s) and No. 2316 with the second portion of 6.8s, on 5 August 1933. This general pattern of services was maintained until September 1939.

'Duke' Nos. 3289 (*St. Austell* until 1930) and 3264 *Trevithick*, run the 'down' Cambrian Coast Express away from Commins Coch on 21 August 1937. The dining car was the third of nine vehicles on this occasion.   *Ifor A. Higgon*

'Duke' Nos. 3289 and 3264 *Trevithick* formed a regular pairing during August and September 1937. Ifor Higgon photographed them working train No. 250 (10.00. a.m. Aberystwyth-Paddington) up the broad and verdant Dyfi valley towards Cemmes Road, 4 September 1937.   *Ifor A. Higgon*

'Duke' No. 3284 *Isle of Jersey* (recently painted green) and No. 3253 *Boscawen* contribute to a stirring picture as they approached Cemmes Road with the 10.15 a.m. from Aberystwyth (TC to Paddington, Birkenhead and Liverpool). 31 July 1937.   *Ifor A. Higgon*

Former 'Earl' class 4-4-0 No. 3200 *Earl of Mount Edgcumbe* coasts past Commins Coch with the nine coach 1.50 p.m. Whitchurch-Aberystwyth express. 6 August 1938.   *Ifor A. Higgon*

(2494)

GREAT WESTERN RAILWAY.

TRAFFIC DEPARTMENT.

WELSHPOOL. STATION,

14th. June 193 5.

SPECIAL STOP ORDER.

To engineman and guard of 3.12p.m.

*Passenger train from Welshpool

to Aberystwyth. 14th. June 193 5.

You are required to call specially at

CEMMES ROAD

for the following purpose.....................
setting down ex Birmingham.

.... STATION MASTER.

This order must be attached to guard's journal.

* Passenger or Goods.

450 pads, 100 lvs. NB 1934 12/33 (2) S

B.R.O. 20079
O.F. 2

London Midland and Scottish Railway Company.

June 12th 19 35.

1.52p.m. Train ex Whitchurch

You must stop at Carno & Commins Coch Halt to-day

to Pick up passengers

Signed ....

To the Driver

Reference to authority Wire

Two 'Special Stop Orders' handed by stationmasters to relevant drivers and guards, authorising special arrangements. The use of an LMS form at Whitchurch is particularly interesting.

IAH Coll.

Major changes, naturally, are usually easier to recall than comparatively minor incidents or figures, which tend to fade rapidly from the memory. Amongst the latter may be noted the lady who ran the refreshment room at Dovey Junction. For years, she travelled down each weekday on the 8.10 a.m. from Machynlleth and spent her working day, between trains, with little to do but admire the solitude of the marshes around Dovey Junction. She was probably pleased to return each evening on the mail. Then there was an unofficial but very useful 'town porter' at Machynlleth, who met each train. He could be relied upon to transport passengers' luggage within the town for a modest fee but, unlike the refreshment-room lady, did not survive the 1940s. He found that many who became self-sufficient during the war gradually dispensed with his services. These and others like them, throughout the country, contributed to the colour of the general railway scene; they went about their work almost un-noticed and virtually, unsung.

SUNDAY PASSENGER SERVICES

Up to 1932, the only Sunday services were the two mail trains, one in each direction, between Whitchurch and Aberystwyth, together with their coast connections between Machynlleth and Barmouth. Then, in 1933, a new train appeared between Birmingham and Aberystwyth. Departure from Snow Hill was at 10.45 a.m. and the route chosen was via Oswestry as, presumably, the signal-boxes along that corridor had already been opened for passage of the mail. After a five minute halt at Oswestry, the train left at 12.41 p.m., stopped at Welshpool and Newtown for a minute's respite at each station, before reaching Machynlleth at 2.18 p.m. Here the train was divided: Aberystwyth passengers reached the coast at 3.00 p.m.; those bound for Barmouth had all reached their destination by 3.28 p.m. A corresponding 'up' service left Barmouth at 2.50 p.m. – the two coast trains 'crossing' at Llwyngwril. The main line service left Aberystwyth at 3.30 p.m. In theory at least, it was

In 1936, the *Earl of Devon* name-plates were transferred briefly from 'Duke' No. 3270 to 'Earl' class No. 3205, before being attached finally to 'Castle' class No. 5048. The unadorned No. 3270 here works the 2.55 p.m. SO Barmouth-Birmingham (Snow Hill) train on 19 June 1938.

Ifor A. Higgon

'Barnum' 2-4-0 No. 3225 works the 'up' mail train out of Aberystwyth sometime during the early 1930s. The first two vehicles were the mail carriers; the leading van was probably new in 1930 whilst the clerestory sorting carriage behind (No. 863) worked this service regularly until replaced by a brand-new vehicle (No. 797) in 1933. Photograph undated but *c*. 1930-33. *Lens of Sutton*

No photograph has yet been discovered of Travelling Post Office (TPO) No. 797 at work on the Cambrian during the six years from its introduction to the outbreak of war. This official view of No. 795 affords an impression, although No. 797 was 7ft shorter than No. 795 depicted here. The nets were carried by No. 797 throughout the six years but were never used on the Cambrian. *WIMM/GW Coll.*

possible to glimpse the seaside here but it would appear that these trains were meant to augment the Saturday through services rather than provide day excursions. They were successful, for they appeared again the following year, the coast portions now being extended to/from Harlech. These arrangements continued largely unchanged in 1936 and the following year, except that the entry in the working timetable referred to the 10.33 a.m. from Small Heath to Aberystwyth and Harlech. In 1938-39, it featured once more as the 10.35 a.m. Birmingham to Aberystwyth (with Harlech TC). It ceased at the end of August 1939 and was not reinstated after the war.

By 1936, a new limited service entered the timetable when a through train for Manchester (London Road) left Aberystwyth at 2.30 p.m. It was confined to three Sundays in August only and stopped at Llandre (to cross the 'down' 10.45 a.m. service from Birmingham), Borth, Machynlleth, Newtown and Welshpool, running on to Llanymynech, Oswestry, Ellesmere and Whitchurch by 5.35 p.m. Arrival at London Road was at 7.00 p.m. There was no corresponding 'down' train from Manchester. The same pattern was repeated in 1937 and 1938 but by 1939 it operated on one Sunday only; August 13.

As ever, the formal timetables do no more than convey a general impression of regular traffic. The services which we find increasingly fascinating today are the extra trains, which are difficult to trace and are now largely forgotten. Their pattern varied considerably and we have no way of assessing their frequency or variety without special printed details. Fortunately, copies of a few weekly Notices of Extra Trains from the 1930s survive and a sample is included here. (Tables VIII and IX) The table from Notice No. CW 19 of 1938 is particularly interesting as it illustrates the need to work trains overnight because no additional paths were available during the hours of daylight. This was not uncommon during congested summer periods pre-war.

Former 'Earl' class No. 3203 makes a brave picture as it storms over Bell's Bridge with steam to spare. 'Concertina' coaches (the first vehicle) were not often found on the Cambrian in as fine condition as this particular example. 10 April 1939.
John Gwyn Dewing

'Duke' No. 3284 *Isle of Jersey* hammers away from Abermule (and rapidly approaches the site of the 1921 disaster – just 100 yds or so to the left of this picture) as it lifts its eight coach load towards Newtown and Talerddig. 10 April 1939.
John Gwyn Dewing

IAH coll.

Whitchurch—Aberystwyth.

Station		1 "A" L.M.S. Camping Special from Coventry. a.m.	2 "A" G.W. Small Heath to Pwllheli. a.m.	3 "A" G.W. Bordesley to Harlech. a.m.	4 "A" G.W. Birmingham to Barmouth.	5 "A" G.W. Tyseley to Aberystwyth. a.m.	6 "A" Relief to 6.0 a.m. ex Birmingham a.m.	7 "A" From Leicester L.M.S.	8 "A" 7.45 a.m. Relief ex Birmingham a.m.
Head Lamps	…								
Welshpool	arr.	12 10	1 42	1 52	2 2	2 25	7 50	8 22	9 52
,,	dep.	12 20	1 47	2 0	2 12	2 30	7 55	8 27	9 57
Montgomery	arr.					2 41			
,,	dep.					2 43			
Abermule	pass						8X12		10X8
Newtown	arr.					2 56	8 19		10 21
,,	dep.					2 58	8 21		10 23
Moat Lane	arr.	12 52	2 20	2 35	2 47	3 6	8 28	8 58	10 30
,,	dep.						8 33	9X16	10X39
Talerddig	arr.						9 0		10 57
Llanbrynmair	arr.						9X5		11 3
,,	dep.								11X7
Cemmes Road	arr.								11 15
,,	dep.								11X17
Machynlleth	arr.	1 32	3 0	3 15	3 27	3 50	9 22	9 37	11 24
,,	dep.	1 40	3 8	3 23	3 37	3 57	9 24	9 40	11 27
Dovey Jct.	arr.	1 47	3 15	3 30	3 45	4 4	9 31	9X46	11 33
,,	dep.						9 34	9a52	11X41
Glandyfi	arr.	To Harlech.	To Pwllheli.	To Harlech.	To Barmouth.		9 37		
Ynyslas	,,						9X46		
Borth	arr.					4 17	9 58	10 9	11 55
,,	dep.					4 19	10 0	10 10	11 57
Llandre	arr.					4 23			
,,	dep.					4 25			
Bow Street	arr.					4 35	10 9	10X16	12 7
,,	dep.					4 37		10 20	
Llanbadarn	dep.						10X11	10X25	12X16
,,	pass						10X17	10X32	
Aberystwyth	arr.					4 45	10 20	10 35	12 25

a—Detach Barmouth portion.

A light engine to leave Oswestry at 11.30 p.m. (Friday) for Welshpool to work the Coventry train forward.

A light engine to leave Oswestry at 7.30 a.m. for Welshpool to work the Leicester train forward.

Table VIII (CW No. 19).

Machynlleth—Pwllheli.

Special Passenger Trains.

		L.M.S. Camping Special from Coventry.	Birmingham to Pwllheli.	Bordesley to Harlech.	Birmingham to Barmouth.	Special Passenger	Special Passenger.
		a.m.	a.m.	a.m.	a.m.	a.m.	a.m.
Machynlleth	dep.	1 40	3T 8	3 23	3 37	—	—
Dovey Jct.	,,	1 47	3 15	3 30	3 45	10X17	11 50
Aberdovey	arr.	—	—	3 44	4 0	10b31	12 4
,,	dep.	2 2	3 29	3 46	4 2	10X32	12 6
Towyn	arr.	2 9	—	3 53	4 9	10 38	12 13
,,	dep.	2 15	3 36	3 55	4 14	10 40	12X21
Tonfanau	arr.	—	—	4 0	4 19	—	—
,,	dep.	—	—	4 2	4 21	—	—
Llwyngwril	arr.	—	—	4 10	4 30	10 52	12 33
,,	dep.	2 27	3 48	4 12	4 35	11X 1	12X42
Fairbourne	arr.	—	—	4 20	4 43	11 9	12 50
,,	dep.	—	—	4 22	4 45	11 10	12 51
Barmouth Jct.	arr.	—	—	4 25	4 48	11 13	12 54
,,	dep.	2 39	4 0	4 27	4 50	11 15	12 55
Barmouth	arr.	2 45	4 5	4 32	4 55	11 20	1 0
,,	dep.	2 55	4 10	4 40	5†10		
Llanaber Halt	arr.	—	4 13		—	—	—
,,	dep.	—	4 15		—	—	—
Talybont Halt	arr.	3 2	4 20		—	—	—
,,	dep.	3 20	4 22		—	—	—
Dyffryn-on-Sea	arr.	3 25	4 27		—	—	—
,,	dep.	3 30	4 29		5†20	—	—
Llanbedr & P.	arr.	—	4 34		—	—	—
,,	dep.	—	4 35		5†27	—	—
Llandanwg Halt	arr.	—	4 37		—	—	—
,,	dep.	—	4 40		—	—	—
Harlech	arr.	3 43	4 47	5 0	—	—	—
,,	dep.	3†48	4 49		5†35	—	—
Talsarnau	arr.	—	4 55		—	—	—
,,	dep.	—	4 57	Empty Train to return to Birmingham	—	—	—
Portmadoc	arr.	—	5 10		5†55	—	—
,,	dep.	4† 8	5 13		—	—	—
Black Rock Halt	arr.	—	5 20		—	—	—
,,	dep.	—	5 23		—	—	—
Criccieth	arr.	—	5 27		—	—	—
,,	dep.	4†18	5 28		—	—	—
Afon Wen	arr.	4†25	5 34		—	—	—
,,	dep.	—	5 35		—	—	—
Pwllheli	arr.	—	5 45		—	—	—

b—Cross 7.55 a.m. Pwllheli.

Loco. Dept. to arrange for the 3.8 a.m. Machynlleth to Pwllheli, 3.23 a.m. Machynlleth to Harlech and 3.37 a.m. Machynlleth to Barmouth to be double-headed.

3.23 a.m. from Machynlleth.—Formed: 10 Eights, two or three leading coaches conveying a party Kidderminster to Harlech, remainder of train conveying parties for stations between Aberdovey and Barmouth. The rear portion to be detached at Barmouth.

5†10 a.m. from Barmouth.—To be utilised to convey passengers for stations between Barmouth and Portmadoc if required.

10.17 a.m. from Dovey Junction. Formation: 5 Thirds, Compo, Van Third, also Barmouth portion off Leicester train. Loco. Dept. to arrange for this train to be double-headed Dovey Junction to Barmouth. Engine and coaches to work second part of 12.20 p.m. Barmouth to Dovey Junction, the L.M.S. coaches to be worked into Machynlleth.

11.50 a.m. from Dovey Junction.—Formed 3 Thirds, Compo and Brake Third, and will convey passengers off the 7.45 a.m. relief ex Birmingham. Empty train to return from Barmouth to Dovey Junction at once.

T.—Train to be examined at Machynlleth and if any passengers for stations between Aberdovey and Barmouth Junction they should be changed into the second train, or if necessary instructions given to the Trainmen to stop to set down as required.

Table IX (CW No. 19). *IAH coll.*

FREIGHT SERVICES

As in the previous decade, a single through goods train in each direction sufficed between Oswestry and Aberystwyth; there were none from Shrewsbury to the coast. Instead, freight trains continued to ply between the major centres/junctions, where the loads were distributed or assembled for forwarding to various destinations. The times of the majority changed little over the years, within a tolerance of 15-30 minutes or so. For example, the Class 'K' goods train which left Machynlleth for Oswestry (for almost three decades from 1936) was universally regarded as the '2 o'clock goods', although its official departure varied over the years between 1.55 p.m. and 2.10 p.m.

In addition to the Aberystwyth-Oswestry through freights, there were other services between Machynlleth, Newtown, Moat Lane, Welshpool and Oswestry, in both directions. Newtown and Welshpool, in particular, were important freight centres, although for different reasons. Newtown was, perhaps, the principal centre dealing in general freight and livestock traffic. In addition, bicycles were produced at the Phillips factory in the town and heavy parcels traffic was generated by the Pryce Jones, Royal Welsh Warehouse. Oswestry and Welshpool also contributed to the general freight and livestock figures, and the latter was well placed for collecting and distributing goods for the Oswestry and Shrewsbury lines. Traffic to and from the Mid Wales line was dealt with at Moat Lane, whilst Machynlleth served the coast, where dedicated services linked certain centres only, such as Towyn, Barmouth or Portmadoc (rather than through trains between Machynlleth and Pwllheli).

GW No. 895 (Cam No. 101) heads a Class 'K' 'up' freight from Machynlleth (1.55 p.m.) to Oswestry. The banking engine was No. 894 (Cam No. 100). 19 April 1939. *Ifor A. Higgon*

'Duke' No. 3253 *Boscawen* requires no banker on the same service on 27 April 1939, seen here approaching Commins Coch Halt.

Ifor A. Higgon

0-6-0 No. 864 on the 10.05 a.m. goods train from Barmouth to Machynlleth, leaves Barmouth Junction on 5 May 1938.

Ifor A. Higgon

Although freight trains were not numerous, those which ran were well loaded and frequently required banking over Talerddig. An interesting innovation emerged in 1939 with the appearance of a Sundays Only through freight train, during the period of the summer timetable, which ran in each direction between Oswestry and Portmadoc. Otherwise, the only goods trains out on the Sabbath were those postponed from the Saturday in an effort to ease congestion on the line.

Given the absence of major industries in the region, it is interesting to note the railway's efforts to encourage such traffic as existed, made evident by its willingness to upgrade goods facilities at even the smallest station or, occasionally, as indicated earlier, where no station or siding existed at all.

Beyer Peacock-built No. 844 approaches Commins Coch Halt with the 1.55 p.m. Class 'K' freight from Machynlleth to Oswestry comprising a typical mixed load of vans, open, lumber and cattle wagons. It was banked in the rear, as far as Talerddig, by Dean No. 2572. 4 June 1938. *Ifor A. Higgon*

LOCOMOTIVES AND ROLLING STOCK

Oswestry acquired an interesting 'new' engine in 1930, in the form of rebuilt 'Duke' No. 3265 *Tre Pol & Pen*. It was not 'designed' in the accepted sense but grew almost accidentally from the fact that 'Duke' No. 3265 lay in 'B' shop at Swindon, alongside 'Bulldog' No. 3365 *Charles Grey Mott*. Kenneth J. Cook, assistant works manager at the time, recalls[11]

The frames of the former were in very poor condition, the design was rather flimsy and fanciful, and I got the idea of building up the 'Duke' on the frames of 3365, mounting a 113 Lot class boiler, using cab, smoke-box and all the 'Duke' fittings including unbalanced crank and its name-plate *Tre Pol & Pen* and number 3265.

So *Tre Pol & Pen* 'evolved' and operated successfully from Oswestry for the next two decades. It soon established the fact that although similar, it was somewhat superior to the old 'Dukes'. As the 'Bulldog' frames were more substantial than those of the 'Dukes' it was also marginally heavier, a decided advantage in view of the latter's tendancy to slip easily. Nonetheless, for some years it was no more than an interesting hybrid and the steady withdrawal of Cambrian locomotives continued throughout the 1930s. The 'Dukes' were still fully employed and largely confined to the main line, although No. 3276 *St Agnes* worked a military special (from Camberley)

to Harlech during May 1930 – and had to return to Barmouth Junction to turn for the return journey. Around this time also, the first 'Duke' is believed to have visited the Ruabon branch, when No. 3262 *St. Ives* worked a 7-coach day excursion from Aberystwyth to Llangollen. Other strangers then on the Ruabon line were two of the new Collett '22xx' class of 0-6-0s; Nos. 2262 and 2270. In August, No. 3603 was amongst the first of the 2-4-2T class to work through to Barmouth Junction; they were not particularly successful and did not stay long.[12]

No. 3265 *Tre Pol & Pen*, the precursor of the 'Earl' class, gathering speed as it worked the 8.30 a.m. Oswestry-Whitchurch train from Cemmes Road towards Machynlleth. 7 August 1937.

Ifor A. Higgon

Cambrian No. 45 (initially named *Rhiewport*) featured in a Newtown & Machynlleth Railway order of 10 January 1863, taken over by Thomas Savin as a result of disagreement with his partner David Davies. Later numbered 900 by the GWR, it was photographed at Barmouth Junction as it worked its way from Machynlleth to Portmadoc, during the period it served there and at Minffordd as station pilot. 6 July 1928.

Ifor A. Higgon

Driver Charles Davies and No. 1043 worked a return Blackpool special from Machynlleth to Barmouth on 13 October 1930 when Barmouth Junction (23.86 miles from Machynlleth) was reached in 37 min. 10 sec. Maxima of 55 m.p.h. between Machynlleth and Dovey Junction, 53 m.p.h. between Aberdovey and Towyn, and between Towyn and Tonfanau, and 57 m.p.h. between Tonfanau and Llwyngwril indicate that the engine was pressed hard over these sections. Photograph undated. *LGRP*

One of the features of the initial Great Western regime down the coast was the regular movement, between Portmadoc and Machynlleth, of the old Cambrian stalwarts numbered 900 and 908 by the GW. They were employed as station pilots at Portmadoc, their principal duty being to shunt the Minffordd exchange sidings. At that time, these were lightly laid and would accept nothing heavier that the little Sharp Stewarts. One worked the yard whilst the other enjoyed an easier time at Machynlleth where, having benefitted from routine maintenance and a boiler wash-out, it undertook a few gentle trips on the Mawddwy branch, before again setting out for Portmadoc. This practice continued from the time of the grouping until 1932, when Minffordd yard was re-laid and could accept the GW '23s'. As far as is verifiable today, the main exceptions to this

pattern occurred during 1923 and 1924 when No. 908, rather surprisingly, shared the duty with 4-4-0 No. 1115 for over twelve months and again, in February 1928, No. 910 entered the lists until the end of April. Nos. 900 and 908 were joined briefly during the spring, 1929, when another small Sharp Stewart 0-6-0 No. 898 helped out and No. 910 served finally in the spring of 1930; otherwise, faithful old Nos. 900 and 908 soldiered on. They were found other duties after 1932; No. 900 (Cambrian No. 45, formerly *Rhiewport*) survived until September 1945, and No. 908 (Cambrian No. 48, un-named) was withdrawn in 1938. The other members of this exclusive 0-6-0 club, Nos. 898 (Cambrian No. 14, formerly *Broneirion*) and 910 (Cambrian No. 51, formerly *Snowdon*) survived until 1947 and 1935, respectively.[13]

'Bulldog' No. 3442 *Bullfinch* (seen here at Chester *c.* 1935) saw service between Chester and Barmouth before the war. During the post-war period it worked several SO trains to Aberystwyth from Shrewsbury. *GBJ Coll.*

At the end of January 1931, Cambrian 4-4-0 No. 98, as GW No. 1043, returned to Machynlleth after a brief visit to Swindon, and worked the 8.20 a.m. Machynlleth-Pwllheli service, virtually until July, when it undertook some duties on the main line. With the commencement of the winter service in September, it reverted to the 8.20 a.m. working, returning on the 4.00 p.m. mail from Pwllheli. The last surviving 'Large Bogie' No. 1110 made its final appearance down the coast, with the Oswestry engineers saloon, before being withdrawn in April. The first part of the year also

saw 'Barnum' class No. 3221 working to Barmouth from Chester/Wrexham, but June brought more 'Bulldogs' to that line in the form of Nos. 3338, 3410 and 3426, and in August, Nos. 3318, 3442 and 3445. Then, on an August Saturday, No. 5187, the first to appear of a 'new' class, worked the second portion of the 1.30 p.m. from Ruabon as far as Barmouth. In September 1931 'Duke' class No. 3283 *Comet* worked an excursion from Machynlleth to Chester via Dolgellau, and the following month, No. 3255 *Excalibur* worked another, this time to Liverpool.[14]

'Aberdare' class 2-6-0 No. 2617 at Barmouth Junction, on the 'goods only' side of the triangle, before returning with the 5.30 p.m. 'up' goods to Wrexham. 31 May 1930. *Ifor A. Higgon*

With locomotive improvements on the main line still dependant on completion of the slow-moving bridge and track renewal programme, new developments again appear to be concentrated down the coast. The principal feature was the completion at the end of March 1932 of a new 55 ft turntable at Pwllheli. The first to take advantage of the new facility was No. 3283 *Comet*; it was quickly followed by *Mercury*, *Merlin*, *Tor Bay* and others. The main trains from Ruabon continued to be operated by 2-6-0s and 'Bulldogs'. No. 3442 *Bullfinch* presented an attractive sight in August, painted green after overhaul; No. 3427 followed in September and No. 3327 *Marco Polo* by December, both similarly treated. Also, at the end of the year, 'Aberdare' class 2-6-0s worked goods turns between Ruabon and Barmouth Junction.[15]

By late February in the new year, a severe snowstorm affected the area, and several lines were blocked. No. 2410, on the early morning Machynlleth-Pwllheli train, became embedded in a drift near Tonfanau and had to be rescued by a snow plough from Ruabon. This was worked by pannier tank No. 1776 and 0-6-0 No. 2511. Eight days later, on Saturday, 4 March 1933, the second tragic Friog cliff disaster occurred when the engine of the first 'down' train from Machynlleth struck a landslide and fell nearly 90 ft to the beach below. Driver John Humphreys and John Price Kenny, his fireman that day (who had only exchanged 'turns' so he could visit his sick mother in Pwllheli), were both killed in the accident. The Board of Trade report indicates that the train was struck by the landslip as it passed; whether this was so, or whether the train ran into the debris of a landslide which may have occurred previously, is still open to some debate. Engine No. 874 was cut up on the beach. Traffic was resumed the following Thursday (9 March) and the GWR immediately set about strengthening the cliff face and constructing the avalanche shelter which still safeguards the line at this point. The first accident here, with

similarly tragic consequences, had occurred on 1 January 1883.

In the autumn of 1933, auto-tank engine No. 4812 arrived at Penmaenpool to work the Dolgellau service but no further 'new' engine-types visited the CWD until 1936. Meanwhile, the scrapping of the older Cambrian engines continued, whilst their GW cousins were assiduously put through the works in order to keep them in good order. The latter may have been old and small but they were kept in fine condition and served the area well, until more powerful locomotives were eventually available.

The damaged roadway at the site of the slip at Friog. The three ropes trailing across the road and down the face of the slip were used by the railway's 'rock-men' who thus had ready access to rail level and, by means of more ropes, to the beach. 9 May 1933.   *WIMM/GW Coll.*

The Friog landslide viewed from sea level. The scarred rock faces, the heap of spoil at the base, together with workmen removing remnants of the locomotive (No. 874) give an impression of the scale of the catastrophe. 9 May 1933.

WIMM/GW Coll.

A notable feature of locomotive operation continued to be the amount of double-heading required during the busy summer periods. This applied equally to passenger and goods services, both on the main line and down the coast. This shortage of adequate power influenced the decision to try 2-6-2T No. 4528 on a goods turn between Machynlleth and Pwllheli as early as November 1924 but, inexplicably, the practice was not repeated until 1936. By that time it must have become apparent that the eagerly awaited new motive power was still some way from materialising. As time advanced and the civil engineer seemed unable to upgrade the Cambrian line quickly enough, K. J. Cook's example of

creative works management in 1930 was remembered, and a 'new' class of 4-4-0s, which Collett called the 'Earls', emerged in 1936. Their story is well-known. The second contribution to finding a quick solution to the motive power problem, particularly down the coast, was to reintroduce a 2-6-2T, so No. 5570 was transferred to Machynlleth and after some forays on the main line, eventually settled down to work the coast where the 45/55xx class of engines were well suited. The combination of power/weight ratio and small diameter driving wheels enabled them to accelerate smartly from the many halts *en route* and they were most effective until the 1960s when they were superseded by the BR class 3 2-6-2Ts.

The remnants of the locomotive were initially removed from the beach to a small wharf, slightly south of the slip and above the high water level. May 1933.

Ifor A. Higgon

A steam crane was then employed to drag and lift fragments to rail level. *c.* April/May 1933.

GBJ Coll.

Almost a quarter of a century after the disaster, the Machynlleth crew of 0-6-0 No. 3200 have every confidence in the engineering work which safeguards the line and enjoy the view as their train is lifted briefly above the seagulls manoeuvering below. August 1957.

GBJ

The 'Earls' hour of glory arrived as a direct result of the Coronation of 1937. Their Majesties King George VI and Queen Elizabeth undertook a tour of Wales in the royal train, which conveyed them from Paddington to Newport, Cardiff and Swansea on 13 and 14 July. The locomotives which then worked the train forward from Swansea to Aberystwyth were 'Earl' class No. 3209 and 2-6-0 No. 6385. After an overnight stop in Pencader tunnel loop, the same locomotives continued the journey to Aberystwyth the following day. Arrival here was at No. 5 platform, as it then was, at 10.20 a.m. Sleeping car No. 461 was then taken out of the royal train formation, and the train transferred to No. 3 platform. Both engines had gone on shed, but No. 3209, now in company of No. 3212, rejoined the train to work forward to Dovey Junction. Here they found classmates Nos. 3210 and 3208, from Machynlleth, waiting to work the train forward to Afon Wen, where the LMS was to take over to Caernarfon, Bangor and, eventually, Euston.

J. M. Dunn, the respected LNWR and LMS locomotive enthusiast who was then working at LMS Bangor, was concerned that the two LMS tank engines due to take over at Afon Wen had not been properly cleaned for the occasion. He recalls the episode at some length,[16] ending his account thus:

> Later on at Afon Wen one can imagine the feelings of the LMS departmental chiefs when the train, all in LNWR lake and spilt milk livery, came in from Aberystwyth headed by two gleaming, brightly polished, spick and span GW engines which were replaced by the two scruffy looking tank engines to take the train forward. After that the Bangor men on the tanks overshot the red carpet at Caernarfon and then stopped short of the appointed place for changing engines at Bangor.

The GW engines may have been 'spick and span' but it is regretted that they had been shorn of their brass name-plates just two weeks before the event. No. 3209 had emerged from Swindon in February that year, when it bore the name *Earl of Radnor*, but sadly, for the little 4-4-0s, one of the personages so honoured by Swindon is said to have objected to his name being carried by a small, old-fashioned, double-framed engine. Within the space of a week, between 25 June 1937 and 1 July 1937, the 'Earl' names were all

'Earl' class No. 3204 *Earl of Dartmouth* photographed after emerging from the works at Swindon on 16 August 1936.
H. C. Casserley

An official photograph, again outside the works at Swindon, of 'Earl' No. 3209 *Earl of Radnor.* 13 February 1937.

WIMM/GW Coll.

Without doubt, the best-known photograph of the LNWR Royal Train on the Coronation Tour of Wales in 1937. 4-4-0s Nos. 3210 and 3208 pass Barmouth Junction *en route* to Afonwen, where the train was handed over to the LMS. 15 July 1937.

Ifor A. Higgon

4-4-0 No. 3210, the leading engine of the royal train, was photographed later that day piloting 'Duke' No. 3259 *Merlin* on the 4.00 p.m. Pwllheli-Machynlleth passenger train. The Royal Coats of Arms were covered for this journey but remained on the engine. 15 July 1937.

Ifor A. Higgon

removed from Nos. 3200-12. Perhaps the recent Coronation had served to emphasise subtle social distinctions within the upper echelons of the court, and the prospect of HM the King observing the names of four respected earls on small engines in Wales during his tour caused a hurried removal of the names at the eleventh hour. The names which would otherwise have been carried by the 4-4-0s on royal duty that year were:

3208 *Earl Bathurst*
3209 *Earl of Radnor*
3210 *Earl Cairns*
3212 *Earl of Eldon.*

Following the removal of the 'Earl' names, it seems a fine opportunity was missed to perpetuate some of the colourful names of earlier Cambrian locomotives. Selecting twenty-nine names from a list which included the likes of *Mazeppa*, *Tubal Cain* or *Minerva* would have been a straight-forward and most pleasant task for someone at Oswestry or Swindon.

CARRIAGES

The appearance of 4- and 6-wheel passenger coaches on the main line virtually ceased during the 1930s and the final years of the decade saw the introduction of increasing numbers of Mr Colletts' fine steel-panelled carriages on most services. The new coaches were particularly popular down the coast, especially when the large windows were on the seaward side of the train. The combination of panoramic vistas and 5/- weekly runabout tickets saved many a holiday, particularly when inhospitable weather ruled out visits to the beach and whole families spent their time on the trains.

Notes

[1]Recalled in Briwnant Jones, G.: *Railway Through Talerddig*, Gomer Press (1990), p. 44.

[2]NLW Facs 687, GW Memo. Book; CWD Improvements 1923-48.

[3]*GWR Magazine*, February 1931.

[4]NLW Facs 687, GW Memo. Book; CWD Improvements 1923-48, and Appendix to the GWR Working Timetable, March 1943, pp. 88-9.

[5]NLW Facs 687, GW Memo. Book; CWD Improvements 1923-48.

[6]ibid.

[7]ibid.

[8]ibid.

[9]Recalled in Briwnant Jones, G.: *Railway Through Talerddig*, Gomer Press (1990), p. 117.

[10]NLW Facs 687, GW Memo. Book; CWD Improvements 1923-48

[11]Cook, K. J.: *Swindon Steam*, Ian Allan Ltd. (1974), pp. 118-9.

[12]IAH Notes.

[13]ibid.

[14]ibid.

[15]ibid.

[16]Dunn, J. M.: *Reflections on a Railway Career*, Ian Allan Ltd. (1966), p. 107.

Chapter 4

The Second World War and the final Great Western years, 1939-47

Nowadays, during the comparatively comfortable years at the close of the twentieth century, it is easy to disregard the deprivation and fear of wartime days – even by those who experienced them.

Few lives were unaffected by the events of 3 September 1939. Controls and restrictions were promptly introduced and a national register was used as the basis for issuing personal identity cards. Ration books quickly followed in the autumn of 1939; food rationing commenced in January 1940. Supplies of heat and light were severely restricted and power-cuts occurred frequently, as limited gas and electricity supplies were diverted to factories which contributed directly to the war effort. In 1939, most homes were heated solely by open fires, and coal was naturally in great demand both on the domestic front and in industry. During the hours of darkness, the need to eliminate stray sources of light resulted in the notorious blackout. The term means little today to a society confident of an abundance of power and light at the throw of a switch but the opposite prevailed during the early 1940s. Street lamps were decommissioned *en masse*, all vehicle headlamps were heavily masked and the doors and windows of all properties were rapidly provided with efficient 'blackout' to prevent the escape of the merest chink of light. Prominent edges of street furniture were painted white – as were the rims of vehicle mudguards – in an attempt to compensate for the absence of street lights. Moving around outdoors during the blackout was a tedious business.

On the railways, station name-boards were painted black or removed entirely, and platform edges were whitewashed as a safety measure; lights, where essential, were adjusted to emit a weak, blue-hued glow. Rolling stock was modified: the gap between engine and tender, normally a blaze of light whenever the firebox door was opened, was covered by a heavy canvas during the hours of darkness, and the edges of carriage windows carried a 3" painted black border to increase the efficiency of the blinds. The normal quota of four light bulbs per compartment was promptly reduced to a solitary shaded blue bulb of much reduced output, a state of affairs which

> # GREAT WESTERN RAILWAY
>
> ---
>
> # Notice to Passengers
>
> ---
>
> **Passengers are advised to take shelter during an Air Raid and not to remain on the station platforms, where there may be a serious risk of danger from falling glass and splinters.**
>
> **J. MILNE,**
> August, 1940.   General Manager.

Wartime poster: Notice to Passengers: air-raid precaution.
Courtesy Ian Coulson

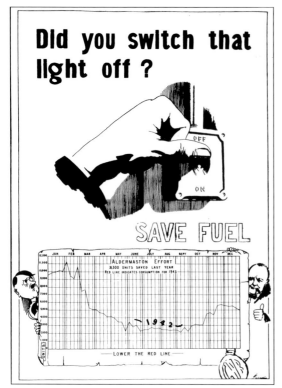

Did you switch that light off?

SAVE FUEL

Wartime poster: staff member A. J. Martin's endeavour to encourage economy of electricity. January 1943.

Courtesy Ian Coulson

remained unchanged until the autumn of 1944 when greater optimism resulted in a gradual relaxation of regulations.[1]

Train and bus services were the principal means of transport in the Dyfi valley, as elsewhere. At the outset, private motorists – few and far between – were allowed a meagre petrol ration, which permitted short local journeys, but this was withdrawn entirely in March 1942 and only essential users, such as doctors or farmers, continued to receive an allowance. Indeed, most of the cars seen around Machynlleth belonged to the farming fraternity – by far the largest section of the community to qualify for what some regarded as an over-generous allowance. The unfortunates,

forced to store their own vehicles for the duration of rationing, were quick to note this comparative affluence and a letter to the *County Times* (10 October 1942) complained of

> ... farmers wasting time and petrol in the town under the guise of attending Sheep Sales. 49 private cars were parked in Maengwyn Street at 2.30 p.m. on 20 September.

The colours and logos of Shell, BP and National Benzole, familiar brands of pre-war petrol, disappeared almost overnight as all pumps were painted a bland grey, appropriately reflecting the anonimity of 'pool' petrol. Essential military convoys passed frequently through mid Wales and although civilian road traffic was generally light, motoring was no less hazardous. At the time, Welsh roads were even narrower and more tortuous than today; their foundations were rarely even and the metalled surfaces were worn smooth in places, as were the tyres of many of the private vehicles still able to use them. Road markings, where they existed, were extremely basic. Most vehicles in those days were prone to be unreliable, whilst a considerable percentage of drivers had never been subjected to a driving test, having obtained their licences before compulsory tests were introduced in 1932. All these factors contributed to a high proportion of breakdowns and/or accidents.

Given such conditions, it was hardly surprising that the railways experienced their busiest period since the First World War. Despite the addition of extra carriages, trains were often packed to capacity. Not only were all available seats occupied but corridors were frequently rendered impassable by a mass of standing passengers and piled luggage, cases and kitbags. People used the trains in their thousands and freight tonnages conveyed by rail during the war were truly gargantuan. The total passenger train mileage operated by the main line railways in 1942, for example, reached 30,000 million; an increase of 50% on pre-war figures. At the same time there was a reduction of 28% in the mileage covered by passenger trains, thus the loading of the trains more than doubled.[2] The railways' true contribution to the war effort has never been fully acknowledged, neither at the time nor since, although it was 'fairly claimed that the British railways . . . were able to place at the disposal of the country at the outbreak of war an organisation which . . . enabled them to meet the full impact of the transport needs of a nation at war'.[3] The railways, undoubtedly, were one of the cornerstones in the fight against tyranny in two world wars but, in terms of reinvestment, they appear to have been poorly rewarded for their effort.

PASSENGER SERVICES

The Great Western's timetable for the summer of 1939 (the last timetable of the greater Great Western) did not run its allotted span from 3 July to 24 September, but ended abruptly on Friday, 1 September, two days before war was declared. The government undertook immediate responsibility for the running of the railways through the Railway Executive, whose first act was to instigate a previously prepared programme which reduced general services and allowed the operation of extra trains for military or evacuation purposes. Amongst the most fascinating trains in the latter category were special arrivals at Aberystwyth conveying containers from the British Museum in London.

The resilience of youth and a sense of some 'grand adventure' is reflected on the faces of these young Merseysiders arriving at Oswestry on 9 September 1939. The recently issued gas masks, in their stout cardboard boxes, were *de rigeur* during the early period of the war. *NLW/Geoff Charles Coll.*

These brought priceless national treasures (including the Magna Carta and paintings from the National Gallery) to Wales for safe storage during the emergency. The first containers, destined for the National Library of Wales, arrived on 25 August, before war was even declared; they continued to arrive until 6 September. Each consignment was accompanied by an escort officer of the British Museum and a railway inspector. Somewhat ironically, it was learned after the war that the *Luftwaffe* used Aberystwyth and the prominent National Library building on Penglais, in particular, as a route marker on bombing sorties between airbases in France and targets on Merseyside.

Evacuation specials featured immediately and prominently in an eight-day programme, code-named EVAK, which had also been planned before the emergency. This was activated locally by divisional superintendents at Oswestry and Chester who simply issued an all-stations telegram, 'EVAK commencing 1 September 1939'. Accordingly, nine 'down' and nine 'up' passenger services were immediately withdrawn between Whitchurch and Aberystwyth (or part thereof), with a further seven 'down' and six 'up' withdrawn on the coast.[4] On Friday, 1 September 1939, Ifor Higgon noted four evacuation specials passing through Barmouth Junction, having arrived via Ruabon. All four were compelled to change engines at the junction, before two trains travelled south as far as Aberdovey whilst the other pair went north, one to Penrhyndeudraeth and one to Criccieth. The evacuation of schoolchildren from Merseyside occurred in several phases but a period of inactivity, often referred to as the 'phoney war', encouraged some children to return prematurely to their homes. These youngsters, in effect, had to be re-evacuated to avoid the air attacks of 1940 and 1941. By July 1940, for example, 68 Birkenhead children and four teachers were already at Machynlleth, but a further 77 were expected together with an additional 200 from Liverpool.[5] Special evacuee trains were also noted by T. B. Owen at Aberystwyth in 1941; some were destined for the town whilst others moved on up the M&M branch (Table X).

Aberystwyth Evacuee Trains				
10/12/41	10.40 a.m.	864 & 2428	Cambrian arrival	Birkenhead – Aberaeron ?
	11.00 a.m.	2223	Carmarthen depart	
	11.50 a.m.	2482 & 864	Cambrian depart	(Light engines)
	1.30 p.m.	3213 & 2482	Cambrian arrival	Birkenhead – Lampeter ?
	2.00 p.m.	3217 & 3254	Carmarthen depart	(8 coaches)
11/2/41	4.00 p.m.	3204 & 3254	Cambrian arrival	(12 coaches)
				(Liverpool – Aberystwyth ?)

Table X   *T.B. Owen*

By the end of September 1939, a more durable emergency timetable was in place. This proved a modest and utilitarian affair and, as far as the CWD was concerned, set a basic pattern which continued with little alteration throughout the war and until 1946 when, at last, some modest improvements were feasible.

Only three through trains ran in the 'down' direction during the winter of 1939-40; a possible fourth involved a break of journey of one hour at Machynlleth, although this inconvenience was rectified by October 1940. These were balanced by four through services in the 'up' direction. With the exception of the 'down' morning mail train, which

OSWESTRY, WELSHPOOL AND ABERYSTWYTH. 87

	Week Days	Sundays
OSWESTRY ... dep.		
Llynclys		
...nt (Salop)		
Llanymynech		
Four Crosses		
Criddleu		
Pool Quay		
Buttington		
WELSHPOOL ... arr.		
LONDON (Paddington) ... dep.		
Birmingham (Snow Hill)		
Wolverhampton (Low Level)		
Shrewsbury ... arr.		
SHREWSBURY ... dep.		
Hanwood		
Yockleton		
Westbury		
Plas-y-Court Halt		
Breidden		
Buttington		
Welshpool ... arr.		
WELSHPOOL ... dep.		
Forden		
Montgomery		
Abermule		
Newtown		
Moat Lane Junction ... arr./dep.		
Caersws		
Pontdolgoch		
Carno		
Talerddig		
Llanbrynmair		
Commins Coch Halt		
Cemmes Road		
Machynlleth ... arr./dep.		
Dovey Junction ... arr./dep.		
Glandyfi		
Ynyslas		
Borth		
Llandre		
Bow Street		
ABERYSTWYTH ... arr.		

Front cover and sample page of the emergency timetable, September 1939.

GBJ Coll.

eliminated the less important stops, trains called at most stations. By October 1942 the number of through services had increased to five each way but none of these extended beyond Whitchurch or Shrewsbury, where changes were always necessary when travelling further afield. Additionally, a change was usually required at Welshpool for Shrewsbury as few trains carried through portions; possibly only the mail trains continued to offer this facility, which was not advertised.

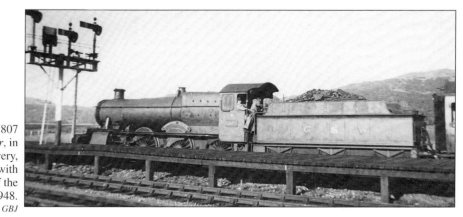

'Manor' class No. 7807 *Compton Manor*, in post-war green livery, at Dovey Junction with the first portion of the mail. 17 May 1948.

GBJ

Collett 0-6-0 No. 3207, having brought the coast portion of the 'up' mail, pauses alongside *Compton Manor*, 17 May 1948.

GBJ

4-6-0 No. 7819 *Hinton Manor* works the second portion of the 'up' mail from Dovey Junction, 17 May 1948.

GBJ

Although an immediate and drastic reduction in services undoubtedly occurred at this time, the change was not quite as severe as the public timetables suggest. Whilst a full programme of summer weekend expresses could obviously no longer be justified, passenger demand persisted throughout the 1940s, wartime or not, and certain services at peak holiday periods continued to run in more than one portion. Tables XI(a) and XI(b)

note most of the traffic observed at Aberystwyth on August Bank Holiday Saturday (2 August 1941) and amply illustrate this fact. These additional trains did not feature in the timetables but covering arrangements were issued to staff via weekly Notices of Extra Trains. This information was usually conveyed to the public through chalked notices at principal stations.

Actual time	Train		Scheduled time
7.30 a.m.	2201	Cambrian arrival (goods)	7.40 a.m.
8.15	3216	" " (1st part)	7.20 a.m.
8.30	3226	" " (2nd part)	"
9.10	3205	" "	9.10 "
10.00	6331	Carmarthen arrival	8.45 "
10.05	3221 & 3213 + 10 coaches:	Cambrian departure (1st part)	10.05 "
10.15	2340	Carmarthen goods departure	-
10.20	3227 & 3205 + 8 coaches:	Cambrian departure (2nd part)	10.05 "
11.05	2201	PU goods to Machynlleth	10.30 "
11.30	2315 + 5 coaches:	Cambrian arrival	11.25 "
12.20 p.m.	6331 + 6 coaches:	Carmarthen departure	12.20 "
12.30	3287 & 3209 + 10 coaches:	Cambrian departure (1st part)	12.45 p.m.
12.45	3216 + 5 coaches:	Cambrian departure (2nd part)	"
1.00	3204 & 3226 + 7 coaches:	Cambrian departure (3rd part)	"
1.15	894 Light engine		
1.30	3222 & 3227	Cambrian arrival (1st part 2.08 p.m or 2nd part of 11.25 ?)	
2.00	3291 & 2345	" " (2nd part " or 1st part?)	
2.20	3220 & 3287	" " (3rd part " or 2nd part?)	
2.45	6351 + 6 coaches:	Carmarthen arrival	12.50 p.m.
2.50	3222 & 2315 + 8 coaches:	Cambrian departure	2.50
3.10	3203 & 894	Cambrian arrival (4th part)	2.08
3.20	2283	Carmarthen goods arrival (1st goods)	
4.50	2283	Cambrian departure	4.50
5.30	2474	Carmarthen goods arrival (2nd goods)	
5.30	7807	Cambrian line goods arrival (Saltney Jc. - Llandeilo Jc.)	
5.35	6351	Carmarthen departure	5.35
6.00	3203, 3222 & 3291	Cambrian departure (Mail) 1st part	6.10
6.20	" " "	" " " 2nd part	
6.30	3221 & 3213	Cambrian arrival	6.30
6.30	3227	Cambrian departure ---- light engine	
6.40	2201	Cambrian departure, goods, to Oswestry.	6.30

The return of No.2201 on the PU goods from Machynlleth was not recorded, nor how the three locomotives utilised on the two parts of the 'Mail' from Aberystwyth were deployed.

Table XI(a): Train arrivals and departures at Aberystwyth on August Bank Holiday Saturday, 2 August 1941.

CAMBRIAN LINE

Departures

7.50 a.m.	to Whitchurch	G1
10.05	to Shrewsbury	H2
10.30	PU goods to Machynlleth	K1
12.45	to Shrewsbury & Whitchurch	F2
2.50 p.m.	to Shrewsbury & Oswestry	L2
4.50	to Machynlleth	P1
6.10	to Salop & Whitchurch (Mail)	O2
6.30	Oswestry goods	E2
7.00	Llandeilo Jc. - Saltney Jc. goods	R2A

Arrivals

7.20 a.m.	from Whitchurch & Salop (Mail)	F1
7.40	Oswestry goods	E1
9.10	from Machynlleth	H1
11.25	from Shrewsbury & Oswestry	L1
2.08 p.m.	from Shrewsbury & Whitchurch	O1
3.00 - 5.30	PU goods from Machynlleth	K2
4.30 - 8.00	Saltney -Llandeilo Jc. goods	R1A
6.30	from Whitchurch	G2
7.00	from Shrewsbury	H3
7.25	from Machynlleth	P2

CARMARTHEN LINE

6.00 a.m.	1st. goods	B
6.55	passenger	C
9.25	2nd. goods	I
12.20 p.m.	passenger	J2
5.35	passenger	M2
7.15	Saltney - Llandeilo Jc goods	R2

8.45	passenger	J1
12.50	pasenger	M1
2.00 p.m. - 5.00 p.m.	1st. goods	N
3.00 - 7.00	2nd. goods	Q
5.00 - 7.00	Llandeilo Jc. - Saltney Goods	R1
8.40	passenger	S (or C2?)

- Characters e.g. G1 represent TBO's personal code to indicate return workings.

- Llandeilo Jc. - Saltney Jc. goods are coded assuming the locomotives worked to Aberystwyth and back. In practice, the locomotives worked through most of the time, particularly after 8.5.1941, an arrangement which avoided delaying the train if the balancing working was late.

Table XI(b): Mondays – Saturdays arrival and departure timetable at Aberystwyth from 28 April 1941.

Table XII is based on part of a Chester Division Notice of Extra Trains for Saturday, 15 August 1942, which reflects the additional traffic on the joint line between Shrewsbury and Welshpool (mostly within the Chester Division). In addition to other information, the notice reveals the introduction that summer of a new SO through train from Shrewsbury to Aberystwyth, achieved by extending the recently introduced SO 3.10 p.m. Shrewsbury-Welshpool service. Again, this was not advertised in the public timetable nor was it operated regularly at first, but ran only in response to demand. Subsequent public timetables for the war period reveal only the SO Shrewsbury-Welshpool service, although in practice there was always a chance that this might work through to Aberystwyth at peak periods.

Table XII

RUABON AND DOLGELLEY LINE—con.

SATURDAY, AUGUST 15th—con.

2-35 P.M. BARMOUTH TO BIRKENHEAD.

A Relief train will run to this train leaving Barmouth at 2-30 p.m. for Chester, calling at the same stations as main train.

To be worked by Engine, Guard and 7 coaches working the 8-10 a.m. Relief, Wrexham to Barmouth.

7-25 P.M. RUABON TO BARMOUTH.

If this train is full, or if the 2-10 p.m. ex Paddington is running 25 minutes or more late, the 7-25 p.m. train must be despatched to time and a Relief train (worked by the engine and coaches of 6-10 p.m. Llangollen to Wrexham) must be run as far as necessary. If run, the Special will return to Ruabon as a Relief to the 7-15 p.m. Mail ex Barmouth, or empty coaches, according to circumstances.

SHREWSBURY, WELSHPOOL AND MINSTERLEY BRANCHES.

SATURDAY, AUGUST 15th.

10-50 A.M. SHREWSBURY TO WELSHPOOL.

A relief Special will run from Birmingham to Aberystwyth in advance of the above train. To run fast from Wolverhampton to Wellington (call for water only) and run thence non-stop via Coleham to Welshpool, then call at Newtown, Moat Lane, Machynlleth, Dovey Junction and Borth. Load 13 vehicles.

10-50 A.M. SHREWSBURY TO WELSHPOOL.

Will work through to Aberystwyth independently of 10-0 a.m. ex Whitchurch. Load 8 coaches. Mr. HIGGINS to further strengthen with one or two Thirds if necessary.

10-5 a.m. ABERYSTWYTH (12-40 P.M. WELSHPOOL) TO SHREWSBURY.

Will be formed of 5 rostered coaches and 3 extra coaches. To return forming 3-40 p.m. Shrewsbury to Aberystwyth.

10-5 A.M. ABERYSTWYTH TO SHREWSBURY.

Will be divided from Aberystwyth to Shrewsbury and extended to Birmingham (RR. to Paddington) as under:—

"A" Headlamps.

	arr. p.m.	dep. p.m.		arr. p.m.	dep. p.m.
Welshpool	—	12 20	Coleham	1 5	
Buttington	12 25		Abbey Foregate	1 8	
Breidden	C S		Wellington	1 21	
Westbury	C S		Oxley North	1 45	
Cruckmeole Junction	C S		Wolverhampton	1 50	

Formation:—Van Third, 5 Thirds, 2 Compos, 3 Thirds, Van Third. Worked from Welshpool by Birmingham Engine and Guard of 8-15 a.m. Relief Birmingham to Aberystwyth.

12-45 P.M. ABERYSTWYTH TO SHREWSBURY.

Will be divided from Aberystwyth to Shrewsbury and extended to Birmingham as under:—

"A" Headlamps.

	arr. p.m.	dep. p.m.		arr. p.m.	dep. p.m.
Welshpool	—	2 55	Coleham	3 40	CE 3 45
Buttington	C 3 0 S		Abbey Foregate	3 48	
Breidden	C S		Wellington	4 0	4 2
Westbury	C 3 X 25 S		Oxley North	4 26	
Cruckmeole Junction	C S		Wolverhampton	4 30	

Load 9 Coaches.

3-10 P.M. SHREWSBURY TO WELSHPOOL.

To be despatched from Shrewsbury immediately after arrival of Relief to 11-5 a.m. ex Paddington. Will work through to Aberystwyth independently of 2-5 p.m. Whitchurch.

To be worked by 8 coaches arriving on 10-45 a.m. Welshpool.

Wartime not withstanding, some of the timetable cuts were difficult to appreciate both at the time and in retrospect. Amongst the more incomprehensible was the withdrawal (from 5 February 1940) of a coast connection to the 'down' morning mail from Machynlleth. This inconvenienced scores of military personnel each day throughout the war. After undertaking long and no doubt tedious night journeys across Britain, passengers found themselves at 6.30 a.m. on a cold and deserted Machynlleth platform, with a wait of an hour and a half for the coast connection. Moreover, the local refreshment room offered no solace as it did not open until 9.00 a.m. This highly unsatisfactory state of affairs persisted until a private citizen, Mr W. G. Kemp of Ivy House (situated some 300 yards from the station) decided to provide service personnel with hot refreshments at his home each morning, throughout the war, and entirely at his own expense. Initially, he undertook the whole process himself, even going down to the station to invite members of the forces to his home, but in later years assistance was provided by the local WVS. Any number between about 30 and 100 servicemen and women accepted Mr Kemp's hospitality each day, until May 1946, when the coast mail was eventually restored to the timetable.

Another omission, which caused some hardship, involved the final 'down' train each evening; this ran from Whitchurch to Llanidloes, arriving there at 9.47 p.m. It was a service which had its roots in Cambrian practices of the previous century but, regrettably for those on the main line, provided no connection from Moat Lane to Aberystwyth (although in peacetime a Saturdays Only train left the junction at 9.15 p.m. and arrived at Aberystwyth at 10.38 p.m.). A balancing 'up' service left Llanidloes for Whitchurch at 6.30 a.m. each morning but again without a connection at Moat Lane. Members of the Machynlleth Town Council, amongst others, complained of this arrangement and approached the railway company, but without success. Aberystwyth line passengers had to wait until the 1946 summer service before an evening train, the 6.30 p.m. from Shrewsbury to Welshpool, was extended to the coast, arriving at Aberystwyth at 9.35 p.m.

Two interesting ticket survivors: a 30 June 1941 *Workman's Return* from Abermule to the Ellesmere Branch (*l.*) and a 19 July 1923 *Limited Cheap Day* issue from Montgomery to Newtown.
Courtesy Ron Jones

Ron Jones, of Newtown, recalls that during the 1940s a second early morning train left Llanidloes for Oswestry and the large Royal Ordnance complex on the Ellesmere/Wrexham Branch. This was usually an 8- or 9-coach formation which picked up workers at all stations *en route*. 0-6-0 No. 2210 was a regular performer on this duty.

The other Llanidloes-Whitchurch service, however, continued unaltered, a direct reminder of earlier Llanidloes & Newtown and Oswestry & Newtown Railway liaisons.

All railways were extremely busy at this time but the Machynlleth-Dovey Junction section was then amongst the most intensively used stretches of single line in the United Kingdom. Had the extra traffic generated by the war been available to the Great Western in peacetime, improvement schemes, such as the doubling of this particular section, would surely have materialised.

As during the First World War, many important military installations were again established in Wales. The largest in the CW Division were at Park Hall, Oswestry and on the coast at Tonfannau where the extensive training camp was home to a REME Detachment (38th), the 37th HAA Regiment and the larger 55th Royal Artillery Regiment. Summer camps had been held here in peacetime but construction of an important permanent base commenced during the autumn of 1939.

Although the war inflicted death, destruction and untold misery on thousands, not all aspects were entirely negative. It is often overlooked, for example, that unemployment – that scourge of the 1920s and '30s – disappeared almost immediately from the area. Civilian workers from as far afield as Harlech, Dolgellau and Aberystwyth were brought each day by train to Tonfannau, and the area's unemployed experienced greater financial stability than they had known for years. Two Crosville buses, usually a pair of the older 'D', 'E' or 'F' series, left Aberystwyth each morning and picked up workers *en route* to Machynlleth, reached in good time for transfer to the 8.10 a.m. coast train. The buses lay idle all day on the forecourt of the nearby Crosville depot, awaiting the evening return trip.

Other military bases were located at Llwyngwril (Royal Marines), Llanbedr (Royal Air Force), Harlech (Royal Artillery and Ordnance) and near Pwllheli, where a camp started before the war was requisitioned by the Royal Navy and established as HMS *Glendower*. A pre-war RAF base was located at Penrhos, also near Pwllheli, and during the early 1940s a small airfield was established at Tywyn. This was used principally by light aircraft, which towed targets for anti-aircraft gunnery practice at nearby Tonfannau, but was also the location of at least three interesting emergency landings.

The wooden signal-box (supplied by the Dutton company in 1890) photographed alongside the 'down' loop at Dovey Junction in 1948. In Cambrian days the area immediately beyond the box was occupied at one time by a signalman's house (generally similar to the bridgeman's house across the river) and by a wooden 'down' platform. The box survived until 1959. 25 August 1948.
H. C. Casserley

Dovey Junction station buildings. The fingerpost declares that the train at the platform offers a service to Welshpool, Birmingham and London. The connection from the coast had yet to appear when this photograph was taken. 25 August 1948.

H. C. Casserley

The first occurred at 5.10 p.m. on 3 October 1941 when RAF Hampden bomber (P5391), piloted by Sergeant T. F. Freeman and attached to 160TU, attempted a forced landing after experiencing engine trouble. The aircraft overshot the runway, crossed the railway line near 89 m.-40 ch. and came to rest on the seashore. Both pilot and crew were unhurt.

A further incident occurred on 8 July 1944 when a USAF Boeing B-17 Fortress (42-31321) attached to the 390th Bombardment Group, then based at Framlingham (Parham), Suffolk, made an emergency landing when returning from north Africa. The aircraft also overshot the runway and encroached on the railway. Miraculously, all fifteen on board escaped injury, although the B-17 was a write-off.

The third incident recorded here occurred at 10.20 a.m. on 26 February 1945 when a RAF Hurricane in the hands of Pilot Officer W. H. Russell attached to 631 Squadron, ran out of runway and nose-tipped on to the railway line. The pilot is thought to have survived.[6]

Conditions at Tywyn were often difficult during winter months as the low-lying runway was frequently waterlogged, a factor which contributed to the eventual transfer of flying duties to the more spacious base at Llanbedr. Tywyn airfield closed in July 1945.

Machynlleth's stalwart yard engine during the war years, No. 1965, shunts Bren-gun carriers. 23 August 1948.

H. C. Casserley

The military camps along the coast generated an enormous amount of extra traffic. During construction of the Tywyn-Tonfannau camps in 1940-41, 0-6-0PT No. 7410 travelled daily from Machynlleth to serve as station pilot and virtually monopolised this duty for over a year.[7] When the camps were fully commissioned, the military population of the Tywyn-Tonfannau area alone was estimated at over six thousand.

As with the Cambrian's troop movements during the First World War, it is probably impossible now to gain a comprehensive impression of the density of traffic to and from the Cambrian coast camps, but the few fragments of information available indicate intense use of the system. Random observations of troop specials by Ifor Higgon at Barmouth Junction include Nos. 3212; 2260+887; and 3287 *Mercury*, on specials to Tonfanau in June 1940. In July, Nos. 3221+2200 and 3204+3214 worked two 12-coach trains on the coast, whilst in August Nos. 3450 *Peacock*+6362 were observed on a 14-coach Ruabon-Barmouth train. A great many others went unrecorded, at all times of the day and night and included several specials of Dunkirk wounded, repatriated to the Cambrian coast camps. Today, there may well be no official record of these trains but there are still those at Machynlleth, for example, who vividly recall meeting the Dunkirk trains and offering cups of tea or bowls of soup to returning troops.

One of the most interesting military specials to arrive at Machynlleth conveyed an Indian artillery detachment, destined for Tonfanau (where unloading facilities were restricted). The precise date, early in the war, was not recorded and no documents regarding this colourful event have been traced but vivid memories remain of nervy and highly troublesome mules being harnessed, with great reluctance, in the spacious station forecourt. Not since the pioneer days of the railway, when the line terminated here, and horse-drawn carriages from Borth, Aberdyfi, Aberystwyth and Dolgellau congregated in the yard to meet incoming trains, could the site have witnessed as many excited animals.

The Indian gunners had an unenviable task, coping with obstreperous mules that had been cooped up for hours in crowded wagons, but the fortunate few who witnessed the event will not easily forget that memorable wartime scene. Yet, despite the soldiers' immaculate bearing, their appearance suggested they were better equipped to deal with some minor skirmish in foreign parts than a panzer division on mainland Europe. The smartly turned out gunners in pith helmets and sand-coloured kit, together with their gleaming though obsolete gun carriages, had obviously come to the United Kingdom for re-equipping and retraining. Nonetheless, a combination of military discipline and railway efficiency soon ensured that unloading was accomplished in next to no time, or so it seemed. The exotic sights and sounds were soon no more than memories. Indeed, when all was quiet after the final departure, at least one young spectator could hardly believe what had just been witnessed. Then, a casual glance at the tarmacadam at the entrance to the station drive revealed heavy scoring from the gun carriages as they had swung around sharply on to the main Tywyn-Dolgellau road, providing instant and welcome confirmation that all was not a dream. Unsolicited verification of this most unusual event was provided over half a century later, in 1993, when Mr John Edwards (then of the Monsanto chemical complex at Acre-fair) unexpectedly volunteered that he too had witnessed this enthralling and colourful event as a young evacuee.

The wartime need for total security still restricts a full and accurate account of such special workings but it is now known, for example, that as preparations for D-Day gathered momentum during the first six months of 1944, at least 31 troop trains entered the CW Division bound for the camps along the coast, whilst a further 26 are known to have worked outward from the same locations: there may well have been more. These trains varied from light formations of five carriages of around 160 tons to heavy 440 ton trains (e.g. five carriages plus 22 carriage trucks) or 13 coach trains with two baggage vans of 420 tons. Rolling stock of all four main-line companies appeared regularly.[8]

Although the Cambrian lines made a valuable contribution to the war effort, only on one occasion, apparently, did they receive any specific attention from the *Luftwaffe*. The incident occurred in 1940, when 'early on Wednesday morning' (possibly 7 October 1940) a German Ju 88 bomber attacked a goods train worked by engineman T. Barr, fireman Newnes and guard C. E. Corbett. The train 'approaching Wales from the West Midlands was machine-gunned but suffered no damage save to a lamp on the guard's van. The train did not stop'![9]

Some indication of the strategic importance of maintaining an operative Motive Power Depot (MPD) at Machynlleth is provided by the fact that the only official air-raid shelters in the town were built alongside the rock siding. They followed the standard 'beehive' pattern constructed elsewhere on the Great Western but, fortunately, they were never used as intended. Eventually, during the 1960s, the rubble surround was removed and at least one of the units was used for a time as a store.

The threat of air raids on Merseyside had diminished by the end of 1944 and some evacuees began to drift home before official provision was made. In due course, special trains were arranged for this traffic but, again, little is known of these although at least one train left Aberystwyth for Liverpool (Lime Street) on Tuesday, 28 November 1944. This picked up at stations as far into the journey as Chirk (where 16 children joined the train) and Wrexham (165 returnees). The few youngsters then still located between Barmouth Junction and Llangollen (19 from Barmouth and Arthog, five from Dolgellau and Llanuwchllyn,

seven from Llandderfel, fourteen from Corwen and ten from Llangollen) were all accommodated in an extra Third reserved for them on the 10.10 a.m. from Barmouth:

> Mr Jones, Ruabon, to arrange for the vehicle to connect rear of the 9.10 from Paddington from Ruabon, to work through to Birkenhead Woodside.[10]

Central Wales proved a haven for many private and public schools during the war years, including Gordonstoun which was rather surprisingly relocated at Lord Davies's home at Llandinam, in June 1940. The Chatelard School (at Aberdyfi), Cotesmore (at Barmouth), Dunluce (Plas, Machynlleth), Holyrood (Aberystwyth) and St Wilfrids (Llanidloes) were amongst other evacuated schools. Some, such as the Chelsea College at Borth and Lapley Grange School, near Furnace, Machynlleth, remained in the area in early post-war days. At holiday time, special travel arrangements were made for each of these establishments, varying from the reservation of a few compartments to whole carriages in the case of the larger schools. In this respect none supported the railway more than the long-established Dr Williams's School at Dolgellau. On Friday, 24 March 1944, for example, 80 passengers left Dolgellau for Birmingham and Paddington, with a further 75 bound for Chester and north-east England:

> Mr T. C. Sellars to arrange for two extra Thirds to be attached rear of 7.18 a.m. Barmouth, also reserve three additional compartments. Coach extreme rear labelled 'Paddington' to be attached front 8.30 a.m. Birkenhead at Ruabon.[11]

Train services were also used on a daily basis by local schoolchildren, and county schools at Aberystwyth, Tywyn, Machynlleth and Barmouth were amongst those served in this way. The numbers attending Newtown warranted the running of a special train which picked up scholars (and shoppers) from Llanbrynmair, Talerddig, Carno and Caersws. Initially, this was worked by Moat Lane men who travelled with Empty Coaching Stock (ECS) to Llanbrynmair (arr. 7.49 a.m.) where the engine ran around before departing at 8.15 a.m. for Newtown, reached at 8.56 a.m. The working of the Newtown School Train, as it was known locally, was transferred to Machynlleth from 1946, with departure at 7.50 a.m. and arrival at Newtown as previously stated. Apart from operating advantages, this also offered the service to the public at

Machynlleth, Cemmes Road and Commins Coch, although no scholars were picked up west of Talerddig. The engine and crew remained at Moat Lane-Newtown each day on shunting duties before returning at 4.35 p.m. with a new all-stations service from Newtown to Machynlleth. Previously, returning passengers had caught a stopping train at around this time but as this was replaced by the newly introduced 3.10 p.m. express from Shrewsbury in 1946, the return working of the morning school set proved most convenient.

Moat Lane Junction, facing Llanidloes (*l.*) and Talerddig (*r.*). 23 August 1948.

H. C. Casserley

A Brecon train occupies the outer face of the main-line island platform at Moat Lane, for the convenience of passengers. Such manoeuvres required additional effort by railway staff but these were much appreciated. The train in the photograph would have arrived from Brecon at 9.42 a.m.: it was due to return at 9.55 a.m. 24 August 1948.

H. C. Casserley

Another pre-war 'up' service was initially worked in similar manner by Moat Lane men, when an ECS Moat Lane-Carno turn served to form an early morning east-bound train which left Carno at 7.35 a.m. This became a Machynlleth turn around 1941, when the stock ran empty to Carno. Machynlleth people who needed to reach Shrewsbury early in the day (usually relatives of local railwaymen, at the outset) soon availed themselves of the opportunity of a 'lift' in the empty stock. Such arrangements, of course, were entirely unofficial and intending travellers, in addition to holding a valid ticket, were advised to secure the guard's 'blessing' for the clandestine portion of their journey well in advance of departure. With their jobs at risk, not all guards were prepared to cooperate and there was little point in arriving in the goods yard on a dark and wet morning to be refused entry to the coaches. Furthermore, as the empty stock was usually stabled in the lower yard and often removed from an accommodating platform, gaining entry to the carriages was a hazardous business for intending travellers. Just occasionally, fortune favoured the

venture and the empty carriages lay adjacent to the old Abercwmeiddew slate wharf, a convenient and welcome departure point under the circumstances. These were probably the only occasions when the wharf was regularly used by passengers.

The appeal of this early morning 'service' was soon acknowledged by the divisional super-intendent's office at Oswestry and from 4 October 1943 the train became an official through working, departing at 6.55 a.m. (from the 'up' platform). The initial two years, however, had provided rare experiences of pulling out of the goods yard 'on the cushions', past heaps of small coal and amidst smells of recently felled lumber awaiting transhipment. Some at Machynlleth can still recall riding in an almost empty train, in total darkness, for over fourteen miles, until Talerddig had been cleared and the compartment lights switched on. Such memories are cherished. From 6 May 1946, the departure was brought forward to 6.35 a.m. and for a period, commencing 7 October 1946, the service was tried from Aberystwyth (dep. 5.45 a.m.) but by the following winter it had reverted to Machynlleth, with departure established at 6.35 a.m.

Although a post-war view, this scene has much of the wartime ambience of the station at Machynlleth. The almost total absence of advertisements (only timetables and 'essential' posters are displayed) and the shuttered bookstall, just visible beneath the canopy supported by black and white pillars – all confirm the date of the photograph, 23 August 1948.

H. C. Casserley

Former 'Earl' class 4-4-0 No. 3216 climbs to the Friog cutting and avalanche shelter with six coaches – 'toplight', clerestory and Collett examples amongst them – forming the 4.00 p.m. from Pwllheli to Dovey Junction on 3 August 1946.

Ifor A. Higgon

No footbridge was provided at Barmouth Junction, where barrow-crossings were the only means of gaining access to other platforms. Around a dozen passengers watch the departure of the Pwllheli train whilst a porter on the crossing and the fireman on the footplate of No. 3220 monitor the situation carefully. 15 August 1946.

Ifor A. Higgon

Wartime Sunday Service

The 'down' morning mail train – more of a newspaper than a mail carrier on Sundays – together with the corresponding 'up' mail in the evening, were the only scheduled services which regularly disturbed the peace of Cambrian Sundays during the war. The 'down' train left Oswestry at 6.30 a.m. and called at Welshpool (7.00 a.m.), Newtown (7.33 a.m.) and Machynlleth (8.27 a.m.), before arriving at Aberystwyth at 9.13 a.m. It was later on Sundays than weekdays and there was no direct connection from Shrewsbury by the joint line. A note in the timetable of 25 September 1939 states, 'Shrewsbury dep. 5.33 a.m. via Oswestry'. Intriguingly, the same timetable offered no Sunday morning service between Gobowen and Oswestry although there must certainly have been a connection. Passengers for coast stations caught the 8.40 a.m. from Machynlleth to Barmouth; the coast mail went no further on Sundays. The main strengths of both these Sunday services lay with the balancing evening trains which carried heavy mail and passenger traffic.

Nowadays, the delivery of Sunday newspapers evokes no particular interest but in some small Welsh towns during the 1930s the salacious content of one or two was enough for them to be considered immoral. Demand was limited; W. H. Smith, the booksellers and newsagents, did not open their Machynlleth shop on Sundays and the 'alternative' newsagent also remained closed, as did Wyman's station bookstall. Nonetheless, Sunday newspapers were available from an entrepreneur who met the early morning train, collected his bundles and borrowed a four-wheel platform trolley to transport his goods to a nearby lock-up garage for distribution. If the mail was delayed for some reason, as frequently happened, a small clutch of the keenest customers gathered at the station where the parcels would be opened and the papers dispersed almost before they had been unloaded.

No. 2464, one of the latter-day stalwarts of the 'Dean' class at Machynlleth, rests 'on the rock' in the company of a classmate and an unidentified 4-4-0, which could be either No. 3200/05 or 09 (which had similar sandboxes). 5 June 1946.
R. C. Riley

0-6-0 No. 892 being prepared at Machynlleth by H. R. Humphreys on 5 June 1946.

R. C. Riley

After the 8.40 a.m. Barmouth connection had departed, the station was closed and the main gates padlocked. The small lych-gate alongside then provided the only entry to the site. This standard GW practice continued throughout the war and into the early 1950s, when it was gradually relaxed. The main gates to the lower (goods) yard were also locked and the practice continued here for a further decade or so.

The yards at Machynlleth – in common with many other country stations the length and breadth of the country – lay dormant on Sundays. Station areas, which were busy and vibrant during the week, were somehow transformed on the Sabbath into an uninhabited, grand-scale 'model' railway where nothing disturbed the tranquillity of sheds, sidings and platforms. Anyone who deigned to venture within its boundaries, however, was rewarded by stimulating sights, sounds and smells. Locomotives, those inanimate hulks which came to life only when coaled, watered and fired by their crews, stood quietly in rows. Some lay in the shed, others on the 'rock' or 'turntable' roads, or 'down the tank'; each siding had its name. Within the shed, glistening piston-rods and slide-bars reflected shafts of sunlight and cooling metal chimed quietly, almost musically, harmonising with the sound of droplets from leaking tenders, dripping into a wet inspection pit. Outside, sun-baked, creosoted sleepers emitted a pungent but pleasing aroma, and if entry was gained into carriages stabled near the cattle pens or down the lower yard, pleasant moments might be spent studying faded views of Marlow or Dawlish, or the Great Western carriage map – that peculiarly compressed view of the company's territories. The station, undeniably, held a particular fascination for some during that enchanting period between the departure of the morning mail and arrival of its evening counterpart.

Occasionally, the tranquillity was disturbed by special Sunday workings, for track maintenance or bridge renewal during the winter. Both signal-boxes could then be opened and, on summer Sundays, further advantage was taken for running seaside specials from several locations on the same day. Troop trains also ran on Sundays and engines were changed at Machynlleth if these were worked to or from the east by a 'Manor' or 'Mogul'. At the time, these classes were still prohibited from the coast.

The early post-war period witnessed much repair and strengthening of vulnerable sections of sea defences, particularly near Tonfannau and Llanaber, just north of Barmouth. Ferocious winds and tides have wrought havoc along these more exposed sections of the coast, ever since the 1860s, and enginemen were frequently drenched by high seas at these locations. The heavy work of strengthening the sea wall justified regular weekend appearances of the Stafford Road steam crane, which manoeuvred huge blocks of stone, some weighing 10 tons or more apiece, to strengthen the sea wall. The engineers relied on sheer bulk in those days; no fancy inter-locking concrete blocks for them. The steam crane was normally brought down by a '63' as far as Machynlleth, where one of the local engines took it to the site. Most of these visitors went unrecorded but No. 6302 (RDG) was noted resting at Machynlleth on 26 February 1948.

Churchward 2-6-0 No. 6302 (RDG) at Machynlleth, 26 February 1948.   *GBJ*

4-4-0 No. 9003 with the 2.00 p.m. 'up' goods at Glandulas, shortly after leaving Machynlleth. 15 May 1948.   *GBJ*

Apart from the signalmen in the east and west boxes, one of the first people to 'book-on' in the evening, before the arrival of the two mail trains, was the steam-raiser. His initial task was to lay oily cotton waste and old wooden sleepers, previously sawn, chopped and nailed into small bundles, in the empty fireboxes of the engines rostered for duty on Monday. The open-structured, tar-soaked firewood and oily waste ensured a high success rate when lit.

The junction was not staffed on Sundays so passengers from the coast changed trains at Machynlleth. The Barmouth portion arrived about 6.40 p.m, after which the coast engine would shunt its stock before going on shed, remaining on stand-by until the Oswestry mail (which departed around 6.57 p.m.) had cleared Moat Lane. Once that had occurred, the enginemen 'booked-off', leaving the steam-raiser to spread the fire from the coast engine on to the prepared piles of firewood and waste. The remainder of that night's duty was spent attending to each engine in turn, slowly building up steam for the morrow. Usually, by about 8.00 p.m., a thick pall of dark, sulphurous smoke, born of the combination of oil, creosote, wood and coal, emerged from the engines, to be carried by the prevailing wind over the rim of the rock and across nearby pastures. Although lighting-up on this scale occurred only on Sundays, the accumulated outpourings from legions of Cambrian, Great Western and Western Region engines, over the years, had discoloured stones, grass and trees – not to mention sheep – on the eastern side of the rock. Alas, since 1967, the rock is cleaner and the grass certainly greener.

A Van Railway demolition train hauled by 0-6-0T No. 819, formerly *Edweade*, one of three Lambourn Valley engines purchased by the Cambrian in 1904. The presence in the train of a wagon from the Ocean Collieries provides a poignant reminder of David Davies's long association with Montgomeryshire's railways. March 1941.

NLW/Geoff Charles Coll.

Dinas Mawddwy station house, 1949.

LGRP

FREIGHT TRAFFIC, 1939-45

Britain's railways were moving slowly but irrevocably towards bankruptcy as the 1930s drew to a close. This parlous situation was attributed to outmoded legislation rather than any particular mismanagement by the railways, and matters became increasingly serious during the 1930s as lucrative passenger and freight traffic was creamed off by the new road competitors.

National freight receipts in the United Kingdom fell steadily during the 1930s and the figure for 1938, compared with 1937, was down by a startling £7 million. During the first five weeks of 1939, receipts fell by a further £1m and a total loss in the region of £10m was forecast by the end of the year. Some of the economies contemplated, such as eliminating all loss-making freight trains, would merely have accelerated the inevitable downward spiral and presented no effective remedy; such measures were seen only as desperate stop-gaps. The four major railway companies, acutely aware of anachronistic legislation which restricted their freedom to compete fairly, formed the Railway Companies Association. This launched a nationwide campaign calling for a 'Square deal for the railways' and exhorting the public to write to their MPs, local newspapers and Chambers of Trade. It emphasised that 'Equality with their competitors is what the railways are striving for . . . with the knowledge that unless they succeed, British railways in their present form will be no more. In their place will be a government-subsidised system resembling all the other railways in Europe and you and I will be paying the subsidy'.[12]

We can now appreciate that circumstances were to change dramatically as the year progressed, the relevance of such matters diminishing as the railways were, once again, called upon to support a nation at war. At the time, roads were totally

```
                                2.      NOTICE NO.34.   21/1/44.

TUESDAY, JANUARY 25TH.


        NEWTOWN FAIR, HORSE SPECIAL, NEWTOWN TO SHREWSBURY.
                        arr.      dep.
                        pm        pm
Welshpool               6.0   OW  6.15  Conveys traffic for North & South
Buttington                    C6/20S        marshalled as under:-
Westbury                      C6/35S        Engine,
Cruckmeole Jc.                C6/44S        L.M.S traffic via Crewe,
Shrewsbury              7-0             G.W.    "     "  Wellington and
                                                          Wolverhampton.
                                       G.W.    "     "  Hereford.


        The engine with guard working this special will return light
Shrewsbury to Oswestry via Gobowen.

        Traffic to be forwarded from Shrewsbury by first available
suitable service, and all concerned to be advised accordingly.
```

Table XIII: Part of a 1944 Chester Division Notice, featuring Welshpool to Shrewsbury only. Any GW traffic for the north would probably have been worked via Oswestry.

W. G. Rear Coll.

GREAT WESTERN RAILWAY
Divisional Superintendent's Office,
CHESTER.

25th September, 1944.

THURSDAY, SEPTEMBER 28th.

SHEEP SPECIAL, MACHYNLLETH ETC. TO DENBIGH L.M.S.
VIA CORWEN.

A special with about 30 wagons of sheep ex
Machynlleth etc. will run in the following times:-

"C" headlamps.

	arr. pm	dep. pm	
Barmouth Jcn.		3.40	To be banked from
Penmaenpool		CS	Barmouth Jcn. to
Dolgelley	3.58	4.28	Garneddwen
Bontnewydd	4.40	X 5. 0	
Drwsynant	C5/19S		
Garneddwen & Stop Board	5.36	P 5.41	Detach B.E.
Llanuwchllyn		5P48	
Bala Jcn.	5.58	OW 6. 3	
Corwen	6.25		

A large engine will be sent from Croes Newydd to
Barmouth Jcn. at 11.45am on September 28th to work the Sheep Special
from Barmouth Jcn. to Corwen. The engine will then proceed to
Croes Newydd shed light.
The Central Wales Division engine which works the
Sheep Special into Barmouth Jcn. will be utilised to bank the
special to Garneddwen Loop if required, afterwards returning to
Barmouth Jcn. light.
Croes Newydd guard to travel on light engines to
Barmouth Jcn. work Special to Corwen and afterwards return with
light engine from Corwen to Croes Newydd.
L.M.S. will work forward by special train from
Corwen at 7-0pm.
Brake van to work home in traffic.
All concerned to note.   (G.13003.L.)

===

Notice No.508.
Messrs.Dolban and Rushton, Croes Newydd;
Inspr.Thorne, Corwen; P.W.Inspr.Bala;
Stations Barmouth Jcn. to Corwen, to   for H.H.Swift.
acknowledge receipt by wire using
code "ARNO.508"

Table XIV.   *W. G. Rear Coll.*

inadequate and could not cope with any large-scale national emergency, least of all, total war. Yet the railways, taken for granted for decades, were expected to play a major role in the ensuing conflict. For probably the last time, traffic was again concentrated on rail, and trains ran, nationwide, loaded to capacity. The railways amply demonstrated that they were able and ready to meet the challenge.

THE CENTRAL WALES DIVISION'S CONTRIBUTION

Initially, freight services continued much as in peacetime, but increased carriage of livestock provided additional revenue. Although not on a daily basis, this traffic assumed greater importance during the war years. More emphasis was placed on home-produced meat and strict food controls led to the grading of all animal stock. The traditional markets at Newtown, Welshpool and Oswestry were obvious grading centres and the *County Times* for 26 October 1940 also noted that 'Machynlleth was now one of the principal grading centres in mid Wales. About 1500 sheep were graded on Tuesday at the mart and a cattle grading day was held on Thursday'. Had it still been peacetime, the railway would surely have wished for 'grading days' on a more regular basis. Special train arrangements for the Kerry (sheep) and Newtown (horse) sales continued; both represented peacetime practices which remained profitable throughout the war. (see, for example, Notice No. 34, Tuesday, 25 January 1944). (Table XIII).

Another interesting pre-war practice which prevailed was the transportation of sheep from hill to lowland areas for 'wintering'. The coastal plain around Harlech was a favoured destination, as was the Vale of Clwyd, exemplified in Table XIV.

Because the population of central Wales consumed more than was produced in the area, one of the characteristics of Cambrian freight operation was that many wagons left the division unloaded. Wartime circumstances increased the need for prompt return of all empty wagons and there has long been a tale, in the Machynlleth area, of a young and inexperienced goods guard who worked a train back along the coast and eagerly accepted all the empty wagons he could find. The result was a train of well over 60 wagons which proved much longer than refuge sidings and loop lines permitted. Chaos ensued. The inexperienced guard imagined he was contributing to the war effort by returning empty wagons promptly but the general disruption was considerable. He was not dismissed but was found other duties!

THE SALTNEY GOODS

The most important freight trains to cross the Division during the war years were undoubtedly the so-called Saltney Goods. These specially introduced 'through goods' trains operated between the large marshalling yards at Llandeilo Junction, east of Llanelli, and Saltney Junction, on the western approach to Chester. At various times they followed (possibly) three different routes between these points. Some are known to have taken the Vale of Neath line to Pontypool Road, Hereford and Shrewsbury. Others are believed to have used the direct LMS route through Pontarddulais, Llandrindod Wells and Craven Arms.[13] The third route crossed the Central Wales Division, when trains went via Carmarthen and the old Manchester & Milford line to Aberystwyth, before proceeding over Talerddig to Welshpool, Oswestry and Gobowen. An interesting feature of the latter was that the designation of travel of the trains, whilst the same at the point of departure and arrival, was 'reversed' whilst on the CWD, mid-way through the journey. That is, a train leaving Llandeilo Junction for Carmarthen and Aberystwyth travelled in the 'down' direction: from Aberystwyth it went in the 'up' direction to Gobowen, where it regained the 'down' main line to Saltney. References to Saltney workings follow the directions taken as they crossed the CW Division.

The Saltney Goods trains were undoubtedly the catalyst which accelerated the introduction of 'blue' category engines to the Cambrian. The largest of these were the 'Manors', although they were not necessarily the most efficient at that time; the shorter Churchward 2-6-0s were equally capable engines. 'Manor' No. 7808 *Cookham Manor*, was officially transferred to Oswestry in April 1946; R. C. Riley's camera recorded it at Aberystwyth shed on the 3rd of that month when it was very much a 'new' engine to the CWD. 3 April 1946.   *R. C. Riley*

No. 7802 *Bradley Manor* at Machynlleth, June 1947.   *GBJ*

The Saltney trains have been shrouded in mystery from the outset. No official documentation has hitherto been discovered to verify or disprove the popular belief that these trains carried live munitions. However, despite a lack of official confirmation, there seems no reason to doubt the supposition. Assuming this to be correct, just how 'live' these munitions were and what form they took is still unknown, as are the initial points where the loads were collated, before the trains were assembled at Llandeilo Junction or Saltney. Furthermore, the final destination/s of this traffic, after arrival at Saltney, is/are not known. At the time of writing, even the direction of 'loaded' or 'empty' workings are not readily apparent, nor indeed whether ammunition/explosives (possibly of different kinds) might have been carried both ways. Munitions trains were usually referred to in official documents as carrying 'Government Stores' and were normally listed as 'special

workings', a term which suggests unusual or spasmodic operation. The Saltney trains, however, although they featured in working timetables rather anonymously as 'Through Goods Class F', were regular services which ran daily in both directions for over four years. They may also have been the means whereby quantities of high explosives were brought into Machynlleth by rail during the period 1940-44, for road transfer to the storage caverns of Braichgoch Quarry at Corris. The Mawddwy branch also saw traffic of this nature, when wagons put off at Machynlleth (or Cemmes Road) were worked especially to Aberangell, with explosives for storage in the Hendre Ddu Quarry chambers. Yet the Saltneys were certainly not the only trains to convey munitions within the CWD. Further east, heavy tonnages imported from America were moved from south Wales ports (notably Barry) to Hookagate (on the Shrewsbury-Welshpool Joint Line) and Llanymynech, for transfer to the old

No. 7808 again, but in an 'atmospheric' shot at Moat Lane. 23 August 1948.   *H. C. Casserley*

No. 7803 *Barcote Manor* works the 10.00 a.m. train from Aberystwyth to Shrewsbury past Machynlleth East Box, and signalman J. Evans.

P. M. Alexander, courtesy C. M. Whitehouse

Shropshire & Montgomery line. Virtually the whole of this charming rural network became an enormous munitions store during the war. Finally, although they were worked independently of the Saltney trains, it must not be overlooked that explosives manufactured at Penrhyndeudraeth went regularly by rail at this time (and continued to do so, until problems were encountered with Barmouth bridge in the early 1980s).

The Saltney trains, however, are especially noteworthy for two other reasons: their points of origin and termination lay outside central Wales (only the First World War 'Jellicoe Specials' come

easily to mind as sharing this characteristic) and, secondly, they were instrumental in introducing 'blue' category engines to the Division.

The precise date of the inaugural working is not known. The CWD Freight Service Timetable from 5 February 1940 contains no reference to them but a confirmed Saltney-Felin Frân (near Llandeilo Junction) through goods train was noted arriving at Aberystwyth behind locomotive No. 6392 on 28 April 1941 – although it is not claimed that this was the inaugural run.[14] The service could have commenced as early as spring 1940 and details of the first of these trains might well have been issued initially on weekly or special notices. There is also a possibility that some of the very first workings could have been hauled by the smaller Central Wales Division locomotives. These would not have been adequate in the long term and Trevor Owen's painstakingly compiled notes of regular Saltney turns (the earliest dating from 28 April 1941) confirm that 4-6-0 'Manors', 2-6-0 'Aberdares' and '63s' dominated this duty from that time. His observations, which furnish us with more detail than we have any right to expect at this late date, suggest that locomotives from both Llandeilo Junction and Saltney initially terminated at Aberystwyth, returning home the same day with the balancing working. This arrangement seemingly applied up to 8 May 1941, when through working commenced. Thereafter, the engines frequently (although not always) returned the following day.

Amongst unusual Saltney power during 1944 may be noted 'Bulldog' 4-4-0 No. 3455 *Starling* and on 21 September 1944, 0-6-0 No. 2216 (CARM) was recorded on an 'up' train at Glandyfi.[15] This, the only recorded appearance of a '22' on a Saltney turn may well have resulted from the failure of a larger engine, as happened occasionally. One of the first '63s' to come on shed at Machynlleth did so as a result of failing on an 'up' Saltney *c.* 1943; the unidentified 2-6-0 lay on the 'rock road' for over a week, awaiting repair.

The weekday services (one 'up' and two 'down') certainly ran between April 1941 and 1944, possibly 1945, but by that time the second daily 'down' train was optional and designated RR – Runs if Required. From 7 May 1945 arrangements changed again as services via Oswestry, in both directions, were listed as 'suspended' although the same timetable lists a Sundays Only Class F Goods which left Oswestry at 2.40 a.m. This train's first scheduled stop was at Moat Lane (4.14 a.m.-4.30 a.m.). and arrival at Aberystwyth was at 7.05 a.m.; intriguingly, there

Churchward 2-6-0 No. 5346 (TYS) leaving Machynlleth with a SO Birmingham-Aberystwyth through train on 12 June 1948. *GBJ*

Coming and going . . . No. 7819 *Hinton Manor*, with assistance from 4-4-0 No. 9027 as far as Talerddig, working the 12.50 p.m. express from Aberystwyth to Whitchurch. This train was the only daily 'up' express for a great many years. 23 August 1948.   *H. C. Casserley*

was no balancing turn in the opposite direction. Also, surprisingly, as late as April 1946, a notice[16] lists the 2.30 p.m. Saltney-Llandeilo Junction (via Oswestry) as RR! However, by May that year, the Saltney Goods seem to have disappeared entirely from both timetables and special notices. Their passing terminated an interesting era when a variey of 'new' locomotives from outside the Division appeared on goods work. Thereafter, during the immediate post-war years, only the summer Saturday passenger trains from the Midlands served to introduce strangers to the Division.

The same train, having passed the camera, progresses up the Dyfi valley   *H. C. Casserley*

The years 1940-42, in particular, must have been fascinating for any railway observer not unduly preoccupied by the war. Rolling stock was frequently diverted from regular rosters to provide special services anywhere across the country. The Southern Region, for example, constantly bemoaned the absence from Southern duties of their useful luggage vans and the LMS similarly objected to their coaches appearing in regular GW sets. Special Notice No. 553 of 19 October 1944 read:

> Every effort to be made to withdraw foreign coaches working in regular Great Western services immediately.[17]

During this period, locomotives also worked away from their 'home' depots, sometimes for months on end, resulting in the appearance of some Welsh engines in London or Cornwall, perhaps, or vice versa. Indeed, as soon as the CW Division was cleared for use by 'blue' category engines,[18] Oswestry took full advantage of the situation and borrowed any available 'strays' for both passenger and goods turns between Whitchurch and Aberystwyth. 2-6-0 No. 7307 was noted at Aberystwyth on Thursday, 15 May 1941, on a pick-up goods from Machynlleth. It had, presumably, worked the first goods of the day from Oswestry to Aberystwyth, a diagram which included a midday all-stations trip to Machynlleth and back (before leaving Aberystwyth with the last 'up' goods of the day). Although not a CWD engine, No. 7307 paid at least a dozen visits in the period up to 5 June 1941. 'Bulldog' No. 3445 *Flamingo* also worked several Cambrian line passenger trains to Aberystwyth that spring, as did No. 7814 *Fringford Manor* and No. 3345 *Sir Watkin Wynn* – a most appropriately named engine in view of the original Sir Watkin's key role during the formation of the Montgomeryshire railways in the 1860s.[19]

Churchward No. 3445 *Flamingo*, amongst the first of its class to operate the Cambrian line to Aberystwyth. Undated.

Real Photograph

No. 3375 *Sir Watkin Wynn* was another 'Bulldog' which had appeared on Oswestry-Aberystwyth services in 1941. Date and location unknown.   *Colling Turner*

Contretemps! 'Bulldog' No. 3450 *Peacock*, working the 1.10 p.m. local to Dolgellau collided with Dean 0-6-0 No. 2525, on a 'down' sheep special, near Barmouth Junction. Damage sustained by No 2525 rendered repair 'uneconomical'; it was withdrawn after the event. 2 November 1945.   *Ifor A. Higgon*

By 1943, however, Oswestry had officially acquired two of the 'Manors' which first entered the Division on Saltney duties; at that time, No. 7807 *Compton Manor* was a NEYland engine whilst No. 7819 *Hinton Manor* was based at CARMarthen.[20] After transfer, the pair shared the working of the Whitchurch-Aberystwyth mail trains. The engine of the 'down' morning mail (Oswestry 4.08 a.m. – Aberystwyth 7.28 a.m.) returned on the 12.35 p.m. from Aberystwyth (Oswestry 3.42 p.m.). The second 'Manor' usually worked the 10.50 a.m. from Oswestry, which reached the coast at 2.03 p.m.; returning home with the evening mail, which left Aberystwyth at 6.00 p.m. (Oswestry 9.20 p.m.). These services were timed to 'cross' at Dovey Junction but as 'down' trains frequently ran late, the two 'Manors' often met at Machynlleth or, if delays were serious, Cemmes Road or even Llanbrynmair. Both these services had direct access to Crewe, with obvious advantages.

Machynlleth's locomotive allocation in July 1942 comprised 24 engines, six 32xx 'Earl' class 4-4-0s, four Dean 'Goods', three each of the Cambrian 8xx and the newer GW 22xx 0-6-0s, and six of the versatile 45/55xx 2-6-2T class. Some variety was supplied by 0-4-2T No. 4865 which shared the Penmaenpool and Dinas Mawddwy duties with a similar CNYD engine (still exchanged on a fortnightly basis); pannier tank No. 1965 normally acted as yard engine and station pilot but occasionally carried out light ballast duties in the immediate vicinity of the station. Perhaps No. 1965's most notable foray on to the main line occurred in September 1945 when, as a result of the 'wash-away' and closure of the Ruabon line at Sun Bank, Llangollen, an ammunition train bound for Trawsfynydd was diverted via Dovey and Barmouth Junctions and worked forward from Machynlleth by No. 1965 and a 22xx 0-6-0.

At this time, Aberystwyth had 13 engines (three '22s', five '32s', two 'Dukes' and three pannier tanks), Portmadoc had seven (five Dean 'Goods' and a pair of 2-6-2Ts) and Pwllheli had five (four 2-6-2Ts and No. 892).[21] The foregoing serves only as a guide, as some engines were exchanged freely between the various sheds. Pannier tanks are not normally associated with the coast line but in addition to No. 7410's stint on the Towyn shunt in 1940-41, No. 2151 enjoyed several trips from Machynlleth to Barmouth Junction, acting as station pilot and banker during the summer of 1947.[22]

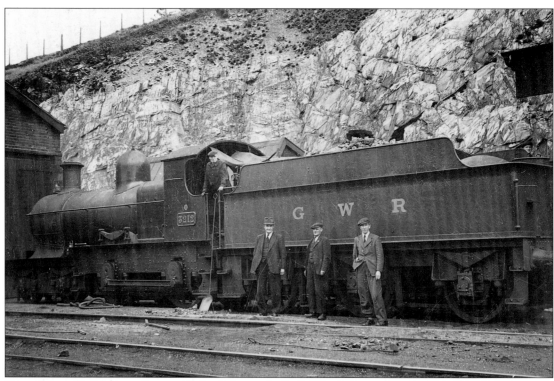

Four of the staff of the Loco Dept. at Machynlleth pose for R. C. Riley in front of No. 3212. *From the left*: W. Lewis, 'Big Bill' (Fitter's Mate); John Vaughan Owen (Loco Foreman); Jimmy James (Chargeman Fitter) and 'Jones y Clarc' (Chief Loco Clerk). 5 June 1946.

R. C. Riley

Collett 0-6-0 No. 2204 at Machynlleth, with Bill Neale (oiling) and R. J. Davies and Archie Fleming on the footplate. 5 June 1946.   *R. C. Riley*

Another Machynlleth group pose alongside yard engine No. 1965: *l-r* J. Evans, ?, Emlyn Jones and George Fleming. Undated.   *R. C. Riley Coll.*

Amongst the more unexpected wartime visitors drafted into the area were the former Midland Railway Johnson 2F 0-6-0s. These worked mainly between Oswestry and Llanidloes although some ventured onto the mid Wales line and one or two picked their way over Talerddig to Machynlleth, but apparently lacked the confidence to go further west; LMS No. 3126 was even listed as a Machynlleth engine when it left the GWR in November 1945.[23] In addition to the Midland engines, LNWR 'Cauliflower' 0-6-0s worked the last 'down' Welshpool goods into Machynlleth on at least two occasions; they stayed overnight and returned with the first 'up' goods the following day. The largest LMS locomotives to work into Welshpool from Shrewsbury at this time were Fowler's attractive 2-6-4T engines.

An excellent but undated photograph of the controls of an open-cab pannier tank loco, looking much as No. 1965 would have appeared.
J. P. Richards

At Harlech, a little-known standard-gauge branch line, or long siding might be a more accurate description, penetrated the sand dunes during the war years and was visited by at least three interesting locomotives: a J94 0-6-0T from the War Department controlled S&MR, and two small 0-4-0 diesel engines, which bore the numbers 70028 and 70226; little is known of them.

The most significant change to CWD motive power, however, had commenced with Oswestry's acquisition of the two 'Manors' in 1943. This development continued in April 1946 when No. 7808 *Cookham Manor* joined the Oswestry fold and two further 'Manors', Nos 7802 and 7803 carried the MCH shed code but operated principally from Aberystwyth. No. 7803 *Barcote Manor* settled-in in

April that year; it was no newcomer to the Cambrian having appeared on the Saltney Goods as early as 3 July 1941, but it was the first '78' noted at Machynlleth on an Aberystwyth working (the 10.00 a.m. to Whitchurch service, balanced by the 3.10 p.m. from Shrewsbury). At that time, the stencilled code of its previous shed (NEY) was still legible on the right-hand cylinder cover so there was then no certainty, for casual observers, that 7803's appearance on an Aberystwyth working was any more than a temporary arrangement. Subsequent events proved it to be an association which endured for nineteen years, until *Barcote Manor* was withdrawn in 1965. Interestingly, No. 7803 was the second Neyland engine to come to central Wales; it followed No. 3259 *Merlin* which was also a firm favourite in both west and mid Wales during the 1920s.

No. 7803 *Barcote Manor*, photographed by 'panning' a simple box camera, on the Derwenlas curve between Machynlleth and Dovey Junction, with the 3.10 p.m. Shrewsbury-Aberystwyth express, on 23 March 1948.   *GBJ*

'Manor' No. 7802 *Bradley Manor* and 4-4-0 No. 9026 work the 'up' SO Cambrian Coast Express, composed of 12.8s, up the Dyfi valley towards Cemmes Road, on 6 August 1949.   *Ifor A. Higgon*

No. 7802 *Bradley Manor*, formerly a Bristol St Philip's Marsh engine, was a newcomer to the area. It appeared on shed at Machynlleth one evening in May 1946 but with a prominent and freshly stencilled OSW on the footplate, behind the front buffer beam. Its continued presence around the depot for a week or so seemed to suggest that perhaps the locomotive foreman rather enjoyed having it around the place; someone certainly appeared reluctant to return it to Oswestry. In due course, *Bradley* found its way to Aberystwyth where it generally earned its keep, on and off, for almost the next two decades. Its first duties were the 7.40 a.m. Aberystwyth-Welshpool train, returning in the evening with the 6.30 p.m. Shrewsbury-Welshpool service, newly extended to Aberystwyth (from 6 May 1946) in response to the requests made initially in 1943. Regular monitoring of the evening 'down' train at this time revealed that it was not long before the OSW code was obliterated and MCH stencilled in its place, on the footplate behind the buffer beam and also on the cylinder covers for good measure. Every effort was made to ensure that *Bradley Manor* did not easily go astray!

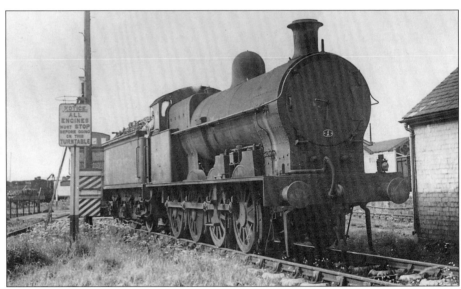

Ex-LNW 0-8-0 No. 48945 at Welshpool, 24 August 1948.
H. C. Casserley

No additional 'blue' category engines were transferred into the CWD for five years or so after 1946. Rather surprisingly, none of the Great Western's 43/53/63 and 73xx classes were acquired during that period although they put in regular appearances on summer Saturday expresses to and from Birmingham and, to a lesser extent, also on the Manchester trains. A most welcome visitor during the mid- and late-1940s was 'Bulldog' No. 3442 *Bullfinch*, normally the Shrewsbury pilot engine at that time. Peacetime, and a gradual return to normality, could have witnessed the completion of the original pre-war plan to convert the remaining 'Dukes' into 'Earls' but upgrading of the main line into a 'blue' route had rendered the original scheme obsolete. The only small change was the renumbering of the class from the 32xx series to a new 90xx group, to allow the new '22s', then under construction, to use the '32' series numbers. Apart from squeezing a few more years of service out of the venerable old 'Dukes' and introducing newer members of the 0-6-0 22xx class, no further development of locomotive matters occurred during the final years of Great Western ownership.

Old No. 3217, renumbered as No. 9017 in 1946, takes water at Moat Lane, with the 7.40 a.m. train from Aberystwyth. 23 August 1948.

H. C. Casserley

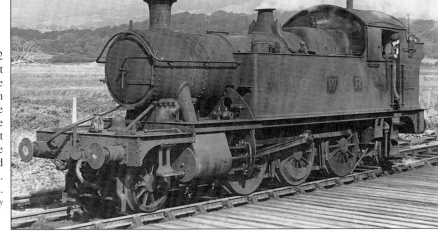

Small 2-6-2T No. 4512 pauses in the loop at Dovey Junction before returning a coast train to Pwllheli. The ignored 'G' on the tank-side suggests that at least one of the cleaners welcomed nationalisation. 25 August 1948.

H. C. Casserley

THE GREAT WESTERN BOWS OUT

The slow pace of post-war recovery permitted few improvements but the first significant timetable changes in five years were introduced for the summer service arrangements of 1946. Regrettably, a return to pre-war traffic density and standards was never achieved.

The popular wartime extension, during peak periods, of the SO 3.10 p.m. Shrewsbury-Welshpool service to Aberystwyth encouraged the introduction in May 1946 of a new daily express in the 'down' direction. This left Shrewsbury at 3.10

p.m. and arrived at Aberystwyth at 6.00 p.m. It stopped only at Welshpool, Newtown, Moat Lane, Machynlleth and Borth and offered good connections at Shrewsbury with the 11.10 a.m. Paddington, and at Machynlleth with the 5.30 p.m. to Pwllheli. The 10.00 a.m. Aberystwyth-Shrewsbury service provided the balancing turn in the 'up' direction, although this was a stopping train. From 1949, three through coaches ran daily to and from Paddington by these services, whilst a pair for Pwllheli reached the coast via Ruabon and Dolgellau.

4-4-0 No. 9021 deputises for a 'Manor' with the 3.10 p.m. Shrewsbury-Aberystwyth, as it ran into Machynlleth station. The Carriage & Wagon examiner stands in the '6ft' whilst his mate makes for the end of the platform. 24 April 1952.   *GBJ*

The dull, 'flat' appearance of No. 3265 *Tre Pol & Pen* contrasts with the well turned-out stock of the 'down' SO Cambrian Coast Express, as it emerges from the Commins Coch curves on 23 July 1949.   *Ifor A. Higgon*

A limited number of through trains were reintroduced on summer weekends, initially as special excursions. Those which ran in more than one portion were decidedly fewer than in pre-war days, but they were still seen occasionally during the high-days and holidays of 1946 and 1947. The SO Birmingham through trains were amongst these, as was a SO Aberystwyth express which left Paddington at 10.10 a.m., introduced on 6 July 1946. It offered no refreshment facilities, as many of the Great Western's dining cars were withdrawn during the war and, having been stored for years in the open, required extensive refurbishment before reintroduction.

Although the frequency of summer Saturday services was not as great as pre-war days, a graphic illustration of the still intensive occupation of the single-line sections was provided one afternoon in June 1948 when the trailing driving axle of faithful old 'Duke' No. 9087 *Mercury* fractured shortly after leaving Cemmes Road. The section was blocked and Cambrian line services were paralysed for several hours. *Mercury* had been returning tender-first to Machynlleth after banking duty and had just passed Abergwydol when the failure occurred. The left-hand wheel dropped immediately within the 'four-foot',

causing the outside coupling-rod bearing to fracture and release the rod as it did so. This, still attached to the leading driving wheel, flailed around with each revolution, being forced into the track and ballast with each complete turn. Fortunately, all other wheels remained on the rails and no one was injured. The section was closed as soon as news of the failure was known and the Machynlleth breakdown train was hurriedly propelled to the scene.

The incident occurred around mid afternoon. Disruption of the intensive summer traffic was total and normal operation proved impossible for the remainder of the day, but the fitters at Machynlleth displayed considerable ingenuity in clearing the line without the benefit of a heavy crane. This was achieved by first dismantling No. 9087's motion. The fractured axle- and wheel-set was then secured in a makeshift 'clamp' consisting of steel bar and bolted end-plates, hurriedly but effectively improvised on site. Engine and tender were then separated; the rear of the engine (complete with the securely clamped wheel-set) was jacked clear of the track and lowered adroitly on top of the tender draw-bar, enabling the tender to accept the weight normally carried by the rear driving wheels, now just clear of the rails. Further

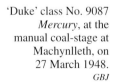

'Duke' class No. 9087 *Mercury*, at the manual coal-stage at Machynlleth, on 27 March 1948.
GBJ

improvisation was required to reconnect engine and tender, before the combination was dragged slowly to Machynlleth at about 5 m.p.h.

Remarkably, the track was not distorted and, apart from some disturbed ballast and a few fractured chairs near the point of failure, was surprisingly sound. Temporary repairs were hurriedly carried out and traffic began to move slowly again that evening, although a 5 m.p.h. speed restriction was imposed and a permanent way inspector rode the footplate of each train between Machynlleth and Cemmes Road to indicate the damaged section to drivers. Trains had been 'blocked back' at stations as far apart as Ynyslas, Llwyngwril and Moat Lane, as they waited for the line to be cleared and for their turn through the bottleneck. Although this incident affected the whole Cambrian system, and probably further afield, it attracted litle publicity and no additional details are currently available.

Many thought this would be the end of *Mercury*, as withdrawal of the 'Dukes' had recommenced after their wartime reprieve, but No. 9087 was taken to Aberystwyth where a replacement wheel-set was fitted. Thus *Mercury* was spared, until withdrawn in July 1949.

The war period and immediate post-war years witnessed categories of traffic not seen on the railways previously nor since. By 1945, for example, a number of GI brides set off optimistically for America and necessitated the compilation of special monthly returns from booking-offices. The practice ceased at the end of 1946 as 'only a few isolated cases are now likely to arise'.[24] 1946 also witnessed the repatriation of German and Italian prisoners of war. It would seem that certain camps were designated to receive POWs for final pre-embarkation preparations; Nantyderry, south of Hereford, appears to have been such a centre. Between January and May 1946 many prisoners who had been allowed to work for local farmers and trades people in central Wales were brought to Newtown and over a period of time, approximately 600 Italian POWs travelled by rail (in reserved compartments on normal Central Wales Division trains) to Shrewsbury, where they transferred to special trains bound for Nantyderry; similarly, around 250 travelled from Oswestry to Gobowen to join the special trains.[25]

A boost for post-war summer passenger figures was provided by the 'new' Butlin's Holiday Camp at Penychain, near Pwllheli, opened on 29 March 1947. This attracted special services from the north-west of England via the LMS at Afon Wen, as well as GW services from the Midlands and Paddington. The latter mainly used the Ruabon-Barmouth route but were worked from the outset by Machynlleth men and engines, as Pwllheli had no spare locomotives or crews. A 'double-home' turn was created whereby two 22xx 0-6-0s left Machynlleth 'light engine' on Friday afternoons and, after an overnight stay at Pwllheli, undertook an early start the following morning with the 9-coach 7.15 a.m. Paddington train, which travelled via Dolgellau to Ruabon. Two of Croes Newydd's '22s' were made available to work a balancing 'down' train (9.00 a.m. from Paddington; 1.13 p.m. from Ruabon). MCH and CNYD thus supplied a pair of '22s' each week, which on alternate weeks, saw a pair of Machynlleth '22s' available to work CNYD turns, and vice versa.[26] An interesting experiment which sought to capitalise on the attractions of the new holiday camp, was a short-lived Pontypridd-Pwllheli service which ran via Merthyr and Talyllyn, Moat Lane and Dovey junctions; a service which partly recalled pre-war Treherbert-Aberystwyth through trains. The Pontypridd-Pwllheli train featured only in the 1948 working timetable as Runs if Required, initially perhaps to gauge public response. As such, it may have appeared only on rare occasions if, indeed, it ran at all, although Harold Morgan witnessed a pair of Dean 'Goods' working a passenger train over the loop at Talyllyn Junction around this time. Regrettably, it does not appear to have generated sufficient traffic to feature in subsequent years.

On 31 December 1947, No. 9017 had the honour of drawing the last GW train out of Oswestry (to Llanidloes).
NLW/Geoff Charles

PARCELS TRAFFIC

It is not easy to appreciate nowadays the sheer volume of parcels handled by the railways in former years. Every town had its goods shed or warehouse and the number of consignments handled was truly phenomenal. Parcels traffic was an extremely lucrative side of the railway business although, in more modern times, it caused many headaches due to damage and pilferage. With all manner of goods moving by rail, there were opportunities aplenty for the light-fingered or weak willed. The carriage of tobacco, which was in even greater demand during wartime, provides a good example. Many consignments went astray and regular claims were made against the company.[27] Losses occurred despite careful control by the railways. Pre-war, in the CWD, at least, bonded goods such as tobacco and spirits travelled in dedicated vans, controlled by one person solely responsible for unloading at the appropriate stations, but problems undoubtedly increased as regular staff were drafted for war service.

The efficient peacetime system creaked and leaked throughout the war and showed no signs of

Smaller stations, such as Montgomery, received only full wagon loads of goods traffic after introduction of the zonal system during 1947. Undated photograph.
Lens of Sutton

145

recovery during the immediate post-war years, as general shortages continued to make certain commodities attractive to petty thieves. The last issue of the *Great Western Railway Magazine* in 1947, carried a piece entitled 'Lost, stolen or strayed – two and a half million pounds' worth of goods in a year' expressing the railway's awareness of the seriousness of the problem. 'Apart from the serious financial loss, the effect has been to cast grave reflection upon the good name of transport services and staff, and throw suspicion on innocent and guilty alike.'[28] This aspect, together with the general contraction of the industry during the 1960s, caused the parcels service to be reduced almost to the point of elimination. It is represented nowadays only by the more limited Red Star service (which, in February 1999, was sold to a private company – Lynx Parcels).

Part loads, thereafter, were concentrated at the major railheads. The bulging walls of the Machynlleth goods shed, however, owed nothing to this extra traffic – it was merely the legacy of early use of rubblestone. 21 July 1949. *WIMM/GW Coll.*

A further view of the sagging goods shed at Machynlleth. The canopy indicates a second road-loading/off-loading point; to the right may be seen a corner of the Loco Stores and office building. 21 July 1949. *WIMM/GW Coll.*

Arrangements for distributing parcels around Machynlleth in the 1940s changed considerably. The GW's faithful old Thornycroft left the area during the war period, either drafted to a place of greater need or scrapped because it had become impossible to maintain. It was not replaced and the service was leased for some years to a private carter, Rowlands and Son.[29] By the mid 1940s, this had reverted to railway control although prevailing conditions decreed that a horse-drawn dray would be more economic than a petrol-driven lorry. When a horse had previously worked the town's parcel service, in Cambrian days, a lean-to stable constructed along the east wall of the warehouse was used, but this had long since disappeared by the 1940s. The Great Western horse used one of the former Corris Railway stables in the lower yard; the carter was Emlyn Jones, of Ffridd Gate.

A major change in the goods department occurred when the GW's zonal distribution arrangements were introduced in 1947. This sought to make better use of rail wagons by ensuring that only complete wagon loads were detached at the smaller stations, but the scheme actually generated extra work for the larger distribution centres which now attracted all the part loads, for final distribution by road. Goods traffic levels at neighbouring Aberystwyth and Newtown had previously justified the use of several delivery vehicles at each centre, whereas a single vehicle had sufficed at Machynlleth until the new arrangements (which required three lorries) came into force. In comparison, no fewer than eight vehicles were required at Newtown. The additional traffic caused congestion at Machynlleth warehouse, which had only one loading bay. A new opening was thus made in the southern wall, enabling two vehicles to be loaded/unloaded simultaneously. This objective was duly achieved but the unstable composition of

the original rubblestone walls must have caused the architects some concern. These circumstances undoubtedly hastened the demise and eventual replacement of the old building in 1960, just three years short of its centenary. Talk of a new warehouse for Machynlleth had been circulating ever since the grouping, but nothing was done when the building was truly needed. Ironically, it was only built when such expenditure, perhaps, was no longer justified. The temporary, precast concrete building erected in the lower yard, while the new building was completed, would have been adequate for the final years of freight operation. Nonetheless, the railway has benefitted in the long term for although the building was leased to a local firm when rail freight services ceased, it has now reverted to railway use and since 1985 has served as the headquarters of the Cambrian section's Building Services & Bridge Department.

NARROW GAUGE.

The fortunes of the Division's narrow-gauge feeder lines varied during the war years. Passenger services on the holiday line to Devil's Bridge ended on the last day of the 1939 summer service (24 September) and was suspended for the ensuing

A general view at Aberystwyth, looking east; the special painting of the platform lamp for the dim 'blackout' days suggests a 1948/49 date. The Oswestry line passed to the left of the engine shed whilst the Carmarthen line, and the line forming part of the locomotive triangle, veered right.
B. Roberts, courtesy J. Peden

five seasons; no freight trains operated. The Vale of Rheidol track runs alongside the standard gauge for a short distance between Llanbadarn and Aberystwyth, and wartime visits to the seaside by main-line trains were characterized by the sight of deepening rust on the narrow-gauge metals on the approach to the terminus. The three locomotives remained out of sight for the duration of the war, tucked away in their own little shed near the harbour; but the coaches were less fortunate, being stored in the open at the station. They remained out of use until the service was reinstated on 23 July 1945.

The former Corris Railway continued with its weekday freight-only service, although this was trimmed from 1943 to thrice weekly trips. An attempt by Machynlleth Urban District Council to encourage the reintroduction of passenger services 'as owing to wartime conditions, the bus company was not able to provide sufficient facilities' was rejected.[30]

The Welshpool & Llanfair Railway, meanwhile, continued to operate a freight-only service; it served a more agrarian area and seemed almost to thrive as road competition was curtailed.

Notes

[1]Chester Divisional Notice No. 506 of 22 September 1944, W. G. Rear Coll.

[2]*British railways in peace and war*, BR Press Office (1944), p. 19.

[3]*Facts about British railways in wartime*, GWR, LMS, LNER, SR&LT (1943), p. 33.

[4]IAH Coll.

[5]*County Times*, 13 July 1940.

[6]per Ian Coulson.

[7]IAH Notes.

[8]W. G. Rear Coll.

[9]*County Times*, 10 October 1940.

[10]CHR Div. Notice No. 622 of 24 November 1944, W. G. Rear Coll.

[11]CHR Div. Notice No. 126 of 21 March 1944, W. G. Rear Coll.

[12]*Ride with me on the Early Bird*, The Railway Companies Association (1939).

[13]CHR DSO Notice 107, 8 March 1944. Special Freight Train Arrangements list included:

> Friday 10 March 1944: 2.40 p.m. Llandeilo Jc. to Saltney to be diverted via Aberystwyth or LMS Central Wales line.

This arrangement may well have operated at other times also, but no supporting documentation has been traced.

[14]T. B. Owen Notes.

[15]IAH Notes.

[16]CHR Div. Notice No. 180 of 13 April 1946, W. G. Rear Coll.

[17]CHR Div. Notice No. 553 of 19 October 1944, W. G. Rear Coll.

[18]Possibly late 1940; the CWD passenger service timetable – from 28 October 1940 & u.f.n. – sanctions the restricted use of 78xx, 41xx, 33/34xx, 26xx and 43xx classes; 'blue' category engines were certainly in evidence by the spring of 1941.

[19]T. B. Owen Notes.

[20]TBO and RAIL 254/98. Both Nos. 7807 and 7819 remained on the Division, virtually to the end of their days: No. 7807 was scrapped in 1964 but No. 7819, a great favourite which still performs on the SVR, paid its old haunts a return visit in 1987. See Chapter 5.

[21]PRO RAIL 254/97.

[22]IAH Notes.

[23]Rowledge, J.W.P.: *GWR Locomotive Allocations*, David & Charles (1986).

[24]CHR Div. Notice No. 642 of 12 December 1946.

[25]W. G. Rear Coll.

[26]IAH Notes.

[27]W. G. Rear Coll., e.g. CHR Div. Notice No. 521 of 8 October 1946.

[28]*GWR Magazine*, December 1947, p. 249

[29]Rowlands & Son: actually the old Thornycroft's driver and his son.

[30]*County Times*, 15 May 1943.

Chapter 5

State Ownership, and the 'Great Western Region'

The state assumed control of the four main railway companies at midnight on 31 December 1947. No one rushed around to over-paint the large letters of ownership on locomotive tenders or freight wagons – as happened to the Cambrian at the grouping – but it was not long before it became apparent that strenuous efforts were being made to expunge all visible evidence of the Great Western and its traditions. A similar situation must have existed with the other main companies but, at the time, it appeared to GW supporters that a particular vendetta, fuelled by jealousy and envy, was being waged against the company. There were undoubtedly those on the British Railways Board who would gladly have eliminated the word 'western' from the region's title, and every vestige

of Great Westernry along with it. In time, many of their aims were achieved, most notably the closure and virtual destruction of the great works at Swindon but, with hindsight, we can also appreciate that the old company had many faithful followers within its ranks. They attained high office in the new administration and put up a stout rearguard action to ensure that many of the finer points of the Great Western survived – even flourished – for over a decade after nationalisation.

The time-honoured name and insignia, however, were gradually obliterated as opportunities arose. Initially, the term 'Railway Executive' was used but eventually new tickets, posters and stationery declared 'British Railways (Western Region)'. During the early months,

Swindon's initial version of British Railways insignia: 0-6-0 No. 2219 on the turntable at Machynlleth; with Neville Pritchard. 24 April 1948.   *GBJ*

Some Great Western tickets survived well into British Railways days; the season ticket between Machynlleth and Towyn was used in 1971, over twenty-two years after the GW had ceased to exist.

GBJ Coll.

2-6-2T No. 4571 at Dovey Junction, 23 August 1948.

H. C. Casserley

locomotive tenders carried the legend 'British Railways' in full, in the GWR's own special shaded lettering, akin to Cheltenham Bold typeface. The first with that legend to appear at Machynlleth was Collett 0-6-0 No. 2219, which was out-shopped in plain, unlined green. The Great Western's stencilled shed-codes disappeared. They were replaced by an extension of an LMS system by which OSW became 89A, BCN became 89B and MCH, 89C.

Amongst those who perpetuated Great Western influence within the new regime were K. W. C. Grand, who succeeded Sir James Milne, the last general manager of the Great Western Railway. On the locomotive side, K. J. Cook succeeded F. W. Hawksworth in 1950 as chief mechanical engineer. Cook was a contemporary of R. F. Hanks, both being one-time Churchward apprentices, although Hanks had by this time left the railway service. Together they exercised considerable influence, in different ways, during the early period of nationalisation; Grand and Cook from within the organisation, and Hanks, as vice-chairman of the Nuffield Organisation, served on the Western Area Board of the British Transport Commission until 1967. This period saw the final development of the steam engine at Swindon and heralded great changes in motive power generally; but, thankfully, it also witnessed the reintroduction of chocolate-and-cream livery for named express trains and the almost wholesale application of lined-green livery for any locomotive ever likely to haul a passenger train. This represented the final manifestation of Great Western principles and pride. It may not have been fully appreciated at the time but we now realise that the old Cambrian line was revitalised during this period, for the 1950s were comparatively good years. They started quietly enough, as materials and supplies were still restricted and food and clothes rationing lingered on, not being finally eliminated until 1953. Nonetheless, new BR Standard class locomotives then began to appear in central Wales and a year

later, from the commencement of the summer timetable on 14 June 1954, the Cambrian line regained an express train which generated pride throughout the Division. Improvements to the line's infrastructure continued as the more vulnerable of the old timber bridges were renewed, one by one. For over a decade, stations, track and rolling stock improved; and a greater number of modern locomotives was more evident, possibly, than at any other time this century.

British Railways Standard 4MT locomotive No. 75024 passes the auxiliary (Merry Weather) pumping engine installed at Craig-y-bwch, just east of Machynlleth. This was used for drawing additional water from the river to augment supplies normally available from the well near the pump-house. The train was the 'first mail' – 2.30 p.m. from Aberystwyth to Welshpool and Shrewsbury. 4 July 1955.　　　　　　　　　　　　　*GBJ*

Although it is easy to focus on glamorous locomotives and express trains, gloss and glamour alone were insufficient for a lasting post-war recovery. The restrictions which threatened the railways in the late 1930s were suspended during the war and largely eliminated with nationalisation, but the threat from road competition remained and increased. Half-hearted experiments were made with road-rail wagons and containers, but the railways had had things their own way for far too long. They appeared ill-prepared and seemingly reluctant to adapt. Far from aggressively seeking new business, they seemed unable to retain that which they had dominated for decades. They displayed little appetite for carrying the battle to the opposition and opportunities to challenge the road lobby were largely ignored.

Bridge renewal, over Afon Carno, between Clatter and Carno. 28 March 1954. *WIMM/GW Coll.*

Work of this nature necessitated complete occupation of the relevant sections of line. Whenever possible, it was carried out on Sundays between the passage of the morning and evening mail trains. Here, the concrete sections for the side parapets are lowered precisely into position; the man with the pinch-bar, inching the crane forward, obviously has a key role in this operation. 4 April 1954. *WIMM/GW Coll.*

The completed bridge. 4-4-0 No. 9017 presents itself for the camera yet again. 29 April 1954. *WIMM/GW Coll.*

During the mid 1950s, no one foresaw that in little more than a decade, the railways' freight business would be annihilated and the network itself decimated. Traffic which the railways had controlled for years was allowed to slip away on to the roads. Just one small illustration is provided by the pit-prop traffic from Machynlleth. This probably appeared insignificant to the railway managers of the day but what occurred at Machynlleth was replicated, in different ways, throughout the network.

Until the mid 1950s, coal wagons had frequently returned to the pits laden with locally grown pit-props. This utilisation of returning empty wagons obviously benefitted both the National Coal Board and the railways. When one

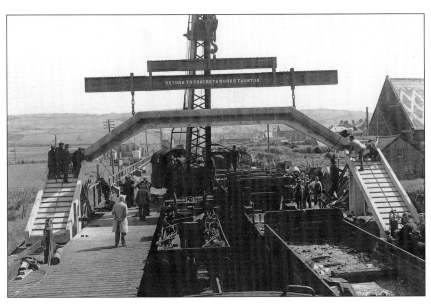

The old lattice footbridge at Borth had become severely corroded by the heavily salt-laden air over the years. It was renewed in concrete on 13 June 1954.
WIMM/GW Coll.

Borth station, with completed footbridge, *c.* 1955.

GBJ Coll.

of the private contractors who hauled the timber from forest to railhead attempted to obtain a better price – by a few pence per ton – for a projected increase in tonnage the railway proved utterly inflexible. The local agent was powerless to negotiate in order to retain the business, so the contractor sold his rather dilapidated lorry – suitable only for short-haul work – and invested in a more modern and powerful vehicle which allowed him to deliver direct to the pits. The traffic was lost to rail and never regained, and wagons returned to the pits unladen.

Parcels traffic similarly withered. Admittedly, there were many more variations and problems with this traffic, particularly loss through petty pilfering and organised theft, which increased

The '2 o'clock' 'up' goods approaching Craig-y-bwch on Thursday 19 July 1953, with 4-4-0 No. 9001 (still with a distinctive 'Duke'-style chimney) and 'banker' No. 4560.

GBJ

154

The appearance of three additional 'Manors' at Oswestry in 1953 released older members of the class for freight duties once more, recalling the *raison d'être* for their introduction to the Central Wales Division in 1940. No. 7819 *Hinton Manor* approaches Machynlleth with the mid-day pick-up goods from Aberystwyth. 22 April 1954. *GBJ*

Photographs of pannier tank engines down the coast are uncommon; here former GW pannier tank locomotive No. 7417 (89C) climbs from Fairbourne towards Friog with the 10.30 a.m. Machynlleth-bound goods from Barmouth. 15 September 1960.

Ifor A. Higgon

dramatically during the immediate post-war years. In answer to a parliamentary question, Mr Alfred Barnes, Minister of Transport, stated that in 1945 the railways paid out £2,525,405 in respect of 641,389 claims, compared with £180,462 in respect of 151,426 claims in 1938; an increase of over two million pounds. The parcels business was so vast that, despite the efforts of railway police and railwaymen of all grades, tracing the culprits

proved a difficult, time-consuming business. Even so, it is hard to understand that some thefts, which apparently occurred on a fairly regular basis, appeared to continue unabated. Some Chester Division Notices reveal that Ogdens, the Liverpool-based tobacco company, for example, suffered regularly in this respect and consequently made frequent claims for loss of goods.[1]

The long-established and most profitable parcels traffic was eventually handicapped by a combination of circumstances, such as low standards of 'economy' packaging and poor security, born of outmoded handling arrangements. Yet, in 1958, British Railways' nationwide parcels service handled nearly 83 million consignments.[2] The more recent Red Star service enjoyed only moderate success in comparison.

Passenger services

Generally, these were in a healthy state early in this period. Although the advantages of car ownership became increasingly obvious and attractive, shortages of material and fuel hindered the mass-ownership of motor cars. The railways were still able to hold sway for a further decade or so – virtually the last time they were able to claim anything like their monopoly of former years. In addition to the Cambrian's basic passenger service, summer Saturday special trains continued to attract capacity crowds anxious to sample holidays at the seaside and forget the deprivation of the war years. Travel abroad was limited. Switzerland was one of the prime destinations of the affluent but there was no mention of low-budget holidays to Costa del Anywhere. Holidays were largely based on what the railways could provide in the United Kingdom. During the peak periods, their services were almost as crowded as during the war and many trains, particularly at weekends, ran to seaside destinations during the late 1940s and early '50s in more than one portion. The Festival of Britain – that 1951 attempt at morale boosting during the grey post-war years – also created extra business for the railways as special trains, reminiscent of the pioneer excursions of the last century, were organised to visit the Festival Exhibition site on the south bank of the Thames in London.

2-6-0 No. 6371 clears Bell's Bridge on the final stage of the climb to the summit at Talerddig, with the 9.55 a.m. Aberystwyth to Shrewsbury train, on 17 August 1957. *GBJ*

4-4-0 No. 9000 tackles the climb to the Friog on 10 September 1953. Not many photographs are thought to exist of trains in service with open doors but apparently careless work at Fairbourne resulted in this record of not one but two open doors on a Pwllheli-Machynlleth service.

Ifor A. Higgon

Churchward 2-6-0 No. 5328 and BR Standard 2-6-0 No. 78005 tackle Wern Bank with the 11.00 a.m. Birmingham-Pwllheli train, on 9 July 1955.

Ifor A. Higgon

THE LAND CRUISE TRAINS.

1951 also witnessed the launch of a touring train in Wales, designated a Land Cruise. It originated on the London Midland Region of BR but made full use of Western Region metals to accomplish an attractive circular tour which encompassed some of the most beautiful scenery in north Wales; it proved extremely popular for a decade. The original train set off from Rhyl along the former Vale of Clwyd line, and Denbigh, Ruthin & Corwen Railway to Corwen. Here, it gained the Western Region line from Ruabon to Barmouth, before returning via Afon Wen and Bangor. During its first season, the Festival Land Cruise, as it was known, ran on Tuesdays, Wednesdays and Thursdays, when there was spare line capacity on BR and at a time of the week when holiday-makers sought divertissement. The regular locomotive at this time was Ivatt class 2, No. 46430.[3] Such was the train's popularity that in 1952 two services, now called the North Wales Land Cruise, were organised; the original continued from Rhyl, whilst a second train started from Llandudno and followed it around the circuit. Both trains spent an hour and a half at Barmouth before resuming the journey northward along the coast, past Harlech and Afon Wen. Each train comprised of six bogie carriages, again drawn by Ivatt class 2 2-6-0s. In 1953, the pattern was repeated except that at least one of the trains, rather predictably, was known as the Coronation Land Tour.

BR class 4 MT No. 75028 (6K) passes Barmouth Junction with the Cambrian Radio Cruise (Rhyl-Corwen-Aberdovey-Bangor-Rhyl). 6 July 1959.

Ifor A. Higgon

Further developments took place in 1954, with the addition of two further trains. The Western Region joined the act and organised a train from Pwllheli. This traversed the same route but in the reverse direction. The Pwllheli train was usually hauled throughout by No. 3207; the fourth train, from Llandudno, travelled in the same direction as the Pwllheli train. The arrangements for 1955 were unchanged.[4]

BR class 4 MT 4-6-0 No. 75026 (89A) passes Bontnewydd with a Western Region Land Cruise train from Pwllheli, bound for Rhyl. 3 September 1957.

Ifor A. Higgon

BR Standard class 4 4-6-0 No. 75033 enters Barmouth Junction with a Welsh Chieftain Land Cruise (Rhyl-Afon Wen-Barmouth-Corwen-Rhyl), 26 June 1959.

Ifor A. Higgon

BR Standard 4-6-0 No. 75020 resting on Machynlleth shed. 1957 *GBJ*

1956 saw a further change of name as the Rhyl train was re-titled the Cambrian Radio Cruise. The second Midland Region train, known as the North Wales Radio Land Cruise, worked south through Harlech and was hauled by class 4 4-6-0s. By 1957, the '75s' appeared more frequently on this train, both from the north Wales coast and from Pwllheli, where Nos. 75006 and 75020 were established for the summer and proved most useful.[5] The itinerary now embraced a trip south from Barmouth Junction to Aberdovey, where the train reversed. The following year, Machynlleth shed again borrowed two '75s' from Oswestry, Nos. 75020 and 75026. They operated Pwllheli Land Cruise trains and occupied themselves with other duties down the coast. In 1959, the Rhyl train was renamed once more, now becoming the Welsh Chieftain; the fare for the round trip remained at 13/- until 1960 but by 1961 it had increased to 20/-. It still appears to have been remarkably good value. The Rhyl train then ran to Towyn via Barmouth and returned by the same route. The Llandudno train also ran to Barmouth, whilst the Pwllheli train, (usually with either No. 75020 or No. 75026 in charge) ran to the north Wales coast via Corwen. Even with diesel power, this circular route would still be popular today but long sections of the line have since closed and 1961 proved to be the final year of operation for these attractive tours.

THE CAMBRIAN COAST EXPRESS (CCE)

Undoubtedly, the train which captured the imagination of most enthusiasts in mid Wales at this time was the Cambrian Coast Express. The summer Saturday through trains which ran between Paddington and the Cambrian coast from 1946 provided a welcome improvement in service.

ACCELERATED TRAIN SERVICE
THE
CAMBRIAN COAST
EXPRESS

LONDON AND ABERYSTWYTH
WEEKDAYS (Mondays to Fridays)   Commencing 14th June, 1954

Principal calling points :-

		a.m.					a.m.
LONDON (Paddington)	dep.	10A 10	ABERYSTWYTH	-	-	dep.	11A 15
		p.m.	BARMOUTH	-	-	,,	11A 0
BIRMINGHAM	arr.	12 10	TOWYN	-	-	,,	11A32
(Snow Hill)	dep.	12 15	ABERDOVEY -	-	-	,,	11A40
WOLVERHAMPTON	arr.	12 35					p.m.
(Low Level)	dep.	12 40	SHREWSBURY -	-		arr.	2 33
SHREWSBURY -	arr.	1 17				dep.	2 40
	dep.	1 23	WOLVERHAMPTON			arr.	3 28
ABERDOVEY - -	-	arr. 3 56	(Low Level)			dep.	3 33
TOWYN : - -	,,	4 3	BIRMINGHAM			arr.	3 55
BARMOUTH - -	,,	4 36	(Snow Hill)			dep.	4 0
ABERYSTWYTH - -	,,	4 5	LONDON (Paddington)			arr.	6 0

A—Seats can be reserved   Refreshment Car facilities available

On Saturdays the "Cambrian Coast Express" will depart from Paddington at 10-50 a.m.
and arrive Aberystwyth at 5-10 p.m.   In the reverse direction the train will leave
Aberystwyth at 9-25 a.m. and arrive Paddington at 4-10 p.m.

Full details of all calling points may be obtained from Stations, Offices and Agencies

The poster which first announced the new Cambrian Coast Express (CCE) service, in May 1954.

WIMM/GW Coll.

The 'down' train left the capital at 10.10 a.m. and reached Aberystwyth by 4.35 p.m., with the coast portion reaching Barmouth, then the northern terminus, by 5.00 p.m. Both 'down' and 'up' services avoided Shrewsbury and ran non-stop between Wolverhampton and Welshpool; there was no dining car. These trains reflected the popularity of the pre-war services and were an immediate success. The times of 'down' services were changed by 1948 when departure from London was at 9.00 a.m. and arrival at Aberystwyth at 4.10 p.m. Pwllheli was the terminus for the coast

portion that year and was reached at 6.22 p.m. The following year, departure from Paddington reverted to 10.10 a.m.; Aberystwyth was reached by 5.07 p.m. (5.10 p.m. in the public book) and Barmouth, the limit of the service along the coast in 1949, by 5.30 p.m. The 1950 timetable reveals a slight improvement in times, with departure as the previous year but arrival at Aberystwyth at 4.53 p.m. (4.55 p.m. in the public time book). 1951 saw departure from the metropolis at 10.50 a.m. with arrival at Aberystwyth by 5.12 p.m. (again, three minutes later in the public book). Barmouth, once more the northern terminus, was reached by 5.30 p.m.

The Cambrian Coast Express

Tariff

The front cover of a CCE restaurant car menu, *c.* 1959.

GBJ Coll.

The trains were laden to capacity and their popularity ensured their reappearance each summer Saturday, although the pre-war title was not restored until the summer of 1950. A restaurant car (BR's term for the Great Western's 'Dining Car') did not reappear until 1953, and then in the 'down' direction only, and only as far as Machynlleth. Return arrangements for this particular car and its crew are not known at this date. It would have been feasible for the car to have been detached here, at the same time as the train was divided into coast and Aberystwyth portions, and returned from Machynlleth at an early opportunity, but it would seem more likely that it continued empty to Aberystwyth, in time for car and crew to return on the 6.00 p.m. mail train to Shrewsbury. Regardless of the arrangements, the experiment proved sufficiently successful for the Western Region to launch a daily restaurant car service between the coast and London the following summer. A new development which surprised many at the time was the continuation of this service during the period of the winter timetable. Thus, for the first time ever, a weekday restaurant car service operated between the Cambrian coast and Paddington throughout the year.

Churchward 2-6-0 No. 6383 (89C) and No. 2217 run the 'down' CCE towards Chapel Crossing, Llanbrynmair. 14 August 1954.

Ifor A. Higgon

BR Standard class 4 4-6-0 No. 75026 and 'Manor' No. 7818 *Granville Manor* head the 'down' Cambrian Coast Express (13.8s) under a road bridge on the A470 at Llanbrynmair, known locally as Pont Lloyd George. 30 July 1960.

Ifor A. Higgon

(*Lower photograph*)
The inaugural 'up' weekday service of the
Cambrian Coast Express arrives at Machynlleth
on Monday 14 June 1954 with nothing more
impressive than a BR class 2 2-6-0 at its head.
The restaurant car is fifth from the locomotive,
No. 78007.

(*Right*)
After changing crews and taking on water and a
banker in the form of 0-6-0 No. 3202, the
inaugural train set off to tackle Talerddig.
Unlike the 'down' service, the 'up' train was
subjected to frequent stops; this, allied to a tight
schedule (for a small engine loaded to 7.8s) and
local crews' initial inexperience of working
restaurant car trains, resulted in much spilled
soup during the opening weeks.

Both photographs GBJ

The inaugural services ran on Monday, 14 June 1954. The locomotive of the 'up' train provided something of an anticlimax when it turned out to be no more charismatic nor efficient than a Standard BR class 2 2-6-0. Rather predictably, it proved inadequate for the task but the 2-6-0s, nonetheless, remained on the roster for the better part of three weeks. Even then, they were not immediately replaced by a more powerful 'blue' category locomotive but by examples of the older '90' class 4-4-0s. Their regime, in turn, lasted around two weeks before a '63' was rostered to the work. 'Manors' occasionally had a hand in proceedings but the GW 2-6-0s were prominent during the autumn of 1954 and for the next few years. The 'Manors' only made the job their own from the late 1950s, after receiving the benefits of improved draughting arrangements developed at Swindon. From the mid 1960s until the demise of steam, the BR Standard class 4 4-6-0s commandeered the duty.

The usual CCE sets comprised 7 coaches each (SE). Initially, two were from Pwllheli and five (including the restaurant car) from Aberystwyth, but operating experience eventually resulted in three coaches working through to Aberystwyth and three to Pwllheli. The restaurant car, which operated from 1954 until the end of the 1961 summer service, usually worked through to Aberystwyth, with the exception of the summer of 1956, when it worked through with the Pwllheli portion. The two portions of the 'up' train were joined at Dovey Junction, but the 'down' train was divided at Machynlleth. The Saturday services continued to use the Abbey Foregate Loop at Shrewsbury and ran non-stop between Wolverhampton and Welshpool. (*see Appendix V for train formation*).

Several of the vehicles used in the 1954 sets had recently emerged from Swindon and were in good condition, but they varied considerably in age and design and the outward appearance of the

4-4-0 No. 9022, and 'Manor' No. 7803 *Barcote Manor* as banker, climb out of Bow Street with a Birmingham-Aberystwyth train on 30 July 1955. Note the tender-to-tender arrangement of banker and train engine had not changed from the 1920s.
T. B. Owen

164

The 'Manors' were establishing themselves as regular CCE motive power west of Shrewsbury by early 1955, a position which was consolidated as a result of modifications to the draughting arrangements carried out at Swindon from 1952; No. 7802 *Bradley Manor* was amongst the earliest to be so treated. On an otherwise bright spring day in May 1955, 7802 managed to 'pick-up' a patch of shade – which accompanied it along the track – as it approached Craig-y-bwch with an 'up' train. *GBJ*

train lacked uniformity. Gradually, however, matters were corrected and both sets comprised of centrally located ex-GW 70 ft dining cars, of diagram H24, sandwiched between examples of the latest Hawksworth-designed corridor coaches. They were painted in the standard BR passenger livery of the day, that is, red below the waist, pale yellow above. Although irreverently referred to as 'blood and custard', this colour scheme had the unexpected advantage of appearing in black-and-white photographs much as the old GW livery. Then, the remarkable hand of Grand, Hanks *et al.* manifested itself through the Great Westernising of the Western Region. It was decreed that certain express trains – the Cambrian Coast Express amongst them – would be turned out in shades reminiscent of the GW's famous chocolate and cream livery, and that locomotives working such services would be painted in Brunswick Green; not exactly the old GW colour, perhaps, but a very acceptable alternative which has managed to confuse many enthusiasts ever since. In addition, locomotives on express work were fully lined, creating a most attractive livery (which equally suited many non-GWR express locomotives).

From the winter service of 1954, the long H24 dining cars were replaced by standard length H25 cars (Nos. 9562-67) which had worked until recently on the Channel Islands boat expresses to Weymouth.[6] Then, in January 1957, the Hawksworth coaches were replaced by new Standard BR coaches. The H25 diners continued

No. 7802 *Bradley Manor* approaching Nawlyn, west of Machynlleth, with the Aberystwyth portion of the 'down' Cambrian Coast Express. February 1955. *GBJ*

and included No. 9563, which was one of several Western Region dining cars refurbished at the Pullman Works at Preston Park. This operated up to 28 October 1957 when, with its companion vehicle (H16 No. 9550 – in chocolate and cream livery), it was replaced by more modern GW dining cars. These were fascinating 12-wheeled composite diners – Nos. 9672 and 9673 displaced from the Cornishman.[7] The latter coach was of great interest and of considerable historic significance. It formed part of a special train assembled during the Second World War for use by high-ranking government and military officials, including Winston Churchill. Possibly the most fascinating user, however, was General Eisenhower, Supreme Commander Allied Forces Europe. The train, code-named 'ALIVE', comprised one LNER and ten Great Western

vehicles which were especially adapted and painted. The train was used extensively by Eisenhower in the United Kingdom before D-Day, and in December 1944 was taken to France (via Southampton) and used on the continent, visiting Belgium, Holland and Germany. No. 9673 ended its days on the Cambrian Coast Express; it was withdrawn in March 1958 and, most regrettably, was not preserved. The replacements for Nos. 9672/3 were examples of the new BR Standard restaurant vehicles, represented (initially) by W1913 and W1914; later examples were W1905, W1910 and W1912.

When the restaurant cars were withdrawn west of Wolverhampton/Shrewsbury, they were replaced on the Cambrian line by a unique BR Standard carriage which carried an automatic buffet,

The 'Manors' did not immediately monopolise the working but shared the turn with GW 2-6-0s, which were well liked by some crews. No. 7310 heads the 'down' CCE over the black bridge at Glandulas, towards Machynlleth, running 'twenty late' on 4 July 1955. The reason for the delay was not discovered. *GBJ*

although this did not prove a success in the long term. It was somewhat under-utilised as it operated only to Aberystwyth, instead of running down to Pwllheli. Unfortunately, the buffet equipment was prone to malfunction and suffered from vandalism. BR did not develop the concept and failed to persevere with the idea.

Interior view of GW Dining Car No. 9672 (similar to No. 9673) as refurbished after the war. Photograph dated January 1946. *WIMM/GW Coll.*

The Butlins Holiday Camp near Pwllheli proved to be extremely popular. Penychain Halt had to be converted into a station, a new signal-box built and the line to Afon Wen doubled to accommodate the special trains to and from the north of England, via Bangor and the LMS, and from London and the Midlands, via Ruabon. If the special trains from Pontypridd, via Moat Lane, and listed in the service timetable for the summer of 1948 did not endure, another through service, between Swansea High Street and Penychain, proved extremely successful; it operated from 1954 until 1963. Interestingly, whereas the 'up' trains returned to Swansea for the first two years, from 1956 they terminated at Carmarthen, until the final year of operation when they ran forward to Cardiff.

Not a microwave in sight! Kitchen view of car No. 9672; same date.

WIMM/GW Coll.

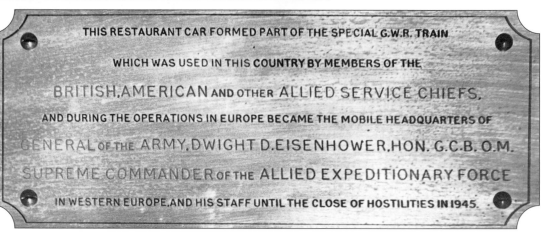

THIS RESTAURANT CAR FORMED PART OF THE SPECIAL G.W.R. TRAIN

WHICH WAS USED IN THIS COUNTRY BY MEMBERS OF THE

BRITISH, AMERICAN AND OTHER ALLIED SERVICE CHIEFS,

AND DURING THE OPERATIONS IN EUROPE BECAME THE MOBILE HEADQUARTERS OF

GENERAL OF THE ARMY, DWIGHT D. EISENHOWER, HON. G.C.B. O.M.

SUPREME COMMANDER OF THE ALLIED EXPEDITIONARY FORCE

IN WESTERN EUROPE, AND HIS STAFF UNTIL THE CLOSE OF HOSTILITIES IN 1945.

The commemorative plaque carried by car No. 9673 after the war. Photograph dated 4 September 1947.

Courtesy Ian Coulson.

Handbill advertising the auto-buffet service.

GBJ Coll.

Interior view of the auto-buffet. 12 February 1962.

WIMM/GW Coll.

Some of the trains which arrived at Penychain via Ruabon created additional work for Machynlleth shed, which supplied a pair of '22' 0-6-0s for the task. These left Machynlleth 'light engine' for Pwllheli on Friday afternoons and worked the Paddington through trains to and from Ruabon. A normal load comprised 9 or 10 coaches and it was frequently around 11.00 p.m. on the Saturday night before the Machynlleth crews returned to base. Between 1954 and 1961 a restaurant car was added to the formation of the 'down' train between Paddington and Barmouth, one of the rare instances when such vehicles worked in service trains over this line. There was

no return duty for the restaurant car, which travelled empty to either Shrewsbury or Chester.

The Central Wales Division was in good heart during the closing years of the decade, despite positive signs that motor transport was beginning to affect railway revenue. Car ownership was increasing, as were the numbers of diesel-engined buses and lorries then replacing earlier petrol-driven examples. Yet, despite these indications, both goods and passenger traffic figures held up remarkably well, particularly during the brief summer months. (Table XV) Services continued much as in previous years, but major changes lay ahead and cut-backs were looming on the horizon during the early 1960s.

Collett 0-6-0s Nos. 2201 and 2210 leave Barmouth Junction with the 1.13 p.m. Ruabon (9.00 a.m. Paddington) to Pwllheli.
Ifor A. Higgon

A BR class 3 2-6-2T, returning from 'banking' duty, waits in the loop at Cemmes Road for a clear road to Machynlleth. Undated photograph.
David Lawrence

Table XV: Machynlleth – Passenger totals and Freight figures 1935-59

	1935	1936	1937	1938	1939	1940	1941	1942	1943
PASS.	24,860	–	–	25,389	21,636	21,892	72,931	50,347	31,956
TONNAGE	–	–	–	–	–	–	18,714	22,267	26,427

	1944	1945	1946	1947	1948	1949	1950	1951	1952
PASS.	32,372	35,705	29,276	25,944	26,037	26,625	21,953	25,483	27,861
TONNAGE	19,448	18,908	16,648	14,769	19,375	20,303	22,603	16,807	17,111

	1953	1954	1955	1956	1957	1958	1959		
PASS.	24,262	24,762	25,622	26,214	25,906	24,640	25,530		
TONNAGE	18,490	16,912	18,377	14,611	15,613	14,594	13,389		

Rail 266

As a result of the Transport Act of 1962, the somewhat unwieldly British Transport Commission was divided into its main components. The British Railways Board was then created and chaired by Dr Richard Beeching; it functioned from 1 January 1963. From this date also, the old Central Wales Division was transferred from the Western to the London Midland Region (LMR). LMR management appeared embarrassed at having acquired the former Cambrian line and merely continued the economies instigated by the Western Region. The Cambrian Coast Express, for example, had lost its restaurant car west of Wolverhampton, since the end of the summer service of 1961, and the programme of cut-back and entrenchment pursued by the new regime quickly created the impression of a run-down railway with little future. After the Divisions's transfer to the London Midland Region the loss of the attractive liveries of locomotives and carriages of the CCE, for example, served only to emphasise the drab appearance of the rolling stock.

The enemy. Wolseley 1500 alongside class 2MT No. 46522, with a Brecon train, at Moat Lane. 8 January 1962.
GBJ

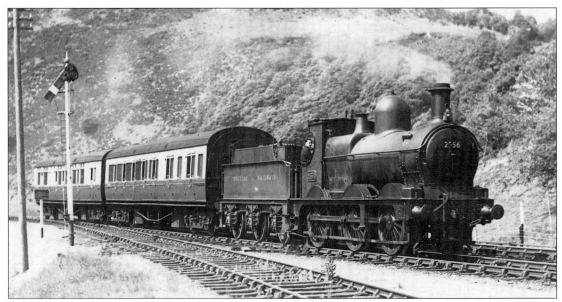

Mid Wales memories: Dean 0-6-0 No. 2556 arriving at picturesque Tylwch with the 2.45 p.m. Moat Lane to Brecon train on 24 May 1952. *Ifor A. Higgon*

Lightweight 2-6-0 No. 46511 – Swindon's adaptation of Ivatt's design – with a respectable load on the 9.00 a.m. mixed freight from Talyllyn Junction to Moat Lane, near St. Harmons. 9 May 1953. *Ifor A. Higgon*

Major economies were already evident in 1962, with the loss of the mid Wales line from Moat Lane. The section south of Llanidloes, to Talyllyn Junction, closed entirely on 31 December that year; that between Moat Lane and Llanidloes remained open for freight until 2 October 1967. The first of the original Cambrian constituents to succumb was the old Oswestry, Ellesmere & Whitchurch section, together with that part of the Oswestry & Newtown as far as Buttington Junction. Passenger services were withdrawn on 18 January 1965 whilst freight services had gone during the previous year, with the exception of the Gobowen, Oswestry, Llynclys Junction section, which remained open to allow access to the quarries there. Although out of use for many years, this physical link remains at the time of writing (June 1999).

Two other major closures in central Wales affected the CWD in different ways. The Ruabon-Barmouth Junction line was scheduled for closure by Beeching, also on 18 January 1965, but, in this instance, nature modified the plan. Exceptionally heavy rain during the week of Monday, 7 December 1964 caused severe flooding at Llangollen, near Corwen and between Llandderfel and Llandrillo, where the foundation of the line was washed away, causing suspension of through services on the afternoon of Saturday, 12 December. During the following week, trains were able to run from Ruabon as far as Llangollen and, further west, between Barmouth Junction and Dolgellau (extended from Monday, 21 December to Bala). Bus services provided a link between the two sections. The heavy rains also caused

The wash-away near Llandderfel, which hastened the closure of the Ruabon-Barmouth Junction line in December 1964. Merioneth County Council then decreed that the track should remain *in situ* for at least two years pending a final decision. Had the stay of execution been ten years rather than two, would there now still be a through service to the coast?

NLW/Geoff Charles Coll.

problems on the Cambrian line at Derwenlas near Machynlleth, between Dovey Junction and Aberdovey, at Caersws and Llandinam and between Newtown and Welshpool. Coast trains ran south from Barmouth Junction only as far as Aberdovey until 21 December and were worked by Machynlleth engines already at Penmaenpool,

Portmadoc and Pwllheli, together with CNYD engines that were west of the damaged areas on Saturday, 12 December.[8] Closure of the Ruabon-Barmouth Junction line had an immediate effect on Cambrian traffic and it was noticeable that trains increased in size and weight as they laboured over Talerddig.

Wash-away near Felindyffryn Halt, on the M & M, south of Aberystwyth. 27 December 1964.   *T. B. Owen*

The demise of the Carmarthen-Aberystwyth branch was also accelerated by the December storms. Again, floods and wash-aways wrought havoc with the permanent way, particularly at the well-known trouble spot near Llanilar. By the afternoon of Saturday, 12 December, flooding was reported there and an inspector, with light engine, set out from Aberystwyth to check the line. This was declared safe for the 5.45 p.m. passenger train from Aberystwyth to Carmarthen. Later, the

inspector went out again, this time running the light engine through to Strata Florida, whence it returned attached to the 5.50 p.m. passenger service from Carmarthen; water was reported on the track in several places. Further inspections, this time on foot, took place the following day. These revealed a severe wash-out near Felindyffryn Halt and, as a result, the line was closed completely north of Trawscoed, on the same disastrous weekend which had seen the end

174

of the Ruabon-Barmouth Junction line.[9] Again, bus services bridged a gap, this time between Aberystwyth and Strata Florida, until official closure which was planned with effect from Monday, 22 February 1965. Between 7 January and 15 June 1966 around a score of engineer's trains recovered track and other materials north of the break. Thereafter, the Carmarthen 'branch' out of Aberystwyth terminated at the Rheidol river bridge. The creamery at Pont Llanio, south of Tregaron, remained rail-connected until October 1970 when the service was no longer required. The creamery at Felin Fach, on the Aberaeron branch, remained true to rail, and milk supplies continued to use the branch to Carmarthen until 1973 when, eventually, all was closed. Only the short section north of Bronwydd Arms – now the Gwili Railway – effectively reminds us of this fascinating branch and once important through route.

The summer timetable of 1965 heralded the closure of the smaller CWD stations to passengers, and diesel multiple units (DMUs) were introduced to cover most of the services. Only the 'down' morning mail and 'up' CCE, together with the 'down' CCE and return evening mail, remained steam hauled. Initially, there was no improvement in journey times despite the elimination of many stops; it still took around two hours to get from Shrewsbury to Machynlleth with, frequently, a further 40 minutes allowed for the final twenty miles on to Aberystwyth. With six services in each direction, the number of through trains remained the same but the format of the new timetable terminated long-established arrangements which had faithfully served travellers to and from the coast for a hundred years. 1965 witnessed the closure of the old steam depots at Aberystwyth and Oswestry.

The red brick Royal Welsh Warehouse of Pryce Jones Ltd., the source of so much rail-borne traffic in the past, forms a warm-hued background as Newtown station welcomes 4-6-0 No. 75021 with the last 'down' CCE from Paddington. 4 March 1967.

T. B. Owen

175

Through trains from the Midlands to the coast continued to feature in the timetables on summer Saturdays; there were half a dozen in 1966, from Paddington, Birmingham and Manchester. A broad comparison of journey times over the years is revealing:

	1922	1939	1967	1990	1998
London- Aberystwyth	6h-05m	5h-35m	5h-21m	5h-15m	5h-09m
Shrewsbury- Machynlleth	2h-10m	1h-55m	1h.55m	1h-31m	1h-12m
Machynlleth- Pwllheli		2h-27m	2h-39m	2h-18m	2h-02m	1h-56m

Portmadoc and Pwllheli steam sheds survived to the end of summer 1966 and Machynlleth lasted a few more months until December; Oswestry Works ceased repairs on 31 December. The few remaining freight trains continued to be worked by steam until December 1966, when diesel locomotives took over. Steam haulage of the morning and evening mail services and the Cambrian Coast Express ceased after 4 March 1967, the final day of the winter service. Pwllheli and Machynlleth survive as booking-on points for guards and drivers, and Machynlleth also has a small number of maintenance staff and is the only diesel refuelling point on the Cambrian.

LOCOMOTIVES AND ROLLING STOCK

The locomotive situation remained remarkably stable during the early years of nationalisation. Occasionally, a fresh '22' might appear to replace a loco withdrawn or taken into works. Machynlleth's four 'Dukes' – *Cornubia*, *Mercury*, No. 9072 (old *Fowey*) and *Thames* – were still in evidence in 1948. In February 'Dean Goods' No. 2323 returned from a heavy general repair, repainted green. At that time this engine was in its 65th year, a remarkable achievement.[10] Cambrian 0-6-0 No. 864 appeared after re-boilering, and painted green; this particular class still made occasional appearances at Crewe, Chester, Carmarthen and Newport, away from the Cambrian heartlands.

'Duke' No. 9054 *Cornubia* at Machynlleth. Driver D. Lloyd Davies (*l.*). 30 July 1948.   *S. W. Baker*

176

Then, during 1949, Machynlleth lost three of the four 'Dukes', leaving only *Cornubia*. The 'Earls' were well represented by Nos. 9003/4/5/9/14/21, in addition to others which appeared from Oswestry and Aberystwyth. No. 9014 returned in July having been re-boilered and painted black and fully lined. On the Ruabon branch the 53-73xx class had almost exclusive control, save for No. 7817 *Garsington Manor*, and Machynlleth and Croes Newydd '22's continued to work in pairs on the Ruabon-Pwllheli Butlins trains. *Cornubia* remained active until withdrawn in June 1950, after 55 years service, at the end of which it held the record for the class with a mileage of over 1,600,000; it had been on the CWD since 1923.[11]

New 'Manor' No. 7822 *Foxcote Manor* works the 12.50 p.m. 'up' express to Crewe and Shrewsbury at Craig-y-bwch, near Machynlleth, 11 September 1951.   *GBJ*

The small '45' and '55' 2-6-2Ts continued to perform well down the coast and the divisions's regular 'Manor' population (Nos. 7807/8/19 at Oswestry and Nos. 7802/3 at Aberystwyth) undertook the heaviest passenger turns on the main line. None could be spared at this time for freight workings but this was to change the following year as ten additional 'Manors' were constructed at Swindon. The first three, Nos. 7820/1/2 *Dinmore*, *Ditcheat* and *Foxcote Manor*, respectively, were sent to Oswestry. They appeared in the lined black livery of the day and were a welcome addition to Cambrian line motive power. Unlike the original twenty 'Manors' which incorporated some parts from withdrawn 2-6-0s, the final ten were all brand-new engines. Their presence immediately released the regular Oswestry 'Manors' for freight duties – the first time for them to appear on CWD goods trains since the wartime Saltney turns. Three other 'Manors', No. 7823 *Hook Norton Manor*, No. 7825 *Lechlade Manor* and No. 7826 *Longworth Manor* put in early appearances on Ruabon-Barmouth trains. In later years, the 'Manors' interchanged sheds several times, particularly between CNYD/CHR and OSW or TYS (Tyseley).

The low evening sun always posed a problem when photographing the 'up' mail at Machynlleth. No. 7822, by now in a rather grimy state, features again at the same location as the previous photograph, but viewed from the other side of the track. 23 April 1952.
GBJ

In March 1951, 'Duke' class No. 9084 *Isle of Jersey*, revisited the division and at the end of June, sister engine No. 9089 (formerly *St. Austell*) renewed acquaintance with the coast line, albeit for the last time, when it worked a 10-coach troop special in company with 'Earl' No. 9017. At the end of the year the first steps were taken to permit 'blue' category engines down the coast when No. 7802 *Bradley Manor* undertook clearance tests between Dovey Junction and Pwllheli on 7, 8 and 9 November.[12] No major problems were encountered but a few months elapsed before the first 'blue' category engine was recorded at work on the coast. This is now believed to have been 2-6-0 No. 7305 which was noted[13] on a Penmaenpool-Tonfanau ballast train on Sunday, 6 April 1952. A week later, on Sunday, 13 April,

another 2-6-0 No. 5395 worked a troop train through Machynlleth bound for Tonfanau; it returned tender-first later that evening. Hitherto, the first instance was believed to have occurred when 'Manor' No. 7823 worked the 6.50 a.m. Barmouth to Dovey Junction train as the result of a locomotive failure on 2 June.[14] On 3 June, another 'Manor', No. 7802 *Bradley Manor*, worked a Sunday schools excursion from Aberystwyth to Chester, via Dovey and Barmouth junctions. This entailed running tender-first between the junctions; the load was 8 bogie vehicles. The following month (1 July), No. 6371 proved to be the first 2-6-0 to work through to Afon Wen, with another 8-coach excursion from Aberystwyth, this time to Dublin. This also would have required some tender-first running between Aberystwyth and

4-6-0 No. 7809 *Childrey Manor* hastens down the Dyfi valley with the 8.20 a.m. Oswestry-Aberystwyth service. August 1962.

GBJ

The Aberystwyth crew of No. 7812 *Erlstoke Manor* wait at Cemmes Road for the arrival of a 'down' train before they can proceed up the bank to Llanbrynmair and Talerddig. September 1961.

John Gwyn Dewing

Dovey Junction. The return from Afon Wen was on 3 July. Later the same month, No. 5395 put in another appearance down the coast when it worked a troop train from Tonfanau to Chester, and returned on the 1.10 p.m. (Birmingham 11.00 a.m.) Ruabon-Pwllheli, as far as Barmouth. Here it was attached to 2-6-2T No. 5507, on the 5.41 p.m. mail to Machynlleth (3.45 p.m. Pwllheli). 'Blue' engines continued to visit the coast as and when required, but a few more years were to elapse before they were regularly rostered over the line.[15]

In December 1952, former Cambrian 0-6-0 No. 849 was allocated to Machynlleth to replace No. 864 which was withdrawn; the latter had been stationed there for a great many years, certainly since 1926. Other members of the class at Machynlleth at this time were Nos. 892 and 894. Venerable old 'Dean Goods' No. 2323 also

remained active but the new year heralded the appearance of two new classes to the division. The first, a class of 25 lightweight 2-6-0s, was constructed (and improved) at Swindon and based on an LMS design by H. A. Ivatt. The first examples were allocated to Oswestry but before gravitating to the mid Wales line, as intended, they undertook running-in turns on local services to Ellesmere and Whitchurch. The second new class to appear was the official BR Standard version, designed by Riddles, but based very much on the Ivatt pattern. The first eight of this latter class went *en bloc* to Machynlleth, for duties down the coast, and must have represented the largest influx of brand-new steam engines ever to descend, almost simultaneously, on the coast line. Two of the Ivatt engines made an early visit down the coast when they worked a ballast train together from Llynclys

The difference of levels between the siding (laid with wartime pattern concrete pots and steel bars) and the main line was most dramatic at Llanbrynmair. Collett No. 3209 makes for Machynlleth with the 'down' Newtown school train. March 1962.

GBJ

'Manor' No. 7818 *Granville Manor*, obviously in fine condition, encounters no difficulty with the four-coach Aberystwyth portion of the 'down' CCE as it climbed Llandre bank in May 1959. *GBJ*

Junction to Portmadoc in January; a strategy which was not repeated as 'Manors' took over such duties later in the year. The similarity of the two 'Mogul' designs prompted Oswestry to conduct simple trials on 18 February 1953, when BR Standard No. 78001 worked the 8.20 a.m. passenger train to Aberystwyth (and the 2.30 p.m. return) and Ivatt class 2 No. 46510 took out the following 9.55 a.m., returning with the the 6.00 p.m. mail from Aberystwyth. The results were never broadcast but – with the notable exception in 1954 – the smaller 2-6-0s did not see extended use on through trains; they rarely featured on any service which called for them to run through from Oswestry to the coast.

The new engines quickly signed the death sentence of some of the older residents. Cambrian Nos. 892 and 894 were withdrawn in April, the former after 50 years service, the latter with 45 years service, and old No. 2323 succumbed in June, withdrawn after an active life of 69 years.[16] At the outset, the Ivatt engines rarely strayed from the Oswestry-Brecon route; although they could also be found on Brecon-Newport trains. No. 46507 was believed to be the first at Newport, but the same engine had found its way to Pwllheli by July. The latter visit, however, was an isolated event. Then, in November that year, a third new class appeared, without fuss or forewarning. One of the earliest visits, if not the first, was by Standard class 4 4-6-0 No. 75020 on 27 November 1953. It worked the 8.20 a.m. 'down' train from Oswestry and the 2.30 p.m. return working; the '75s' had arrived. They quickly displaced the 'Manors' from Oswestry, with the exception of No. 7819 *Hinton Manor*. The next dozen years or so were to witness considerable exchanges, at various times, of 'Manors' and '75s' between the Cambrian sheds and the Northern Division sheds at Chester and Wrexham (Croes Newydd) but two engines, generally, remained faithful to their original routes; No. 7819 to the CWD from Oswestry and No. 7817 *Garsington Manor* to the Northern Division's line from Ruabon/Croes Newydd. The end of the year was notable for the rather unusual working by a GW '63' of twelve ballast hoppers from Arenig to Llanilar, via Barmouth and Dovey junctions.

1954 commenced with 'Manors' dominating at Aberystwyth and '75s' at Oswestry; Machynlleth was well stocked with 'Earls', now frequently called '90s', as a result of the 1946 renumbering, small 2-6-2T engines of the 45/55xx classes, '22s/32s' and the eight BR class 2 2-6-0s. Cambrian No. 849 was laid-up over the winter but re-entered traffic for the summer service. It worked through until October, when it was withdrawn, along with Nos. 855 and 895. No 'blue' category engines worked regularly down the coast at this time, although casual visits on troop trains or ballast specials continued. In May, No. 75005 was noted on a troop train at Towyn and in August, what is believed to be the first visit by a '75' to Pwllheli took place when No. 75023 arrived there with a train of ballast hoppers.[17]

The most unexpected rostering of any CWD locomotives, however, occurred when the little BR 'Moguls' found themselves in charge of the 'up' Monday-Friday Cambrian Coast Express. Their time in the limelight, rather predictably, was brief; the task was beyond their capability and they survived a mere 2-3 weeks. The 'down' train, from the outset, was worked by '63s' or 'Manors'.

No. 7818 moves to be coaled and watered at Machynlleth as the inaugural DMU excursion returns from Aberystwyth to Llandudno. Sunday, 8 September 1957. *GBJ*

Locomotive matters then continued with little change in 1955, when the most notable event was the rail strike during late May/early June, which almost brought train movements to a halt. On the coast, three 'up' and three 'down' trains were managed but none were worked to Barmouth by Northern Division engines, although CWD engines provided a sketchy service. The introduction of the summer service was delayed until July.

182

No. 7819 *Hinton Manor* coasts into Machynlleth station with an Ellesmere-Aberystwyth excursion. 18 August 1957.

GBJ

The following year, 1956, saw further developments on the locomotive front as the numbers of 4-4-0s started to decline. In January, there were around a dozen at Machynlleth but this was reduced to half that number by May. They were replaced by '22s' and the new '32s'. Some of the BR class 2s were also transferred out of the Division. 'Blue' engines appeared more frequently down the coast from the commencement of the summer service on 11 June. One diagram now involved an exchange of Northern and Central Wales Division 'blue' engines. The locomotive of the 1.01 p.m. SO Ruabon-Pwllheli then worked the 6.45 p.m. Pwllheli-Machynlleth and was available, as required, during the following week. On Saturday it worked the 1.35 p.m. Dovey Junction-Pwllheli, before returning with ECS to Barmouth and departing 'light engine' for Croes Newydd, which would be reached around 8.00 p.m. Initially, Machynlleth's No. 6335 alternated with a Croes Newydd '63' but, later, 'Manors' also

appeared. When winter service commenced in September, all the 4-4-0s were placed in store at various sheds; by the end of the first week in October, none remained in service.[18]

Special passenger trains did not cease entirely with the ending of the summer service, but they were now inclined to run in the reverse direction. Instead of bringing visitors into the area, they travelled away from the region, often to the shopping areas of Merseyside. A popular plan was for one train to start from Machynlleth and meet another at Barmouth Junction, which would have worked down the coast from Portmadoc or Harlech. After combining to form one train they worked forward to Chester, for Liverpool or Manchester. Such excursions, although not frequent, featured regularly over the years. In February 1957, for instance, No. 4377 worked five coaches from Machynlleth to Barmouth Junction to meet No. 2244 which had worked south with five more.[19] In May 1957, 'Manor' No. 7806

Talerddig station in August 1962. The '63' which banked the CCE to this point was detached here, allowing No. 7823 *Hook Norton Manor* to continue alone to Shrewsbury. *GBJ*

The Cemmes Road signalman presents the token for a 'down' train, 23 May 1963. *John Gwyn Dewing*

4-4-0 No. 9005 in store at Llanidloes, 11 June 1957.

Ifor A. Higgon

Perhaps the length of David Davies's 'monstrous train' of 1863 (*Railway Through Talerddig*, p. 54) was never exceeded on the N&M section, but this Sunday school excursion from Aberystwyth to Shrewsbury was typical of many 14-coach trains which were evident on post-war summer Saturdays. Nos. 7814 *Fringford Manor* and 7802 Bradley Manor (leading) approached Cemmes Road on 7 June 1960.

Ifor A. Higgon

returned to Machynlleth in resplendent condition after a visit to the works; it worked regularly down the coast for over two years, until transferred to Newton Abbot on 23 June 1959.[20]

The two '75s' (Nos. 75006 and 75024), loaned to Machynlleth by Oswestry to cover the Land Cruise trains from Pwllheli during the summer of 1957, were obviously welcomed and useful additionally on through services during the hectic weekend periods. They returned to Oswestry when the Land Cruise trains ceased. The summer service again saw the '90s' brought out of hibernation but

by September, they too had returned, save No. 9021, which remained active throughout the winter. Perhaps it is best remembered for sharing the working of a second portion of the 'up' CCE on Christmas Eve. It had worked its train from Barmouth to Dovey Junction, where it combined with 'Manor' No. 7819 *Hinton Manor* on the Aberystwyth portion, before the pair set off for Shrewsbury. The main train (also 10 coaches) was worked from Dovey Junction to Shrewsbury by another 'Manor' No. 7828 *Odney Manor* with BR class 2 No. 78005.

No. 7823 *Hook Norton Manor* and a uniform set of coaches form the 'down' Cambrian Coast Express as it approached Machynlleth in August 1960. *GBJ*

2-6-2T No. 5510 runs hurriedly around its train standing in the 'Aberystwyth' siding at Machynlleth (even though most trains which used it left for the coast). The end vehicle in this view is Hawksworth Bk/3rd No. 2202, now restored to full Great Western livery by the Great Western Society at Didcot. April 1960. *GBJ*

No. 9021 continued in service during the following spring and again piloted the CCE over the Easter period but perhaps the most significant event of 1958 had occurred in February when a DMU Special Test Train ran across central Wales. On Tuesday, 18 February, a 3-car Cross Country set left Cannock Road at 7.32 a.m. for Ruabon and Barmouth (arr. 11.26 a.m.). It then worked from Barmouth (calling at all stations) to Dovey Junction, before returning to Barmouth by 5.05 p.m. After an overnight stop, it set out the following day (8.40 a.m.), again calling at all stations and halts to Pwllheli (arr. 10.45 a.m.).

Departure from Pwllheli was at 11.15 a.m., when it travelled via Barmouth and Ruabon, *en route* to Cannock Road. A week earlier, the same unit had worked from Cannock Road, via Shrewsbury and Aberystwyth, to Carmarthen; then, after another overnight stay, it returned to Cannock Road the following day, 12 February.[21] It seems regrettable that the opportunity was not taken to exploit the flexibility of DMU operation by instigating all-year-round through services between Shrewsbury and Carmarthen, for example, or between Caernarfon and Carmarthen. But old traditions and practices died hard.

Driver Neville Pritchard controls the flow of water as the tanks of BR class 3 No. 82034 are replenished at Moat Lane, whilst working the Newtown school train back to Machynlleth. 22 September 1962.   *F. K. Davies*

In 1958, however, steam was still supreme and a variety of locomotive types traversed the Cambrian lines, particularly during the summer months. GW '63s' Nos. 6371 and 6392 were regular performers down the coast, together with No. 7339 of the former '93' class, which had undergone weight modification allowing them to

operate on 'blue' routes. These locomotives, which combined power and reasonable comfort within a compact wheelbase, seemed well-suited to the coast lines but they were not introduced in any great numbers; their usefulness obviously ensured they were equally welcome elsewhere.

187

Allocations of main line engines changed yet again when, during the summer, Oswestry's '75s' were exchanged for the Northern Division's 'Manors' – with the notable exception of No. 7817 *Garsington Manor*, which remained at CNYD. This meant that OSW '75s' were no longer available to help out with the Land Cruise services. The Pwllheli trains were then worked by a pair of '22s', a state of affairs which prevailed until the first week of August when Nos. 75020 and 75026 were found for Machynlleth. Later in the month, No. 75006 replaced No. 75020 but by the end of the Land Cruise programme, the Standard class 4s had disappeared once more, leaving No. 7806 *Cockington Manor* as the only regular 4-6-0 representative. The end of summer activity also saw most of the '90s' returned to store, the exceptions being No. 9013 and 9021 which were withdrawn from Machynlleth; this left only six members of a class which formerly numbered twenty-nine.[22]

Moat Lane station sign was in fine condition when photographed *c.* 1961.

John Gwyn Dewing

No. 7806 *Cockington Manor* and 2-6-2T No. 4575 rest at Machynlleth on a June Sunday in 1957.

GBJ

No. 7806 *Cockington Manor* and a light load leave Barmouth Junction as they make for home with a Pwllheli-Machynlleth train. 30 April 1959.   *Ifor A. Higgon*

The smaller engines were adequate for the lighter, winter duties. Indeed, during February 1959, a fairly regular pannier tank working again took place between Machynlleth and Barmouth, echoing earlier visits by Nos. 2151 and 7410. Machynlleth acquired No. 7405 during January that year and during February, at least, it frequently worked a morning goods train to Barmouth, returning with the 3.25 p.m. passenger train. It remained on Machynlleth's books until November, when it left for Oswestry, but before then, in October, it was joined for a while by classmate No. 7434. During June, Standard class 4s Nos. 75020 and 75026 returned once more to Machynlleth (from Tyseley) but this time on permanent allocation. 'Earl' class No. 9005, formerly *Earl of Devon*, which had lain in store at Llanidloes since the end of the summer service in 1957, was condemned in July 1959. The same month saw two classmates travelling together for the last time along the valleys of the Mawddach and the Dee, when Nos. 9004 and 9014 took the ten-coach 7.20 a.m. Pwllheli-Paddington train as far as Ruabon. The '75s' on this route had dwindled from five examples to one, an indication that they were not received kindly in Wrexham and Chester; the GW 'Moguls', which had increased in number, were much preferred.[23] The five surviving '90s', which had assisted with the summer traffic, were put in store in September, for the last time. If the old brigade was fading away, there appeared to be no shortage of newcomers prepared to establish themselves in their place. The next new class to appear on the Cambrian took the form of BR Standard class 3 tank No. 82005; it first worked out of Machynlleth on 27 August.[24]

Stanier 2-6-2T No. 40086 ascending Friog bank with the 10.35 a.m. Barmouth to Dovey Junction train. 9 July 1960.

Ifor A. Higgon

Stanier 2-6-2T No. 40085 on the turntable at Machynlleth, July 1960.

GBJ

In January 1960, yet more usurpers arrived when four Stanier-designed ex-LMS 2-6-2T engines appeared in Machynlleth. Nos. 40085/6, 40110 and 40205 were refugees from the recently closed Rhosddu Shed at Wrexham and had formerly worked between Wrexham and New Brighton. They were not in particularly good condition and found little favour amongst enginemen. Two were immediately transferred and Nos. 40085/6 had also left for Oswestry and Shrewsbury by the end of the summer. The British Standard class 3 was better received; No. 82031

arrived in January and was joined soon after by Nos. 82000 and 82020. But this was not the end of new motive power, for March saw the introduction of yet another new type although, in this instance, its appearance was fleeting. Little Ivatt class 2 2-6-2T No. 41240 might have been fine for the lighter loads encountered during winter months, but local footplatemen knew instinctively that the heavier summer loads would tax both men and machine. They had suffered enough with underpowered locomotives; No. 41240's trial down the coast was not successful. When summer

For a few years at the end of the 1950s, the 'down' Newtown school train was extended from Machynlleth to Aberystwyth. 4-4-0 No. 9017 attacks the 1 in 75 grade out of Borth with the 4.20 p.m. from Newtown. July 1958.

GBJ

arrived, only two of the 4-4-0s in store were returned to traffic, No. 9017 to Machynlleth and No. 9014 to Croes Newydd; both lasted until October, with No. 9017 surviving still, albeit in foreign parts. Machynlleth had lost all its small tank examples of the '45' class, but the slightly larger 55xx variety were well represented at the start of winter service; No. 4575 did not quite

make it, for it was withdrawn in August. Nos. 5510/45/53 and 5555, however, survived although by January, only No. 5555 remained, but it too was transferred within a month. In February, a new locomotive diagram came into force which granted Oswestry locomotives regular access to the coast lines. These were usually the small class 2 2-6-0s which worked the early morning (2.30

191

a.m.) goods train from Welshpool to Machynlleth. Instead of returning with the 2.00 p.m. 'up' goods, as in the past, they worked the 1.28 p.m. Dovey Junction to Pwllheli passenger train, and 5.30 p.m. return.[25]

Sometime during the early 1960s an interesting newcomer invaded the old N&MR territory when a Fowler 2-6-4T worked the 3.40 p.m. from Shrewsbury through to Machynlleth. It would normally have been changed at Welshpool but a motive power crisis caused it to work over Talerddig to Machynlleth. After turning and servicing, it returned the following morning with the 4.30 a.m. goods to Newtown, where it would have shunted for a few hours, as required, before continuing to Welshpool with the 10.05 a.m.

Fowler 2-6-2T No. 40008 on the Welshpool turntable. 23 August 1954.   *H. C. Casserley*

BR Standard locomotives at Machynlleth. *From the left*, 2-6-4T No. 80080, and 2-6-0s Nos. 78000/7. Shrubbery surrounding the air-raid shelters is just visible behind No. 78007. August 1962.   *GBJ*

2-6-0 No. 6392 climbing out of Fairbourne with the 'up' Cambrian Coast Express. 15 April 1961.   *Ifor A. Higgon*

freight.[26] Locomotives at this time, particularly Oswestry's class 2s, generally sported green liveries, with the exception of those repaired at Crewe, which appeared in lined black livery. This period also saw increased numbers of the GW 2-6-0s down the coast; Nos. 6336, 6339, 6353 and 6395 were regular performers, the latter resplendent in fully lined livery.

The influx of British Railways Standard locomotives continued in 1962. A dozen or so of the class 3 tanks were seen during the summer and the withdrawal of GW engines gathered pace, as if in readiness for the transfer to the London Midland Region at the end of the year. On 29 April, a new cyclic roster was introduced, commencing with a 'down' local (6.55 a.m.) from Wrexham to Barmouth, the engine then worked the 1.58 p.m. Barmouth to Machynlleth local; the following day, it worked back to Wrexham via Welshpool. 'Manors', '63/73s' and '22s' were used by CNYD. From the commencement of the winter service, Machynlleth and Salop sheds also contributed to this arrangement.[27]

During the spring, Nos. 75020 and 75026 entered the works, to emerge in June and July, respectively, both in green livery and sporting double chimneys. They had been joined at Machynlleth, in the meantime, by No. 75021. No. 6368 also arrived to replace No. 6336 for the summer service and in July a transfer took place of BR Standard 2-6-4Ts from the London, Tilbury & Southend section. Several arrived at CNYD, SaLoP, OSW and MCH sheds and worked all over the lines hitherto covered by 'blue' route engines; Nos. 80079 (CNYD) and 80101 (MCH) were among the early arrivals.

In February/March 1963, there was yet another interchange of locomotive stock between Croes Newydd and Aberystwyth, when the class 4s ended up at Wrexham and three 'Manors' were transferred to Aberystwyth. The five then working from Aberystwyth were Nos. 7802/3/19/21 and 28. A few Ivatt class 2s were also drafted to Machynlleth after closure of the mid Wales line on 31 December 1962, making a total there of four. The '75s' at the home depot were changed that year, with Nos.

75002/4 being used down the coast. Five of the large 2-6-4Ts, eleven of the class 3 2-6-2Ts and three '22s' completed Machynlleth's compliment.

Over the years, various versions of the Royal train have visited mid Wales but perhaps the most memorable of recent times was the visit of August 1963, when no fewer than five 'Manors' and an Ivatt 2-6-0 were prepared for the occasion. No. 7812 was the 'spare' engine in charge of the breakdown crane, No. 46521 was used at Harlech to provide overnight heating and to draw the train out of the refuge siding the following morning, and the four 'Manors' used on the train itself were Nos. 7819, 7822, 7827 and 7828.

The most important administrative change during 1963, as a result of regional boundary changes, meant that Machynlleth's 89C code was removed from the Western Region lists, to become 6F on the London Midland Region register from 9 September.

Special care was always called for when alighting at Llanbrynmair, particularly during the blackout, as the 'down' platform was bisected by a minor road. The signalman stands with the token for the next section to Cemmes Road as 2-6-4T No. 80135 runs alongside with an Aberystwyth train.
c. 1963.

David Lawrence

0-6-0 No. 2204, fitted with a snowplough and fully fuelled in readiness for winter weather at Machynlleth. December 1958.
GBJ

The 'rock' road at Machynlleth had probably never held such distinguished company. *From the left*: 'Manor' Nos. 7828, 7827, 7819 and 7822 receive last minute attention before royal train duties on 9 and 10 August 1963. 9 August 1963.   *T. B. Owen*

Nos. 7827 *Lydham Manor* and 7828 *Odney Manor* with the royal train from Aberdovey, at Morfa Mawddach (as Barmouth Junction was known after 1960). 10 August 1963.
Ifor A. Higgon

As 1964 advanced, so did the threat of dieselisation. The GW presence diminished visibly; only the 'Manors' at Aberystwyth and 0-6-0 Nos. 2236, 2268 and 3208 at Machynlleth provided any reminder of former glories. This trio represented the final GW engines to be stationed at Machynlleth. The summer service brought yet another change, this time to SO Birmingham and Paddington through trains to and from the coast. These were now routed via Machynlleth and Welshpool, instead of via Ruabon, as previously. The new 10.55 a.m. Pwllheli-Birmingham (previously the 11.10 a.m. via Ruabon) service picked up at all stations as far as Machynlleth which, with the normal load of 8/9 coaches, entailed some hard work for the crew of the '75' normally rostered. Time was often lost in frequent 'drawing-up' at stations *en route*. The through Paddington train now left Pwllheli at 10.35 a.m., again usually headed by a '75' but occasionally by a class 4 with class 3 tank assisting. 4-6-0 No. 75012 was transferred to Machynlleth to assist with the summer traffic.

BR Standard types and former WR class 2s covered all normal duties on the Ruabon branch; CNYD possessing eight or nine '75s', three or four class 4 tanks and two of the Ivatt 465xx class. From 4 May, all freight traffic ceased on the Ruabon line. Although the Birmingham and Paddington through trains were diverted, the 11.00 a.m. SO Ruabon-Pwllheli and the 1.25 p.m. SO

Barmouth-Ruabon continued. The 6.55 a.m. passenger from Wrexham to Barmouth and the 2.25 p.m. Barmouth-Machynlleth etc., were still worked by the usual variety of engines – 'Manors', 75xxx, 80xxx and 465xx from CNYD, OSW and SaLoP sheds – who completed their cycle via Welshpool.[28] From 4 May also, freight services down the coast, including Aberystwyth, were reduced to one 'down' and one 'up' service per day. On the main line, there were two Shrewsbury-Machynlleth freights, one of which ran no further than Welshpool on Saturdays. A third SX service, which is detailed under 1966, ran no further than Newtown. Commencing with the timetable from 7 September 1964 to 13 June 1965, all Cambrian line trains – passenger and freight – were operated to the 24-hour clock although, surprisingly, the adjacent Chester area adhered to a.m. and p.m.

Seasonal decorations adorn No. 7802 at Aberystwyth. 24 December 1958.   T. B. Owen

No. 7801 *Anthony Manor* on
freight duty at Welshpool,
28 December 1964.

T. B. Owen

4-6-0 No. 7812 *Erlestoke
Manor* approaches
Commins Coch and
coasts around the sharp
curve which could be
relied upon, always, to
deliver an extra little kick
if approached at anything
above the stipulated
speed. 30 May 1963.

B. J. Ashworth

1965 (coincidentally, the number of the little yard engine at Machynlleth, for many years) proved to be significant in the story of the Cambrian lines; it was the year the steam engine had to acknowledge that its days were numbered. From 18 January, diesel multiple units began to operate passenger services between Shrewsbury and Aberystwyth and between Machynlleth and Pwllheli. Also on this date, Whitchurch-Buttington Junction and Morfa Mawddach to Bala sections closed. Freight services were still steam-hauled; Machynlleth had sufficient engines to cover the remaining duties, whilst the mail and Cambrian Coast Express remained steam-hauled, with Shrewsbury shed supplying the locomotives, which initially included the 'Manors' formerly at Aberystwyth. 1965 also witnessed the final appearance of former Great Western engines on the Cambrian. Collett No. 2236 continued in use at Machynlleth until withdrawn in May, whilst two other former 89C '22s' had gone further afield; No. 2268 was withdrawn from its role as snow-plough at CNYD and No. 3208 was withdrawn from Llandudno Junction, where it had similar duties.

The summer service, which commenced on 14 June, attracted three other BR recruits to assist with the additional traffic, Nos. 75013/28 and 55. Then suddenly, in July, all the class 4 2-6-4T engines were rather dramatically condemned. From that time the '75s', with small 2-6-0s Nos. 46521 and 46446 and a few Shrewsbury 'Manors', remained in sole charge. The latter were in a sorry state; none looked cared-for and several ran without name- or number-plates. By the end of the year, all were withdrawn although, miraculously, several former Cambrian line 'Manors' survive and are now preserved in fine operating condition.

'Manor' No. 7809 *Childrey Manor* near Glaspwll bridge, with Pumwern farm across the river. August 1962. *GBJ*

Closure of the Ruabon line and the end of steam operation ensured that Barmouth would no longer witness this kind of activity. 28 November 1964.
T. B. Owen

An unidentified 'Manor' makes its way across the Mawddach estuary on a cold but calm winter's day in January 1950.
John Gwyn Dewing

1966 opened with the redesignation of the Welshpool-Newtown section as a 'Permitted Red' route, the first official indication being traced to Supplement No. 2 of the working timetable (3 January 1966, until further notice) which stated:

Add – The speed of any train worked by a permitted engine of the 'Red' Classification must not exceed 50 m.p.h. at any point in either direction between Welshpool and Newtown, with a further restriction of 15 m.p.h. when travelling over Bridge 147 between Abermule and Newtown, 44¼ and 44½ m.p.

This new directive primarily affected the daily Shrewsbury-Newtown freight which conveyed Presflo cement wagons to Llanidloes, for the construction of the Claerwen dam. This was the duty which introduced the final batch of 'new' steam motive power to the Cambrian when former LMS class 5 4-6-0 and class 8F 2-8-0 engines were noted on several, separate occasions by Messrs Ron Jones and E. H. Stephens at Newtown. Ivatt Nos. 46446 or 46521 from Machynlleth were usually on hand to complete the final leg of the journey to

Llanidloes. Empty wagons were returned to Aberthaw (dep. Newtown 11.55) on Mondays and Thursdays only. On other days, the locomotive returned LE, and tender-first, to Shrewsbury. One unidentified 8F was even observed at Moat Lane by T.P. Dalton whilst class 5 Nos. 44931, 45031 and 45145, together with 8F No. 48131, were noted by E. H. Stephens at Newtown. From 9 December 1966, the cement train was hauled throughout by No. 46508 until, finally, a D51xx class took over.[29]

BR class 4 No. 75047 approaches Bell's Bridge with a clear exhaust and steam to spare, with the 'up' CCE. 30 April 1966.   *GBJ*

No. 75029 passes the site of the old East signal-box at Machynlleth in November 1966.   *GBJ*

Standard class 4 No. 75004, with the 'up' coast CCE, slows to pick up passengers at Portmadoc. 7 June 1965.

T. J. Edgington

'New' locomotive types appeared until the end of steam; Standard class 4 2-6-0 No. 76040, with the 10.30 a.m. Pwllheli-Paddington, crosses a Pwllheli-bound DMU at Towyn. 2 July 1966. *T. J. Edgington*

Apart from these interesting workings, the BR class 4s were in almost total control of Cambrian steam during the last full year. The CCE and the mails were generally steam-hauled to the end; some '75s' and No. 46521 remained at Machynlleth to cover the coast and Shrewsbury engines. With the exception of through trains, most passenger services within the Division were dominated by DMUs; the SO 13.45 Aberystwyth-Shrewsbury provided an exception by being loco-hauled on 9 July and 20/27 August. Type 2 locomotives were in evidence at Machynlleth but at this time they were mainly for crew-training purposes only, although, later in the autumn, they undertook occasional goods turns; Nos. D5079 and D5080 were early examples. As the summer service approached, what appeared to be the final batch of steam reinforcements arrived. Right at the last, they included a class new to the old line – the BR Standard class 4 2-6-0, represented by Nos. 76038/43 and /86. The additional '75s' were Nos. 75024 (the last locomotive to pass through the shops at Oswestry Works), 75047 and 75052. But even then, these were not adequate for the intensity of summer Saturday traffic on the Cambrian and were augmented by further examples of both classes, which worked down from Birmingham and Shrewsbury. Most trains operated as single loads but some along the coast section, including the 10.30 SO Pwllheli-Paddington and the 08.05 Birmingham-Pwllheli were double-headed. A new train was the 06.35 SO from Knowle & Dorridge to Barmouth, which was usually hauled by a '76' with a load of 4 or 5 coaches. The return service left Barmouth at 12.40. Only one Saturday train was diesel-hauled; the 08.35 Manchester (Piccadilly) to Barmouth,

returning at 14.28. A D69xx Type 3 normally provided the motive power. The load of eight coaches was divided at Machynlleth, with the diesel continuing to Barmouth. The process was reversed on the 'up' journey.

The summer service finished on 3 September and with it ended the Paddington-Pwllheli through coaches of the Cambrian Coast Express. Thereafter a DMU connected with the main train for the few months it had left to run. The last steam-hauled freight train down the coast ran on 6 December 1966, with No. 75047 in charge. From the following day, Type 2 diesel locomotives took over the roster, working from Crewe to Pwllheli and back.

The era of the steam engine thus came to an end in central Wales, after more than a century of faithful service. Undoubtedly, it has disappeared as a regular spectacle but the survival and continued success of the main line between Shrewsbury, Aberystwyth and Pwllheli must now be regarded as the most important factor.

Collett 0-6-0 No. 2276 struggles single-handed towards the summit at Talerddig and, with help from sunshine and shadows, contributes to a dramatic souvenir of steam days. 8 January 1962. *GBJ*

David Davies and his men would recognise this location and, no doubt, would be much impressed by No. 7819 *Hinton Manor*, as it blasted its way through the cutting. However, the significance of the blue window, indicating the location of the auto-buffet, would elude them. 24 May 1963.

John Gwyn Dewing

Notes

[1]CHR DIV Notice No. 369 of 25.7.47. Details include claim from Ogden's of Liverpool for a lost parcel to Camelford, Cornwall comprising: 5 lbs St Bruno + 1 lb Jugger; 5 lbs Redbreast Flake, plus 3 lbs Headway Flake. Total claim £36 3s 9d.

[2]*Facts and Figures about BR*, Staff Edition (1959), p. 15.

[3]IAH Notes.

[4]ibid.

[5]ibid.

[6]IAH noted Nos. 9526/7 (H14) with 9536 and 9540 (H15) during 1924-27, and 9562 (H25) post-war.

[7]H57 Diagram, *Railway Observer*, February 1958.

[8]IAH Notes.

[9]T. B. Owen.

[10]IAH Notes.

[11]ibid..

[12]ibid.

[13]ibid.

[14]Briwnant Jones, G,: *Railway Through Talerddig* Gomer Press (1990), p. 121.

[15]IAH Notes.

[16]ibid.

[17]ibid.

[18]ibid.

[19]ibid.

[20]Machynlleth Shed Register.

[21]IAH Notes.

[22]ibid.

[23]ibid.

[24]Machynlleth Shed Register.

[25]IAH Notes.

[26]per Ron Jones.

[27]IAH Notes.

[28]ibid.

[29]E. H. Stephens, in *Railway Modeller*, March 1967.

Chapter 6

The Diesel Years: a pictorial essay, 1967-99

Modernisation of the Cambrian did not occur overnight: it continues as a gradual, on-going process. Certain aspects of the old railway outlived others; motive power, for example, changed during the 1960s but a further twenty years or so elapsed before modern signalling methods became apparent. Nowhere has the revolution been more evident than in the stations themselves. The vast majority have disappeared, as we knew them, and Machynlleth is currently the only manned station on the line (with the addition of Barmouth during the summer period).

The equipment installed in the present booking office at Machynlleth would perplex any Victorian relief clerk beamed down from above but such a being arriving at Fairbourne, portrayed here in 1965, would have made himself at home in next to no time, although the small, white plastic hairbrush – just below the right-hand side of the ticket cupboard – might well have puzzled him. February 1965.

WIMM/GW Coll.

Token exchanges by hand were usually quite 'gentlemanly' affairs, though one or two exceptions are known. However, all seemed well here as the fireman of No. 7812 *Erlestoke Manor*, on the 'down' CCE, picked up the token from Moat Lane West to Caersws on 3 June 1965.

B. J. Ashworth

The official maximum speed for token exchange was 15 m.p.h. which was usually rigorously observed by crews unused to the procedure, although Cambrian regulars more than doubled that figure. In this exchange at Caersws, the fireman of No. 7812 knows he has placed the token from Moat Lane neatly on the arm of the setting-down post and, like any good sportsman, has his eyes firmly on the 'ball', in this instance the waiting Caersws-Carno token protruding from the next post. 30 May 1963.

B. J. Ashworth

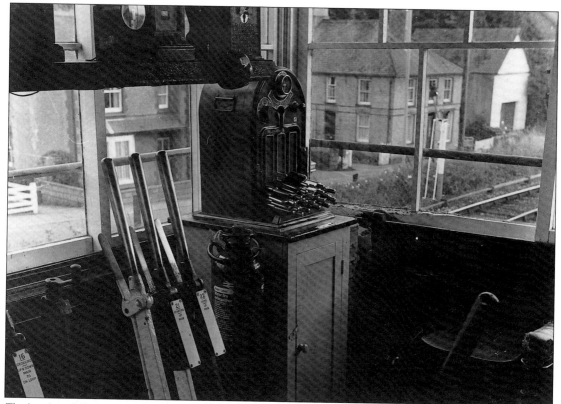

The interior of Cemmes Road signal-box showing the instrument controlling the section to Machynlleth East. Apart from the plastic/formica lever tabs and the BR fire extinguisher, this view could have been taken at any time during the 50 year life of the box; regrettably, the original print carries neither photographer's name or date. *GBJ Coll.*

Old traditions survive into the 1990s. Flowers, cabbages, beans and tomato plants surround the crossing-keeper's hut at the entrance to a camp site (largely on the foundations of the war-time Royal Marines establishment) at Llwyngwril. *c.* July 1991. *GBJ*

'Normal movement of traction units must cease when water is higher than 1" below the underside of the head of the running rail. Emergency running at 3 m.p.h. is permitted . . . to a maximum of 4" above the top of the rail.'
Supplement No. 2 to the Working Timetable of June 1964. Dovey/Dyfi Junction, on 27 June 1966. *T. J. Edgington*

The turntable at Machynlleth was cut up *in situ*. This small road-mounted crane removed the central pivot. The date was not recorded but the turntable was removed within eighteen months of the end of steam.
Neville Pritchard

One of the most interesting items of rolling stock at Machynlleth in recent years was the former Midland Railway saloon No. 2234. It arrived on the 4.17 a.m. freight train from Crewe on 5 September 1970. The locomotive is shunting the remainder of the train which accompanied the saloon. 5 September 1970.

Andrew Dow

A broader view of No. 2234. 5 September 1970.
Andrew Dow

The largest locomotive to traverse the Cambrian was former LMS 4-6-2 locomotive No. 6203 *Princess Margaret Rose*. After withdrawal from main-line service it lay 'preserved' at Butlin's Holiday Camp at Penychain. By 1975, efforts were being made to remove it for restoration to main-line running condition but as the Bangor-Afon Wen line (its means of entry into the area) was then closed, special dispensation was granted to allow one journey along the Cambrian coast. Here, class 24 diesel No. 24.053 leads the way from Penhelig, along the deviation line to Dyfi Junction and eventually to Derby. 11 May 1975. *Ifor A. Higgon*

Diesel-era Dyfi Junction, with the 18.00 Aberystwyth-Wolverhampton (*l.*) and the 18.30 to Pwllheli (*r.*). 20 September 1981.

J. A. Peden

A pair of diesels, Nos. 25. 265 and 25.287 pass the derelict Glandyfi station (since restored as a private house) with the 10.10 Aberystwyth-Wolverhampton service on 18 September 1984.

J. A. Peden

Although the signalling had been rationalised, an oil depot constructed on the site of the carriage sidings and no main line steam locomotive had been near Aberystwyth for five years, two of the little Vale of Rheidol engines managed to re-create some of the atmosphere of steam days. June 1972.

GBJ

Freight traffic was not as dense in more recent years although it endured and the yard at Aberystwyth still had a nicely 'used' appearance. June 1972.

GBJ

The same day, narrow-gauge No. 9 *Prince of Wales* attempted to compensate for the lack of main line steam as it set off through the old loco yard, bound for Devil's Bridge. June 1972.

GBJ

Tywyn yard remained active until freight was withdrawn in 1983. Use of a telephoto lens emphasises the seemingly abrupt change of level in the 'down' platform, viewed through the footbridge. June 1978. *GBJ*

The four oil-storage tank wagons on the left rest on a short length of unconnected track, whilst the small trees (extreme left) obscure one of the air-raid shelters constructed at Machynlleth during the war; the second may be seen more clearly, between the storage tanks and the DMUs. Freight storage sheds and PW buildings were in use at this time. The old turntable road lies extreme right. June 1979. *GBJ*

View from the footbridge at Machynlleth, showing the central signal-box and former loco and goods sheds. The lower yard, though bereft of wagons, looks remarkably neat and gives the impression it could cope with an influx of wagons with ease. April 1984.

GBJ

Buffer stops at two of the sidings in Machynlleth's lower yard were constantly destroyed by the weight of wagons. The unusual solution was to 'ground' two old 'iron mink' vans, filled with concrete and fitted with simple guides to keep them on the rails, at the ends of the sidings. They were resilient and were periodically dragged away from the end of the track by a pair of engines, as required, but this was their final resting place. June 1984.

T. B. Owen

Although general freight was withdrawn in 1983, timber from Scotland was still being unloaded at Welshpool two years later, on 15 June 1985.

J. C. Hillmer

Two views of Machynlleth in DMU days. Class 101 (4-car) arrives with the 08.38 Pwllheli-Birmingham (New Street) service. 15 June 1985.

J. C. Hillmer

The same units await departure. The large building (*l.*) was built on the site of the old Corris Railway. The former 1960-built goods shed, now serving the Building and Maintenance Department, stands on the right. 15 June 1985.

J. C. Hillmer

The damp and dismal morning of 11 July 1986 gradually improved as the royal train arrived at Machynlleth with HM The Queen. When it came to a halt the locomotives extended beyond the starter signal, to permit the vestibule of HM's saloon to rest opposite the main entrance. After the usual formalities and HM's departure, the train was 'set back' to allow the two locomotives to run around.

GBJ

No. 37.430 *Cwmbran* and No. 37.426 *Vale of Rheidol/Y lein fach* run past the royal saloon. 11 July 1986.

GBJ

Nos. 37.429 and 37.426 cross Barmouth Bridge with the 07.40 Euston-Pwllheli through train on 26 September 1987.

J. C. Hillmer

Nos. 37.426 and 37.429 enter the loop at Harlech with the return 15.30 through train from Pwllheli to Euston. The semi-derelict pens in the former goods yard are reminders of livestock traffic in the past. 26 September 1987.

J. C. Hillmer

Steam returned briefly to the Cambrian in 1987. No. 7819 *Hinton Manor* and a former inspection saloon provided on some of the trains, rest at Machynlleth. July 1987.

GBJ

No. 7819 *Hinton Manor*, a Cambrian line favourite of many years standing draws the empty carriage stock from the coast siding into the station at Machynlleth, before setting off for Pwllheli with one of the first steam-hauled passenger trains for twenty years. 26 July 1987.

GBJ

218

No. 40.122 struggles unaided on Llandre bank with a train from London on 5 September 1987. Class 40s were not frequent visitors; the train was already half-an-hour late and enthusiasts on board – not to mention their fellow passengers – were not impressed.

R. W. Kidner

Diesels No. 37.688 *Great Rocks* and un-named No. 37.380 pause at Newtown with the 06.20 Birmingham (New Street) to Aberystwyth train, on 25 June 1988.

J. C. Hillmer

Two 'Sprinters' cross at Welshpool; No. 150.118 (*l.*) with the 11.25 Aberystwyth-Shrewsbury and No. 150.113 (*r.*) with the 11.15 Birmingham (New Street) to Pwllheli trains. 26 July 1991. *J. C. Hillmer*

Welshpool abandoned, with tracks removed and construction of the town's bypass well advanced., 19 July 1992. *GBJ*

Welshpool realignment, with the loop for the new island platform (behind the central stanchion of the new footbridge) and the short (and only) refuge siding alongside, on the right-hand side. 19 July 1992. *GBJ*

HST special working to Pwllheli, near Llangelynin. 11 May 1991. *T. B. Owen*

No. 37.421 works the last 'up' loco-hauled Sunday train from Aberystwyth (15.07) at Borth. 12 May 1991.

T. B. Owen

Trevor Owen secured this unusual and dramatic view of No. 37.418 working the last Aberystwyth-Stanlow (empty) oil train at Bell's Bridge. 28 April 1993.

T. B. Owen

The single-track bridge at Cilcewydd, replaced by the Cambrian just before the grouping.   *GBJ Coll.*

The newer (and one-time double track) bridge was declared unsafe for trains during early 1994 and emergency arrangements became necessary. Temporary stations were quickly erected at either end of the bridge, the track was severed and the space originally occupied by the 'down' line was resurfaced as a footpath.

In this view, a group of passengers on the bridge are transferring from an Aberystwyth/Pwllheli service to their Central Trains connection. February 1994.   *J. Horsley Denton*

223

Two trains face each other, separated only by a pair of buffer-stops and the severed track on the bridge; coast line train in the foreground. February 1994.

J. Horsley Denton

The view from the 'coast' platform, looking east. 7 February 1994.

T. B. Owen

This view, looking west from the 'Welshpool' platform, provides welcome evidence that parcels were still carried. Passengers, on the left, are transferring to the waiting 'coast' train (158.791). The red brick building, formerly Cilcewydd Creamery, was once rail-connected. 7 February 1994.

T. B. Owen

A further visit by the royal train occurred on 31 May 1996, when class 20.301 and 20.302 worked forward from an overnight stop at Machynlleth, past Nawlyn towards Dyfi Junction and Aberystwyth. *T. B. Owen*

The same pair, now with No. 20.302 leading, return the royal train across the 'humped' bridge over Afon Clettwr, on Cors Fochno. 31 May 1996. *T. B. Owen*

A final reminder of some of the glories of the Cambrian line. A GW camp coach offers peace and serenity at Glandyfi, whilst the little station still hoped optimistically to attract ramblers to the attractive Llyfnant Valley nearby. 6 September 1962.   *John Gwyn Dewing*

An immaculate No. 7818 *Granville Manor* approaches Llandre with a 'down' Cambrian Coast Express. May 1959.

                                                                                                                                                           GBJ

Appendix I

This takes the form of a list of some of the 'blue' category engines noted by Ifor Higgon in the Barmouth Junction/Morfa Mawddach area, 1927-55.

In March 1927, 0-6-0 pannier tank engines Nos. 1824 and 1863 tested Barmouth bridge for 'blue' category engines. In October that year, the process was repeated with unidentified 2-6-0 and 39xx type engines. The tests were continued in 1928 and 1929, using 2-8-0 freight engines Nos. 2879 and 2853, as noted below.

Ruabon-Barmouth.

2-8-0 28xx		Date first noted		Additional notes
2879	-	1928 October	28XX operated	1st clearance test. *
2853	-	1929 August 13	to Barmouth	2nd clearance test.
2878	-	1937 November	Junction only.	1st on normal duty. +
2898	-	1939 April		
2899	-	1939 December		
2888	-	1940 June		
2871	-	1940 July		
3821 (OXY)	-	1940 September		
2880	-	1940 September		
3823	-	1940 December		also 3821, 3823, 2878, 2879 and 2899 this month.
2806 (WES)	-	1941 January		
2895 (OXY)	-	1941 September		last identified 28xx
28**	-	1944 December		unidentified 28xx

* No. 2879 appeared in December 1940 as NPT engine, and
+ No. 2878 appeared in December 1940 as BAN engine.

4-4-0 'Bulldog' class

No.	Name	Date first noted	Additional notes
3314	*Mersey*	1928 August	
3445	*Flamingo*	1929 March	also August 1931
3421	-	1929 March	also May 1947
3360	*Torquay*	1929 August	
3426	-	1930 January	
3423	-	1930 January	
3442	*Bullfinch*	1930 April	also August 1931
3369	*David McIver*	1931 January	also August 1931
3338	*Swift*	1931 June	also August 1931
3410	*Columbia*	1931 June	also August 1931
3318	*Vulcan*	1931 August	

APPENDIX I (continued)

4-4-0 'Bulldog' class

No.	Name	Date first noted	Additional notes
3427	–	1932 September	
3327	*Marco Polo*	1932 December	
3359	*Tregeagle*	1933 December	
3403	*Trinidad*	1934 March	
3358	*Tremayne*	1934 November	
3450	*Peacock*	1935 February	Regular appearances
3342	*Bonaventura*	1937 March	
3399	*Ottawa*	1939 January	
3366	-	1939 January	
3455	*Starling*	1944 December	Worked Saltney Goods
3377	-	1946 April	also May 1946
3454	*Skylark*	1950 June 16th	Worked 3.45pm (7.8s)

2-6-0 'Aberdare' class		Date first noted	Additional notes
2664	-	1928 January	Worked goods to/from
2617	-	1928 January	Barmouth Junction only
2600	-	1928 February	
2673	-	1928 March	
2604	-	1928 March	
2642	-	1928 April	
2612	-	1928 April	
2633	-	1928 May	
2618	-	1928 September	
2659	-	1928 October	
2658	-	1929 February	
2665	-	1930 June	regular visitor to 4/46
2641	-	1933 January	
2679	-	1933 February	
2620	-	1934 December	
2638	-	1935 October	
2619	-	1937 October	
2660	-	1938 March	appeared until 10/45
2623	-	1939 September	
2608	-	1939 December	
2648 (PPRd)	-	1940 October	
2662	-	1944 November	last recorded 26xx.

APPENDIX I (continued)

2-8-0 ROD type			Date first noted	Additional notes
3024	-	2-8-0 ROD	1936 December 28	
3008	-	operated to	1937 February	
3024	-	Barmouth	1937 March	
3001	-	Junction only.	1937 April	
3030	-		1937 April 3	
3016	-		1937 October	
3039	-		1938 March	
3021	-		1939 May	
3032	-		1940 November	
3028	-		1942 April	Last 30xx visit

43 – 73xx class 2-6-0

These appeared in great numbers over the years. A figure of *c.* 160 (from No. 5364, the first noted in August 1927 to No. 5378 recorded in August 1955) can only be regarded as a most conservative total, as IAH did not set out to log each and every locomotive seen.

'Manor' class 4-6-0	Date first noted	Additional notes
7805 *Broome Manor*	1938 31 Oct and 1 Nov	Conducted clearance tests
7817 *Garsington Manor*	1939 February	
7813 *Freshford Manor*	1939 April	
7806 *Cockington Manor*	1940 January	
7812 *Erlestoke Manor*	1944 September	
7800 *Torquay Manor*	1946 August	BAN
7804 *Baydon Manor*	1948 May	
7802 *Bradley Manor*	1948 November	
7825 *Lechlade Manor*	1950 December	
7823 *Hook Norton Manor*	1950 December	
7826 *Longworth Manor*	1950 January	
7827 *Lydham Manor*	1950 February	
7808 *Cookham Manor*	1953 April	
7819 *Hinton Manor*	1953 July	
7821 *Ditcheat Manor*	1953 July	
7811 *Dunley Manor*	1953 July	
7801 *Anthony Manor*	1953 September	
7828 *Odney Manor*	1953 December	
7807 *Compton Manor*	1954 January	
7820 *Dinmore Manor*	1954 February	
7822 *Foxcote Manor*	1954 April	

Appendix II

LOCOMOTIVES WHICH WORKED OUT OF MACHYNLLETH SHED, 1958 & 1959
Copied from the official shed Register by Gwyn Roderick.

1449 ex.EXE 9.9.58	4549	6305 CARM
1636	4560	6307 TYS
2200	4564	6310 CARM
2201	4575	6318 CNYD
2202	4588 OSW	6320 82B
2204	4599 to SDN 26.3.59	6325 TYS
2210 OSW	5507	6329 CARM
2211 CNYD	5510 ex.SDN 10.4.59	6331 OXY
2217	5517 to SDN 6.12.58	6335
2219	5540 ex.Bristol 9.59	6340 84F
2231	5541	6342
2232	5553 ex.Bristol 8.1.59	6344
2233	5556	6348 86A
2234 SALOP	5565 ex.Bristol 12.9.58	6349
2235 OSW	5570	6353
2237		6363 82B
2239 OSW	5726	6368
2244		6371
2251		6377
2255	4377	6378
2264		6387 SALOP
2274	5309	6392
2275 OSW	5312	
2280 ex.GLO 20/6/58	5318	7308
2281	5319	7310 CNYD
2285	5322 TYS	7313 CNYD
2286	5324 SALOP	7317 TYS
2287	5336	7325 CNYD
2289 ex.Works:on loan	5345	7328 SRD
2294 CARM	5362 SALOP	7329
2298	5369 TYS	7338 85A
3200 OSW	5386	7339 CNYD
3201		
3202		7405
3204 OSW		7434
3207 84G		
3208		
3209		

7801	46503	75020
7802	46504	75024
7803	46505	75026
7806	46507	
7809	46509	78000
7810	46510	78002
7814	46511	78003
7819	46512	78005
7821	46513	78006
7823	46514	78007
7824	46523	
7827	46524	82005 first working
7828	46527	27.8.59
7829	46527	
9004 CNYD		
9013		
9014 CNYD		
9015		
9017		
9018 CNYD		
9021		Total 148

Appendix III

844, 49, 55, 64, 73, 84, 87, 92, 93, 94, 95, 96
1787, 2151
2200*, 01, 04, 10, 14, 16*, 17*, 19, 23*, 54*, 55, 60, 71*, 72*, 73*, 83*, 84*, 91*, 98*
2315, 23*, 27, 40*, 45, 54*, 62, 83, 86,
2404*, 07*, 11*, 17, 31*, 36, 37, 38*, 46*, 47*, 49, 60, 66*, 68, 74*, 76, 82, 83,
2525, 29*, 35, 36, 46*, 52, 54, 56, 62*, 72, 76
2612, 22, 25, 31, 36, 37, 39, 43, 49, 51, 52, 60, 62, 76, 77, 79
3200, 01, 02, 03, 04, 05, 07, 08, 09, 12, 13, 14, 16, 17, 21, 22, 24, 25, 26, 27, 28
3254, 65, 72, 73, 87, 91
3375, 3435, 45, 46*
4358*, 65, 75, 77, 81
4501, 13, 39, 49, 55, 75
4812, 59, 74
5310, 23, 24, 30, 39*, 47, 55, 71, 92, 95*, 99
5517, 24, 41, 60, 70
5816, 5819
6304, 07, 09*, 10, 11, 13*, 14*, 21, 25, 29, 30, 31*, 33, 34, 38, 42, 43, 48, 49, 51*,
6352, 53, 54, 55, 59, 62, 65, 67*, 71*, 74, 80, 82, 83, 84, 86, 89, 92, 96, 97
7306, 07
7401, 06, 10
7803, 06, 07*, 13, 14, 16*, 19*

Locomotives marked with an asterisk* predominated on Carmarthen line duties at this time, but individual examples e.g. '22s' and Dean 'Goods' also ventured occasionally on to the Cambrian line; some 'blue' engines thus indicated featured also in Llandeilo-Saltney goods trains.

Drawing on T. B. Owen's notes, it is possible to trace the operation of No. 7803 through Machynlleth on Saltney turns from 3.7.41; No. 7807 from 30.7.41 and No. 7806 from 27.9.41. No. 7814 appeared on Cambrian line passenger turns on 17.12.41 and No. 7807 was first noted on passenger duties from Oswestry on 1.7.1942 when still a NEYland engine; it was transferred to OSWestry in April 1943.

Appendix IV

MACHYNLLETH MOTIVE POWER DEPOT 89C *c.* 1949/50
List courtesy of Gwyn Roderick

Paybill No.	Name	Enginemen
1	T. W. Jones	Bill Welshpool
2	C. Davies	Charlie Davies
3	L. J. Roberts	Llew Roberts
4	R. S. Williams	Dick Williams
5	W. E. Neale	Bill Neale
6	R. H. Edwards	Dick Edwards
7	R. J. Pugh	Bob Pugh
8 (Chargeman)	E. E. Owen	Ernie Owen
9	G. E. Parry	George Parry
10	E. J. Cudworth	Ted Cudworth
11	R. L. Edwards	Len Edwards
12	H. R. Humphreys	Hughie Humphreys
13	D. L. Davies	Dai Lloyd Davies
14	G. Evans	Griff Evans
15	G. Fleming	George Fleming
16	D. C. Pryce	Dan Pryce
17	E. Owen	Ellis Owen
18	W. J. Jones	Bill Merthyr
19	O. B. James	Burton James
20	E. Humphreys	Evan Humphreys
21	O. Evans	Ogarth Evans
22	J. Ll. Pugh	Jack Pugh
23	E. Pugh	Ted Pugh
24	W. E. Field	Bill Field
25	E. Evans	Emlyn Bach
26	J. T. Royles	Jack Royles
27	R. H. Ingram	Dick Ingram
28	O. Bebb	Ossie Bebb
29	H. R. Benbow	Harry Benbow, Llanidloes
30	T. G. Aldridge	Tom Aldridge, Caersws
31	T. F. Callow	Fred Callow
32	W. Davies	Bill Davies, Caersws

Passed Firemen and Firemen

41	D. A. Rees	Alun Rees
42	D. E. Lewis	Dewi Lewis
43	D. Hughes	Donald Hughes
44	G. Parry	Glyn Parry

Paybill No.	Name	Enginemen
45	A. Fleming	Archie Fleming
46	S. C. Lloyd	Syd Lloyd
47	W. P. Hughes	Will Abercegir
48	R. L. Owen	Bob Harlech
49	C. Evans	Cledwyn Evans
50	E. Evans	Teddy Evans
51	A. Aldridge	Arthur Aldridge
52	I. T. Lloyd	Ieuan Lloyd
53	W. L. Putt	Bill Putt
54	N. W. Pritchard	Neville Pritchard
55	E. P. Edwards	Teddy Edwards
56	D. E. Evans	Dafydd Dinas
57 (Steamraiser)	H. Evans	Haydn Evans
58	E. Jones	Edmund Bach
59	R. J. Davies	Bob John
60	D. G. Pugh	Gwynfor Pugh
61	D. O. Bowyer	Dai Bowyer
62	R. L. Davies	Ronnie Davies
63	D. M. Evans	Murray Evans
64	D. P. Myles	Dai Myles
65	T. Evans	Tom Llanegryn
66	H. T. Davies	Trevor Pennal
67	T. G. Pugh	Cards.
68	L. Jones	Les Bullock
69		
70		
71		
72	J. D. Evans	Jacob Evans
73		
74		
75	L. T. Lloyd	Llew Lloyd

Fitting Staff

Chargeman Fitter	J. H. James	Jimmy James
	Fitter A. Griffiths	Alf Griffiths
	Fitter G. Cawley	George Cawley
	Fitter G. Edwards	Gomer Edwards
	Fitter R. A. Caffrey	Dick Caffrey
Fitter's Mates	E. J. Holt	Evan John Holt
	T. H. Holt	Tom Holt
	W. Davies (Craneman)	Bill Davies
	W. Jarman	Billy Jarman
	W. Lewis	Big Bill
	P. Smythe	Paddy Smythe
Firedroppers & steamraisers		
	E. Caffrey	Ernest Caffrey
	F. Jobson	Fred Jobson
	D. Roberts	Dennis Roberts
Coalmen		
	R. D. Rowlands	Dick Rowlands
	R. J. H. Arnold	Reggie Arnold
	V. Humphreys	Vic Humphreys
Storemen		
	J. H. Evans	Jack Rhydymain
	I. O. Hughes	Iorrie Hughes
	G. Barton MM	George Barton
Boilersmith	W. E. Griffiths	Bill Griffiths
Mate	J. Price	Jackie Price
Boiler Washer	J. Arthur	Jimmy Arthur
Tube Cleaner	J. Jones.	Jack Clark
Plant & Machinery		
	E. M. Jones	Evan Maldwyn
	E. Jones	Evan Jones
Foreman	J. V. Owen	John Vaughan Owen
Supervisor	T. James	Tom James
Supervisor	J. Lloyd	Jack Lloyd

Appendix V

THE FORMATION OF THE CAMBRIAN COAST EXPRESS

Week commencing 14 June 1954

Paddington departure

SX 10.10 a.m.	Van 3rd	Pwllheli	
	Composite	Pwllheli	
	Brake compo	Aberystwyth	
	3rd	Aberystwyth	
	Diner	Aberystwyth	
	Composite	Aberystwyth	
	Van 3rd	Aberystwyth	
SO 10.50 a.m.	Van 3rd	Aberystwyth	H
	Composite	Aberystwyth	H
	Brake compo	Aberystwyth	J
	3rd	Aberystwyth	J
	Diner	Aberystwyth	J
	Composite	Pwllheli	J
	Van 3rd	Pwllheli	
	3rd	Pwllheli	
	3rd	Pwllheli	
	3rd	Pwllheli	
	3rd	Pwllheli	
	Brake compo	Pwllheli	

H denotes regular SX Pwllheli coaches
J denotes regular SX Aberystwyth coaches, illustrating a change of destination at weekends

Appendix VI

MACHYNLLETH LOCAL DEPARTMENTAL COMMITTEE (LDC) AND THE 'LINKS'

The work of each shed, or Motive Power Depot, was carried out by a series of enginemen subdivided into groups or 'links', each link possessing its own specific turns or duties. The links were formulated through discussion between management and the Local Departmental Committee (LDC) which represented the men at the depot, and were implemented by mutual agreement – various proposals being made by both sides. Every depot had its own LDC.

Any insurmountable problems at a local level were referred to Sectional Council No. 2. who, if they could not deal satisfactorily with them, would pass them on to the head offices of both unions, i.e., the Associated Society of Locomotive Engineers & Firemen (ASLEF) and the National Union of Railwaymen (NUR).

The Machynlleth LDC meetings were conducted in the members own time usually, but not always, on Sundays and at a variety of venues in the town, ranging from the refreshment room at the station, to the former Corris Railway building, the Town Hall or the Owain Glyndŵr Institute. The cost of hiring each room was paid by each union in turn. Two sample sets of links are included here, representing winter service 1927 and summer service 1946.

WINTER 1927

Meeting at the Town Hall, 25 Sept. 1927 at 8.00 p.m. Bro. W. Evans in the chair. NUR to pay for the room.
Links operating from October 1927.

No. 1 Passenger Link

Book on at	4.15	for	5.15 a.m.	Coast Goods
	3.15	for	4.15 a.m.	Passenger
	5.00	for	6.10 a.m.	Coast Mail
	6.15	for	8.20 a.m.	Passenger to Aberystwyth
	7.45	for	8.20 a.m.	Passenger to Pwllheli
	1.07	for	1.40 p.m.	Passenger to Pwllheli
	3.00	for	6.00 p.m.	Passenger and Banking

No. 2 Goods Link

Book on at	2.45 a.m. for 3.45 a.m.	Goods
	2.45 a.m. for 3.45 a.m.	Banking
	6.05 a.m. for 7.05 a.m.	Goods
	7.45 a.m. for 8.45 a.m.	Goods
	10.00 a.m. Banking	
	10.29 a.m. for relief of 7.45 a.m. Goods men	
	no specific time	Early Ballast
	no specific time	Relief of Early Ballast
	1.55 p.m. for 2.10 p.m.	Goods

No. 3 Link

Book on at	6.45 a.m. for 7.30 a.m.	Yard
	2.15 p.m. for 2.30 p.m.	Yard

No. 4 Link

4 o' clock Shed.

SUMMER 1946

Machynlleth Links operative from 6 May 1946. Meeting at Owain Glyndŵr Institute, Thursday, 18 April 1946 at 7.45 p.m. Note that a.m. and p.m. are not indicated on the original; all present were obviously well aware of the turns involved and the notes are copied as written.

No. 1 Link

6.45	Aberystwyth and 12.0 back
7.15	Pwllheli
3.30	Barmouth and back
4.30	Portmadoc
6.35	Newtown
12.35	Relief to 12.0 ex Aber. and work to Salop

No. 2 Link

4.40	Coast Goods
1.35	Welshpool Goods
7.15	Towyn
12.30	Banking
7.25	Newtown School Train
10.38	Relief Towyn
7.30	Spare
9.57	Banking
3.00	Aberystwyth
10.42	Relief to Newtown Shunt

No. 3 Link

6.0	Shed
4.0	Banking
6.45	Preparing
10.38	Towyn shunt
4.40	Assist Goods
1.0	spare
4.0	Goods Newtown
5.0	Shed
5.0	Yard
11.15	Dinas Mawddwy

No. 4 Link

8.15	Yard shunt
3.45	Yard shunt

Bro W. E. Neale in the chair; NUR to pay for the room.

Bibliography

BAUGHAN, Peter E.: *North and Mid Wales*, Regional history series, David & Charles (1980).

BEHREND, George: *Gone with Regret*, Jersey Artists (1967).

BRIWNANT JONES, G.: *Railway Through Talerddig*, Gomer (1990).

BRIWNANT JONES, G.: *Great Western Corris*, Gomer (1990).

CHRISTIANSEN, R.: *Forgotten Railways, North & Mid Wales*, David & Charles (1976).

CHRISTIANSEN, R. & MILLER, R.W.: *The Cambrian Railways, Vols I & II*, David & Charles (1967).

CLARK, R. H. & POTTS, C, R.: *Historical Survey of Selected G.W. Stations*, Guild Publishing (1987).

CORRIS SOCIETY: *Return to Corris*, Avon Anglia (1988).

COX, C. & KRUPA, C.: *The Kerry Tramway*, Plateway Press (1992).

COZENS, Lewis: *The Corris Railway*, Cozens (1949).

COZENS, Lewis: *The Van & Kerry Railways*, Cozens (1953).

COZENS, Lewis: *Mawddwy Railway*, Cozens (1954).

DALTON, T. Patrick: *Cambrian Companionship*, Oxford Pub. Co. (1985).

DUNN, J. M.: *Reflections on a Railway Career*, Ian Allen (1966).

GASQUOINE, C. P.: *The Story of the Cambrian*, Woodall, Minshall, Thomas & Co. (1922).

GREEN, C. C.: *Cambrian Railways Album, Vols I & II*, Ian Allan (1977/81).

GREEN, C. C.: *North Wales Branch Line Album*, Ian Allan (1983).

GREEN, C. C.: *The Coast Lines of the Cambrian Railways, Vols I & II*, Wild Swan Publications (1993/5).

HARRIS, Michael: *GW Coaches from 1890*, David & Charles (1985).

HARRISON, Ian: *GWR Locomotive Allocations 1921*, Wild Swan (1948).

HILLMER, J. & SHANNON, P.: *Diesels in North & Mid Wales*, Haynes OPC (1990).

HOLDEN, J. S.: *The Manchester & Milford Railway*, Oakwood (1979).

JOHNSON, Peter: *The Cambrian Lines*, Ian Allan (1984).

JONES, Elwyn V.: *Mishaps on the Cambrian Railways*, Severn Press (1972).

KENNEDY, R.: *Steam on the Cambrian*, Ian Allan Ltd. (1990).

KIDNER, Roger W.: *The Cambrian Railways*, Oakwood (1992).

LLOYD, M.: *Private Owners on the Cambrian*, Welsh Railways Research Circle (1998).

PETO, W.: *Register of GWR Locomotives, Vol II, Manor 4-6-0s*, Irwell Press (1996).

POCOCK, Nigel & HARRISON, Ian: *GWR Locomotive Allocations for 1934*. Wild Swan (1987).

R.C.T.S.: *Locomotives of the GWR*, Pt 10, RCTS (1966).

ROWLEDGE, J. W. P.: *GWR Locomotives Allocations; First & Last Sheds, 1922-1967*, David & Charles (1986).

SIMMONS, Jack & BIDDLE, Gordon (eds): *The Oxford Companion to British Railway History*, Oxford University Press (1997).

Journals:

Issues of *The Railway Magazine, Trains Illustrated, Railway World, The Great Western Railway Magazine.*

Newspapers:

Cambrian News, Western Mail, Montgomeryshire County Times, Y Cymro.

Index